More Than Just A Flag

MONICA F. HELMS

BOOKS

Edited by Laurence Watts

Front cover photograph by Brian Groff.

ISBN: 0578465869
ISBN-13: 978-0578465869

CONTENTS

FOREWORD

When I think of Monica Helms, I think of sincerity, humor, and compassion. I first met Monica in Phoenix, Arizona, in April of 2000, when I was speaking at a workplace-related conference she attended. After I had delivered my talk, she approached and asked to speak with me. We sat in the hotel lobby and I listened as she told me of some of her personal goals and her worries as a trans woman with children to support. She wanted to make a difference. I could tell that she would.

The story of Monica's life, as she tells it here, is honest and gritty, without grandstanding or self-indulgence. She isn't trying to prove anything. Instead, she shows us her struggle and her introspection in a straightforward way that intertwines with the increasing visibility of the transgender community and the advent of our community's participation in the political life of the United States.

I am honored that she invited me to write this foreword, and I want to tell you why. Yes, she mentions me as one of her influencers and notes my presence in a few historical contexts, but she didn't mention one particular experience that had an emotional impact on me. Of course, she needn't take note of my feelings in her book; this is her story, and she may even remember what I'm about to tell differently than I do, but I'm telling the story anyway.

In 2001, when the HBO-produced film *Southern Comfort* was exhibited in a special screening in Atlanta, in conjunction with the then well-established transgender community conference of the same name, Monica and I sat together in the audience. I had known Robert Eads, the trans man whose final year of life is documented as he battles ovarian cancer - detected too late to treat because too many doctors refused to examine his transgender body. Once Robert had a diagnosis, his life's mission was to make it to the next Southern Comfort Conference to say goodbye to all his friends. *Southern Comfort*, directed by Kate Davis, is a beautiful and powerful film, and as we had approached the theater Monica was worried that it was going to be too difficult to watch. Monica had never met Robert, but we both knew his close friends, who were also in the film. As we took our seats, Monica asked a woman on the other side of her if she had any extra tissues. I braced myself for a rising tide of emotion.

The film didn't disappoint. Like Monica's story, the film has humor and pathos and interactions with other important people, and when the reality of Robert's death is conveyed to the audience, Monica collapsed onto my shoulder and sobbed uncontrollably. I put my arms around her, knowing nothing I could do would console her pain, and she gradually recovered. The depth of her feeling was palpable, genuine, and justified, but what struck me was her courage in expressing it. Sure, many people were crying in that theater, many who had known Robert even longer and better than I had, but there was something about Monica's intensity, something about her ability to face reality, something so very loving and hopeful and forgiving in Monica that felt—in that moment and still today—unique.

This is the passion for life and the willingness to live it fully that Monica brings to her autobiography, and it exemplifies the spirit with which I hope all her readers will approach her story, the events of her life, and her intersections with transgender history. In many ways, Monica's story represents the hopes and dreams of all transgender people, and I pray her self-effacing wisdom will touch us all.

Jamison Green.

INTRODUCTION

Most transgender narratives center on the author's struggles with identity, and most end shortly after that identity is resolved – usually with transition, and often just after gender-confirming surgery. Life, of course, does not end with reinvention. I, a reader of many of those autobiographies, have often been left wondering: now what?

We are lucky to have memoirs by Kate Bornstein, Jennifer Finney Boylan, Aleshia Brevard, Jan Morris, and others who have described their adventures after coming to terms with themselves. These are tales of complex, interesting and productive lives. We need more. I am happy to introduce another such long-after-transition tale, this one written by Monica F. Helms.

In 1999, Monica Helms designed the transgender flag, the original of which now resides at the Smithsonian Institution in Washington, D.C. She is best known for that, but she did much more than create a flag. She served honorably as a submariner in the U.S. Navy, married and fathered two sons, had a career as a telephone operator, and is now married for a second time. Since the early 1980s, she has been intensively involved in trans community-building and activism.

Monica earned her bones as an activist in 1993 and 1994, when she was involved in creating a union at the telecommunication company Sprint, which did not want its workers unionized and did whatever it could to dissuade organizers. She was trained in union-building by the AFL-CIO and testified against Sprint in Federal court. Several years later she transitioned on the job at Sprint, paving the way for other trans people at the company.

Even before Sprint though, Monica was an activist. In 1983, she was one of six founders of the Alpha Zeta (for Arizona) chapter of Tri-Ess, the Society for the Second Self, an organization for heterosexual cross-dressers. Monica notes that five of the six, herself included, eventually transitioned gender roles, a common occurrence among Tri-Ess members.

Monica served honorably as a submariner in the U.S. Navy at a time when women were not allowed on submarines. She has been successful at re-introducing herself in submariner circles and has lobbied extensively on behalf of transgender veterans. She is co-founder, with Angela Brightfeather, of the nonprofit Transgender American Veterans Association and was the organization's founding president. In 2004, she presided over the first march by transgender veterans to the Vietnam Memorial and the laying of a wreath in honor of transgender veterans at the Tomb of the Unknown Soldier. Monica retired from TAVA in 2013.

Some of her other achievements:
- Before TAVA's launch in 2003, Monica was active on the board of directors of the nonprofit National Transgender Advocacy Coalition.
- Monica was Georgia's (and the South's) first transgender delegate to the Democratic National Convention. She has been active in lobbying state legislators in Arizona and Georgia, and the U.S. Congress.
- Along the way, Monica managed to pick up three college degrees, two in television production. She maintains a channel on YouTube with some 250 videos.
- Monica has six books available for purchase on Amazon. Five are science fiction, three of which – perhaps unsurprisingly – involve submarines.

Monica has lived and is living a full life. This memoir documents all that she has done, and the grace with which she did it. How wonderful it is that it doesn't stop in the 1990s with her gender transition!

Dallas Denny.

1 – ALL ABOUT ME

When a person reaches a certain point in their life, like I have, they spend a lot of time thinking back to the Good Ol' Days, assuming they had any. With me, the Good Ol' Days haven't stopped. I feel like I have lived enough life for three people, yet I still crave more.

For some time now, people, especially from the transgender community, have suggested that I need to write down my life story. I have resisted this for many years. I've already written six books and have learned the hard way that, for me, writing books only becomes a labor of love when you reach the final few chapters. Up until then, it's just a labor of pain. Because of my age I've also wondered whether I have enough time left to finish such a story. I already had chunks written down, but I knew it would take time to cut away, edit and add to what I already had. I knew that Monica's story dwelled in there somewhere. It would just take time to do her story justice. Something told me I needed to finish this now.

As my life has progressed, I've found that I'm both man and woman, neither a man nor a woman, and sometimes both at the same time. I am not confused, rather I believe I'm enlightened. I feel that I have been blessed to see life through the eyes of a man and the eyes of a woman. It has given me an amazing viewpoint of the world. As such, I believe I am an *amalgamated person.*

An amalgamation is "the process of combining or uniting multiple entities into one form." In metallurgy, in an amalgam or alloy, the elements do not chemically combine, but mix together to form a stronger byproduct. I feel that the amalgamation of male and female in me has helped to make me a stronger person. I identify as female, but I'm more of a bigender person. This allows my brain to float between multiple worlds, or solidly take on one role or another. Sometimes I am a man and a woman at the same time, or I can change in a nanosecond, then change back just as fast.

I can easily see that once I'm gone people will say, "She created the Transgender Pride Flag." My life will be distilled down to that one moment in time and nothing else I ever did will matter. I know I should be grateful to be remembered at all but, while designing the Flag may have been the single most important act of my life, it's not the only thing I accomplished.

I'm delighted that the Flag has been a force for good, but I confess that this outcome happened more or less inadvertently. I created the Flag because it represents my feelings about gender and my pride in being transgender. If no one ever used it, I would be happy to still own the original, but fate had other plans. Now the original is in the Smithsonian and the Flag is used all over the world. It will remain a mystery to me why it caught on as well as it has. I have tried to encourage its use, but the truth is there are as many reasons why trans people like using it as there are trans people. As an activist, I have always tried to unite trans people. The Flag does just that. It makes us one large family.

For those people who wish to know about the other things I have done with my life, they can read this book. I give credit to those I have worked with over the years, many of whom helped to mold the person I have become. There are many people to thank for the positive impression they had on my life, but the people who had a negative attitude also helped me. They showed me how not to act.

The outcome, my life, is detailed here in these pages. I want people to see that my life was *More Than Just a Flag.*

2 – IN THE BEGINNING

I don't remember anything about how I came into the world, but I've also never met anyone who does. However, I like to think that this is what went down just before being born:

"Helms! Front and center!"

"I'm here, St. Christopher, sir."

"Looks like we're about ready to send you to your assignment."

"That's great, sir. I've been in the Soul Waiting Room since before the War of 1812. Playing cribbage with Napoleon's former soul is getting boring. I think he cheats."

"You should consider yourself lucky. Some souls have been waiting for their assignment since The Boss Lady's Son died on Planet Earth." St. Christopher made the Sign of the Cross. "Looks like we'll have a lot of souls being assigned shortly. The people of this particular world just finished another war, so when all the soldiers and sailors come home, there'll be a boom in babies."

"Wow. Sounds like an exciting time to be born, sir."

"Maybe. You'll have to judge for yourself."

"So, sir, can we go over my assignment one final time?"

"Sure." St. Christopher opened the Big Book and checked the information next to my name. "Says here you're going to be born to a couple in Walla Walla, Washington, in the United States of America."

"And, I'm going to be a human girl, right?"

"That's right. Your name will be 'Monica Helms',"

"Then, it's all set? You don't see any problems, do you?"

"Now, what makes you think there's ever any problems?"

"You know. Rumors go around, mostly from the old souls who've had previous assignments."

"Those are just 'old soul' stories. The Boss has a plan for everyone and She's not about to tell anyone, including us at the Soul Repository Center."

"Mistakes aren't made?"

"Come on, now. You've been here long enough to know She doesn't make mistakes."

"Well, I was just wondering."

"I have your assignment right here. We don't know what happens once you step through The Doors and see The Boss before your birth. It's been that way since we started. If She wants, She can make adjustments to your assignment. That's Her prerogative. After all, She's The Boss."

"Okay. So, when do I leave?"

"Shortly. I suggest you say your goodbyes."

"Even my soul mate?"

"Yes, especially her. Keep in mind, she won't be born until 1974, twenty-three years after you."

"Is a year very long?"

"Don't worry about it. You'll be fine."

"Thank you, sir." I paused. "I have one question."

"Yes?"

"Do you have an assignment for Napoleon's old soul?"

St. Christopher smiled. "Let's just say, if you happen to read the March 1969 issue of National Geographic, check out page sixty-five. He'll be the third naked native woman from the left."

I smiled.

"Hey, your name is flashing! You have to go, now!"

"To The Doors?"

"Yes, hurry! You can't keep The Boss waiting!"

I turned and ran toward the huge doors at the end of the massive room where all souls have to go to be sent to their assignments. I would soon become a human girl. I couldn't wait. I'd heard they got a lot of neat stuff at Christmas. I wanted an Easy Bake Oven.

As I reached The Doors, they swung open. Thousands of souls poured through and stood in line so The Boss could send them all to the right places. As I got closer, I saw a vast emptiness in front of the line. It seemed to grow larger and larger the closer I got. Then it happened: I saw Her.

"Monica Helms!" Her voice boomed.

I felt scared. "Yessss, ma'am?"

"I have a new assignment for you."

"A new assignment?" What could it be?

"Yes. You will be a special person, but those around you will not know it. I'm doing this for a reason."

"But...."

"Enjoy your life, Robert."

"Robert?! But, that's a boy's na...."

Everything went dark.

The darkness quickly turned into a harsh, bright light. My brain suddenly became overloaded with all kinds of new and strange sensory inputs. I felt wet, cold, hungry, and felt the effects of gravity.

Then I felt something I really didn't like. A sharp pain came from the bottom part of my new body. I opened my new mouth and let out a loud scream. That surprised the hell out of me. *Did that come out of me?* I wondered if I could do that again.

Before I tried, I felt another sharp pain, this time on the backside. I screamed again.

"Congratulations Mary, you have a healthy baby boy."

A boy? I was really a boy? I reached down between my legs. *Sure enough, I got one of those thingies only human boys are supposed to have.* I began crying.

"Look, he's touching himself. How cute."

I screamed again.

Goddess, I don't want to be a boy. You made a mistake.

She didn't respond.

"Would you like to hold your new son, Mary?"

"Yes, please."

The doctor placed me in the arms of a warm and wonderful person.

"Hi, I'm your mother."

My mother? Wow. I came from her? I'm going to like this person. Maybe she can turn me into a girl.

Most people these days think of God in the male gender, and in the early years of my life I felt the same. In truth however, I have lived most of my life as an agnostic. Then, when Darlene came into my life, I started to believe in a female god: The Goddess. When I first wrote this chapter, I used "God" as The Boss. Later, I changed the character to The Goddess to better reflect how I feel today.

3 – EARLY MEMORIES

My earliest memories as Robert started around 1954, at the age of three. Several things happened that year that would shape the future Monica. My parents bought a house just west of the city limits of Phoenix, in an area that later became Maryvale. My parents and I moved into a corner lot, one of the first houses built in the area, and had the distinction of being the first residents of Maryvale. My mother lived in that house for the next 61 years, remaining after my father died in 2004. Eventually she moved out at the end of 2015 because of her health. My sister Julie and her husband moved her into an apartment attached to their house and my mother has been much happier since she moved there.

The house and surrounding area could not have been more perfect for my development as a child. People initially used the field opposite my house to raise cattle, but, two years after we moved in, the cows had been removed, leaving a great field for me and the other local kids to play in. On the other side of the field, next to a two-lane 43rd Avenue, grew several tall trees, perfect for climbing.

After we moved in, the neighborhood quickly filled with families, many with children around my age. The boys played all kinds of games that boys played in the 1950s, and I loved them all. I had numerous toy guns and rifles. We had dirt in the backyard that made perfect roads for my toy cars and truck. My parents bought me Lincoln Logs and plastic bricks, both of which pre-dated LEGOs. They would let me build all kinds of wonderful things in the dirt. After it had rained, the street corner where our house sat would flood along the gutter, creating a mini lake, perfect for floating toy wooden boats. On a recent trip back to Phoenix, it rained during my visit there and, once more, even after all these years, a huge lake formed along the gutter. I loved being a boy in that house.

An early event that helped shape my life occurred when the birth of my baby sister, Carrie, happened in 1955. I felt proud be her big brother, so much so that I brought other kids in the neighborhood over to our house to see her. Of course, a few years later, she became an annoyance. No surprise there, right? Then, three years after my first sister, my second sister, Julie, came into my life. Then two years after that, a brother, Dennis, whom I had prayed for. My parents even allowed me to name him. The house quickly became crowded.

When I recall my childhood, I remember, at the age of five, praying to God and asking him to turn me into a girl. I have no memory of what caused me to think that, but it happened shortly after my first sister came on the scene. Somehow, I knew I wasn't built right. Because I grew up in the Catholic religion, they taught me from an early age that if you wanted something, you prayed to God for it. Catholics made God sound like a spiritual Sears catalogue. Or, for those of you who didn't grow up in the 1950s and 60s, Catholics made God seem like Amazon, with the Catholics being His Prime members. You prayed for something and got it two days later with free shipping.

Although the Catholic God eventually did answer my prayer to turn me into a girl, it took Him 41 years. Maybe for the Catholic God that might be "Two-Day Delivery", when it absolutely, positively has to get there in four decades, or less. It probably would have happened sooner if I had prayed to the Goddess.

When some people talk to me today, they say that being trans is a choice and that, while growing up, outside forces influenced me. I ask them how does a five-year-old get influenced by outside forces when he couldn't read and had no Internet in the year 1956? They don't know how to respond to that.

In 1957, I started first grade. All the girls at my school wore pretty dresses and had their hair done beautifully. By contrast, I wore boring slacks, a button-down shirt and had my hair cut short. I envied them. I remember wanting to wear dresses. I remember wanting long, flowing hair. But no. Society in 1957 couldn't handle a six-year-old boy wanting to live life as a girl. Nowadays, some enlightened parents are allowing their sons to express themselves as girls, or their daughters to live their true selves as boys, but that didn't happen when I grew up.

Although I wanted to look like a girl, I still wanted to play boys' games, wear my Davy Crockett hat, and play with boys' toys. One of the boy activities I couldn't get into however, principally because I lacked the requisite skills, was sports. I did play Little League for a short time, but not very well. Why? Because I threw the ball badly. In high school, I tried out for baseball, but the first time a pitcher threw me a ball, to see if I could be a catcher, I got hit in the eye. I cried, and as we all know, "There's no crying in baseball." So much for that sport.

During my school years, my father repaired engines as an Air Force jet mechanic. He could make or fix anything. Over the years, he expanded our house with a dining room, a utility room, and an entertainment room. He also extended the master bedroom. He was always working on something around the house.

My father taught me how to use hand tools early on and didn't hesitate in allowing me to use power tools when I got older. This gave me the opportunity to make things myself, which I found incredibly fulfilling. Eventually, my mechanical aptitude would allow me to become a machinist's mate in the Navy, where I worked in the engine room on submarines. Even today, building something from scratch takes me into a world of serenity. I am thankful to have passed on this love of building to my two sons, and I have no doubt they will in turn pass it on to their own sons. It's a legacy that I am immensely proud of.

During my school years, my parents enjoyed taking our family on camping trips in various parts of Arizona. We visited many places in the Grand Canyon State, but Fort Tuthill, just south of Flagstaff, became our favorite campsite. As a kid, camping gave me a chance to explore, fueling my curiosity. The boy in me could never quite get enough of forests, lakes, and rivers. Mother Nature became my friend and still is today.

We also made trips to California, going to the beach, Sea World, Knots Berry Farm and, back then, a new place called Disneyland. My father bought a Regular 8 movie camera and took movies of the places that we went. Those movies still exist today. My parents loved taking us out and watching us have fun. They nurtured both the boy and the girl in me, though they didn't know that at the time.

Germany – 1961 to 1964

People in the military rarely stay in one place for very long. My father had been stationed at Luke Air Force Base, Arizona, for seven years, when the Air Force decided he had been there long enough and he needed to be sent elsewhere. In 1960, around the time of the birth of my brother, Dennis, my father received orders to go to Bitburg Air Force Base in Germany. They wanted to station him there for three and a half years and they would allow him to take his family with him. Little did I know how important this part of my life would become, for my development both as a boy and as a girl.

Just a few days into 1961, we started a cross-country car trip through the southernmost U.S. states, before eventually driving along the East Coast. This is because our family could only get to Germany from New York City. I had a great time following our progress on maps and seeing a part of the country I had no recollection of seeing before. The road-trip appealed to the explorer in me. Our final destination would be Pawtucket, Rhode Island, where my mother's parents and family lived. Before arriving there, we spent a short time in Newport News, Virginia, to visit my father's family.

About a week later, we arrived at my Italian grandparents' home, the very house my mother was born and grew up in. We lived there for about five months, while my father flew to Germany to get things ready for our arrival. I enjoyed my grandparents' home and the feeling of belonging that it gave me. My grandparents made me feel welcome and I loved being around them. I became immersed in my Italian heritage and I loved it.

I had a lot of cousins in Rhode Island. Some lived in the same house as my grandparents. My aunt and uncle, who lived next door, had three girls, one my age and two older than me. For the first time in my life I had close female relatives I could use as role models. At the age of ten, I had no idea why I needed them as role models, but nevertheless that's exactly what they became. Had I been able to spend more time with them, my inner girl may have come out sooner than it otherwise did.

Then, after five months in Rhode Island, we flew as a family to Frankfurt, Germany, on board a commercial propeller airplane. The flight took seventeen hours. Goodness knows how my mother survived the flight with four children in her care, one of them just seven months old.

Erdorf, Germany

When we arrived in Germany, we moved into a house my father had found for us. We would live there temporarily until we could move into base housing. The Air Force called living off-base in Germany "living on the economy", because you were surrounded by and intermingled with real Germans, rather than being on base and taken care of by the military.

Our house sat in a picturesque little town called Erdorf, located 6.9 km north of Bitburg, the location of my father's Air Force base. At ten years old, I loved to explore. I couldn't have asked for a more perfect place to live. Tucked neatly in a valley of beautiful hills, with the Kyll River running through it, Erdorf had an air of mystery about it. We arrived in the summertime and I couldn't wait to see what Erdorf had to offer.

A century-old mill sat alongside the Kyll River, its waterwheel slowly turning in the river's gentle flow. Nearby, a train station, built in 1871 of red sandstone in the Gothic Revival style, stood along the Eifel Railway tracks. In the weeks that followed, my sister and I would wait at the train station for a bus to take us to school on base.

Exploring the area around Erdorf became one of my daily endeavors. A cherry tree grew close to our house and, in addition to sampling its fruits, I stole strawberries from a neighbor's garden.

During my walks in the forests and fields around Erdorf, I discovered many rusting items hidden in the grass. I found an old flat iron that would have been heated on a stove and used to press clothes. I also found both a spent military shell and a live shell in one of the nearby fields. My father took the live shell to the base, where I presume he disposed of it safely. I also found a WWI bayonet in an open field. An expert told me it came from WWI and not WWII based on its design. In the forest just outside of the town's limits, I discovered a couple of dark and dank war bunkers.

When winter came, we had a great time sliding down hills in our sleds, building snow people and having snowball fights. We also witnessed how the Germans celebrate Christmas and learned a couple of local Christmas carols. Winter had a downside however. I quickly realized that I hated cold weather, and still do. Walking down the hill to the train station, to go to school, felt bearable, but walking back up again later in the day sucked.

My family established several long-lasting friendships when we lived in Erdorf and I remember my time there fondly. When I look at current pictures of the small town on the Internet, it doesn't appear to have changed much over the years, which pleases me.

Bitburg Air Force Base

When the time came for us to move into base housing, I discovered that the change brought with it a whole new set of adventures. Also, as I grew older and navigated puberty, I began to notice girls more and more.

I remember all of a sudden being aware, almost overnight, that some girls had bumps on their chests, although a few of my friends warned me that some girls enhanced their attributes with tissue paper. Slowly, the idea of kissing a girl turned into an obsession for me. Even so, while in Germany, the closest I got was holding hands with a girl and slow dancing with some others at a school dance.

I played Little League at the fields near our building and it became a great place to hang out, even when our team didn't play. I remember a slightly older kid finding reasons to bully me. It had to do with my last name, which no one could ever pronounce correctly.

His bullying went on for weeks, until one day I decided I'd had enough. I made a fist and swung my arm around and at him, cold-cocking him in his face. He never bothered me again. Around then, I started saying to myself that my name would one day mean something. I didn't realize it wouldn't be the name I received at birth.

In my spare time, I explored the base, though it didn't have nearly as much appeal as the countryside that surrounded Erdorf. During our time there, my father drove us to a number of nearby places. We lived less than 100 kilometers from Luxemburg, so we would cross the border for visits. We did the same with Belgium, usually on a Sunday afternoon. I remember eating wonderful French fries in Brussels, and later I discovered that the Belgians typically fry them in animal fat.

We visited relatives stationed in France, but we never made it to

Paris. We also spent a week in the Netherlands seeing the windmills, tulip fields and the city of Amsterdam. I really enjoyed exploring Madurodam, a 1:25 scale town that had model replicas of famous Dutch landmarks, historical cities and large developments. It became the first time I'd seen anything like that, and it probably inspired me to build so many model replicas later in my life.

As well as visiting several German cities during the time we lived there, we spent two weeks driving through Switzerland and Italy, all the way down to Rome, before returning home via Austria. We camped at a campsite in Verona, the city in which Shakespeare set *Romeo and Juliet*. We also visited Pisa, climbing the windy, worn, white marble steps to the top of the Leaning Tower. There, I stood on the same spot where, 375 years earlier, Galileo had allegedly dropped two iron spheres of different weights to show that mass had nothing to do with the speed of descent.

In Rome, we threw coins in the Trevi Fountain, toured the Coliseum, and visited the Vatican. My mother, a deeply religious Catholic woman, wouldn't have countenanced leaving Rome without seeing St. Peter's Basilica.

Mom has a story she always loves to tell about our visit to the Vatican. She loves to remind me that, just before we entered St. Peter's, I got sick. She tells me that was God giving me a sign to be a good boy. Once inside the Basilica, the history of it overwhelmed and amazed me. Pictures cannot do the interior justice, such is its rich, incredibly ornate and atmospheric decoration. After a couple of days in Rome, we headed north to Venice, before returning home.

I enjoyed my time in Germany greatly. I think in total I must have visited about nine different countries, and numerous ancient cities and sites in each. I also developed as a child while there. I learned to build plastic models, received my first microscope and telescope, and started to enjoy science and music.

It wasn't all sunshine and roses, however. My grandmother passed away shortly after we arrived, which necessitated my mother flying back alone to attend the funeral. I also remember my father being called onto base when the East Germans began building the Berlin Wall and, on the evening of November 22, 1963, remember hearing on the radio that President Kennedy had been shot. We celebrated my brother's third birthday that day, which is one of the reasons I remember it so vividly.

4 – THE GIRL IN THE SHADOWS

While I enjoyed my time in Germany, doing all the things boys are meant to enjoy, secretly lurking in the shadows of my developing mind sat the girl I should have been. She waited patiently for the right moment to make herself known. With only a brief appearance at age five, when I prayed to God to make me a girl, she laid dormant for years. Only after puberty did she once again begin to stir.

At the age of 12, my parents started trusting me to watch my brother and sisters, while they went out with friends. They loved to go out square dancing and, one evening, while my siblings slept in their beds, I found myself aware of the Girl in the Shadows. At her urging, I went into my parents' bedroom and looked through my mother's dresser drawers. I found several of my mother's cotton panties and bras, neatly stacked in piles. The Girl in the Shadows wanted to try them on. I wanted to try them on. When I did, they felt exciting to wear and somehow perfect.

Over the next few years, this became a ritual. Whenever I found myself alone at home, and nothing else occupied my time, I would head for my mother's dresser. The Girl in the Shadows slowly inched her way into the light and into my conscious mind. Sure, a number of things happened that shoved her aside from time to time, but she always returned. She never went away and slowly she became part of my life.

Wichita, Kansas

After my father finished his tour of duty in Germany, the Air Force sent him to finish out his career at McConnell Air Force Base in Wichita, Kansas. I didn't care too much for the endless flatness of Kansas, having lived in Arizona and Germany all my life. I ached to see even a small bump on the horizon to indicate a mountain. Any mountain. The land where Dorothy lived would be my home for the next two years. But, "No place like home," would never be a place I could ever consider being my home.

Several things stood out about Kansas that I remember vividly. Because of its flatness, I could ride my bicycle anywhere without much problem. However, the constant wind made it difficult at times. I put miles on my bike visiting friends and going places. We had to hide from tornados a few times. I got more into science and took my first drafting class, discovering that I had a natural talent for it.

My hormones continued to ravage my body. I would spend hours looking at the girls at school. I studied them more and more, with my study slowly evolving into lust. Unfortunately, I never went on a date or even kissed one the whole time we lived in Kansas. I don't think they found me attractive. I may have been shy, but what thirteen- or fourteen-year-old boy isn't shy?

The Girl in the Shadows came out now and then, but not as often as she had in Germany, because I simply didn't spend much time home alone.

In the summer of 1966, my father retired from the Air Force and we moved back to Phoenix to live in our old house. For the five and a half years we had been away, my parents had rented the house out. By the time we came back it needed a lot of repairs.

Phoenix, Arizona – High School Years

Boy, did I really luck out. When we moved to Kansas, I attended eighth and ninth grades. In that state, middle schools consisted of seventh, eighth and ninth grades, so when I arrived I didn't attend the lowest grade, the grade that gets picked on all the time. High schools in Kansas consisted of tenth, eleventh and twelfth grades.

When I came back to Arizona however, I started high school as a sophomore in a school that consisted of four grades. So, once more I managed to avoid being in the lowest grade and thus avoided the hazing that freshmen always get. This helped to shield the Girl in the Shadows from some potentially vicious attacks. We all know how brutal kids can be. I didn't appear effeminate, but kids saw me as a puny boy and those are always targets for the bigger kids.

Not too long after starting my sophomore year at Maryvale High School, I joined the astronomy club where I met a freshman by the name of Dann Frank. He and I had a similar interest in music and we became best friends, something I sadly regret to this day. In those early years however, we had a great time together.

On an astronomy club field trip to Lowell Observatory, Dann and I got in trouble when the group stopped on the way back to visit Oak Creek. Dann and I wandered away from the group and began hopping rocks in the creek. Everything seemed fine until Dann threw his shoes onto a nearby rock, thinking he would easily be able to retrieve them. The frigid water made that nearly impossible however. Having already lost track of time, this made us even later, and by the time we returned to the bus our teacher became very upset with us. As punishment, he kicked us both out of the astronomy club.

Dann and I remained friends however, and we became pretty much inseparable. Together we rode our bikes all over Phoenix, saw movies and worked on a number of joint projects.

Maryvale High's sophomore biology teacher had a side business selling biological supplies, including animals for dissection. One summer, he gave Dann and me the job of catching crayfish in the local canals. To help us, he gave us a trash bucket, rubber gloves and a permit from the city that allowed us to work in the canals.

With our music playing, we would climb down into the canal and reach under the vegetation that grew along the water's edge to find the many holes where the crayfish lived. We wore our rubber gloves loosely so the crayfish would bite onto our gloves rather than our fingers. Once we caught one, we'd throw it on the adjoining road. Sometimes, we would come out with two or three attached to our gloves. We received three cents apiece for every crayfish we caught. One day, we pulled out 760 of those little snappers, for a total of $22.80. Not bad for a couple of young teenagers back in 1967.

Another time, we took a bus 20 miles across town to see *2001: A Space Odyssey* on the massive screen at the Kachina Theater, located in Scottsdale.

Dann and I both liked science and each of us loved watching the television broadcasts of NASA launching astronauts into space. The power of the rockets impressed us no end and inspired me to want to launch some rockets of my own. After some initial research, I discovered that just a short bike ride away was a company called Centuri that sold model rockets. So, Dann and I gathered up some money and rode to Centuri to see what they had.

Back then, two companies sold kits to build model rockets: Centuri, in Arizona, and Estes, in Colorado. Estes still exists today, having bought out Centuri, providing safe and educational model rockets for kids of all ages. We made our purchase and on March 27, 1967, Dann and I launched our first model rocket, a Centuri Javelin. The reason I know the exact date is because I kept a record of every launch we did, which I still do today.

Launching model rockets would become a hobby that I took into adulthood and even passed on to my two sons. On two different Fourth of July holidays, I even started a small brush fire in the field next to my house. The launch of that very first rocket in 1967, though, set in motion a series of events that would eventually lead me into the Navy and on to submarines.

My love for building and launching model rockets also led me to create the model rocket club at Maryvale High School in my senior year. This became the first time I ever founded and ran an organization. I didn't have any amazing organizational or people skills, but at a high school club my deficiencies went unnoticed. Anyway, kids joined the club so they could build and launch model rockets, not because they had some desire to change the world.

The model rocket club didn't help me develop leadership skills, but through it I did meet several people who became life-long friends. Well, they stayed life-long friends until I started my transition. These people influenced me and the direction my life would take. One person, Winfield, had a father who had spent time on board aircraft carriers during World War II, and who relayed exciting tales of his adventures. The Navy sounded to me like a branch of the military that provided a lot of skills that could be useful once a person got out. He got me thinking.

One of the other hobbies my friends and I got into was playing pinball. On a trip to Portales, New Mexico, for our first model rocket meet, Dann, Winfield and I discovered a pinball machine in the rec center of Eastern New Mexico University. The album *Tommy*, by *The*

Who, had just come out and we listened to it on our trip there. The machine drew us to it and we couldn't resist. Pinball, then later arcade video games, became a big part of our lives. Pinball ended up becoming all-consuming for Dann because later in his life he even sold and repaired them.

High school itself didn't provide me with any notions about what I wanted to do with my life. Some of my friends knew what they wanted to do, but I didn't. Dann's own life began to take a nasty turn. This started when he found himself in trouble with the law for stealing car radios. So, after high school I started taking classes at a local junior college, but nothing really inspired me or provided me with the vocation I felt I needed.

Then in 1970, with the Vietnam War in full swing, the government held its second draft lottery and my number came up 79.

"Oh, shit. My draft number is low. What am I going to do?"

Unexpectedly, the summer of 1970 found me staring down the barrel of the draft and at the prospect of being called up relatively soon. Spending time in the jungles of Vietnam didn't inspire a sense of the kind of adventure I craved. Quite the opposite. I enjoyed camping in the woods and mountains of Northern Arizona, but my survival skills didn't include dodging bullets and watching out for booby traps. I needed a plan.

The grades from my first year of junior college sucked and likely meant I couldn't get out of the draft with a college deferment. Heading to Canada didn't appeal to me, because I've never liked snow and didn't own a car that I could drive there in. Besides, I grew up in a family with a strong military background, so draft-dodging didn't cross my mind. My grandfather, my father, all my uncles and one aunt, had spent time in the military and none of them had lost their lives in a war. Nevertheless, I didn't want to risk becoming the first family member to die in combat. I decided I needed to be proactive, and something I had thought about earlier came to mind. I decided to join the U.S. Navy.

5 – "HEY, SAILOR. NEW IN TOWN?"

When I approached a Navy recruiter in late July 1970, I hoped to learn a skill that would serve me well once I left the Navy. Earlier, I had read that NASA would be experimenting with nuclear-powered spacecraft, so I figured that a career in nuclear power and propulsion might mean I could work for them once I got out. However, NASA eventually dropped the program, and fate had different plans for me.

I signed up to go through the Naval Nuclear Power Program and to eventually serve on submarines. Visions of *Seaview* and *20,000 Leagues Under the Sea* danced in my head. I couldn't wait to look out of that big window at the front of the sub. Boy, would I be in for a shock about the reality of submarine life.

In spite of being a wimp as a kid, military training got me into the best shape I have ever been in. During Boot Camp I received my draft notice. The Chief told me to toss it in the trash.

After Boot Camp, I had to go to my Machinist's Mate 'A' School in Great Lakes, Illinois, in the dead of one of the coldest winters they had experienced in a long time. I don't remember a lot from then, except seeing the group *Chicago* in Chicago, and visiting bars in Milwaukee. I also remember reading *The Hobbit* and *Lord of the Rings* for the first time. I have never since been as enveloped in a series as with those books.

On the other side of Lake Michigan lived a man in Benton Harbor, not too much older than me, who served with my father in Germany. He even traveled with my family on our two-week tour to Italy. During my stay, I took a bus to Benton Harbor to visit him and spend some time with some girls he knew, who were around my age.

The drinking age in Illinois at the time was 21, compared to 18 in Wisconsin. As such, many sailors would take the train to Milwaukee when we could, stay at the YMCA, and at night go drinking in the bars. A new obsession entered my life, one that would keep me from discovering my gender-identity issues for a few years longer. I obsessed over losing my virginity. Yet, try as I may, I never connected with the right woman during my entire time stationed at Great Lakes.

My next stop would be Vallejo, California, to begin training in the Navy's Nuclear Power Program. This first part of the program consisted of school classes, where they taught us condensed courses in advanced chemistry, physics, heat transfer, electronics, mechanics, nuclear reactors and math. I did fine in most of the courses, but in others I struggled more than I ever have in my life.

Because of my inability to make the grade, some of the instructors sent me to mandatory night-study, where I had to work late into the evening. Because of all the studying, I didn't eat well during those days and as a result my health began to fail. My immune system weakened and I caught mononucleosis. This debilitating disease sent me to the hospital for two weeks, and then back home to Arizona for a month of rest and relaxation. In the beginning of my time at home, I felt so weak that I would sleep for 12 to 14 hours at a time.

Believe it or not, catching mono became one of the best things that could have happened to me at the time. It also turned out to be one of the major turning points in my life, much like launching my first model rocket. Once I had recovered, I returned to the base at Vallejo, bought a 1966 Ford van, and had to start over with the next class of sailors going through the Nuclear Power Training School. I worked in the Administration Office until the new class started and, second time around, I did much better in the courses than I had previously.

Had I not gotten sick, I would have probably failed Nuclear Power School and then been sent to a surface ship as a regular Machinist's Mate. The disease gave me a second chance at the school, setting my path in the direction of finally getting stationed on a submarine. I credit a lot of my independent thinking to my service on submarines, but I still had a way to go before I would see the inside of one. I also believe The Girl in the Shadows benefited from my time as a submariner.

Before I entered the next phase of my training, I had a chance to take some leave in Phoenix. I jumped at the chance when I found out that my friend, Dann, would soon be released from lock-up. To surprise him, I waited at the door of the jail and stood there when he walked out.

Subsequently, he and I spent some time together and he even rode up to Idaho Falls with me to my next duty station. Our interaction must have made him rethink his life, because he decided to sign up for the Navy when he got back to Phoenix. He eventually became an ejection-seat mechanic on the new F-14 Tomcat. Later, he witnessed history while serving on the USS Enterprise during the evacuation of Saigon at the end of the Vietnam War.

The Navy sent me to Idaho Falls to start my Prototype Training. I know what you're thinking: what is the Navy doing in a landlocked state like Idaho? Well, in the isolated mountains of Idaho, the Navy had mock-up engine rooms from two classes of submarines and a surface ship. This allowed them to train sailors in the actual operation of equipment associated with nuclear reactors in a way that best simulated at-sea conditions.

I met several new and interesting people in Idaho Falls. One 18-year-old woman, Pat, invaded my life and went on to cause me nothing but headaches. Even today, thinking about her still makes me shiver. For a short time, I rented a room in a boarding house where several other Navy people also lived. Pat lived there with her boyfriend, another sailor going through Prototype School.

Pat loved having sex but had one big requirement. A man would have to have nine inches or more before she would have sex with him. Apparently, the man she lived with met her requirements, but that didn't stop her from fooling around with other men while he worked.

In Idaho, we worked rotating shifts, which had a habit of screwing with our sleep patterns. However, with this rotation we would get four days off every four weeks. That gave me a lot of time to ride my new dirt bike, visit places like Yellowstone National Park and, of course, chase women. When I moved into the boarding house, I quickly found out that Pat's boyfriend and I had different shifts. It meant that when Pat stayed home alone, I got the chance to talk with her at length about a number of things and we got to know each other well.

Early in our friendship, the conversation drifted toward the subject of sex. It became apparent that both Pat and I obsessed about it, but for different reasons. Pat was always looking for her next conquest. I didn't qualify, right off the bat, because she didn't want to be my first, me being a virgin still. Her length requirement would have disqualified me had she known Mother Nature had short-changed me.

Prototype School didn't leave me with many memories, but Idaho Falls did. I met some wonderful people, had a V8 engine put in my van, and began a new hobby of off-road motorcycle riding. The freedom of riding the hills and lava fields of Eastern Idaho gave me a tremendous, liberating feeling, one that I sorely miss in my old age. I know that I can purchase an off-road motorcycle and get back into the pursuit as a woman, but the cost is prohibitive for me these days. Plus, my balance isn't what it once was and probably means I can no longer ride safely. But, the memories of those times still make me smile today.

So, in August of 1972, I left Idaho Falls without having experienced the beauty of making love with another woman. Yes, you read that right. Another *woman*. Having lived as my true self now for over 21 years, I have now had the chance to re-evaluate my interactions with women as a young man. Looking back, I know that as a man I could dance, openly flirt, hold hands and even kiss women in public. Physically, I could have had sex with a woman, the same as any other man. Emotionally however, I felt different from other biological men. I now understand why, even though at that time I had no idea.

The Navy had one more school for me to attend before they sent me to the fleet. For eight weeks, I attended Submarine School in Groton, Connecticut. This meant I would get the chance to travel across the U.S. for the first time on my own, which I did in my 1966 Ford van, with my Husqvarna motorcycle stowed in the back. Being stationed in Groton gave me the chance to visit my relatives in Rhode Island and Boston.

One of the most interesting parts of Sub School happened when they had us take on the Water Tower. (Insert dramatic music here.) The school had a massive tower that stood over 50 feet tall and had a tank of water inside. At the bottom, they had built a submarine escape trunk where trainees would rise to the surface. Sailors had to pass the Water Tower test before they could be stationed on submarines.

The day they took us to the Water Tower, they gave us a device that looked a lot like a Mae West life jacket with a hood. Five of us crammed into the escape trunk and the instructor began the pressurization. Before he reached equalization pressure, the pain in my head became too much to bear. I had a cold, which made it impossible for me to equalize, so the instructor aborted the test to let me out. Blood dripped from my nose. I thought I would wash out, but the instructors decided to give me a second chance a few days later.

One week later, I once again faced the Water Tower, but this time everything went well. I placed the hood over my head, stepped into the water from the escape trunk and swam to the top hollering "Ho, ho, ho" all the way up. The design of the hood allowed the expanding air in the vest to blow into the hood so the wearer could breathe. To ensure that the person rising from the trunk released depressurizing air from their lungs, they had to say "Ho, ho, ho." If anyone didn't do so, divers stationed at various levels would stop the person and make them release air from their lungs. Holding it in could cause a person's lungs to burst. That didn't sound like fun.

With the Water Tower test completed, I had passed Submarine School. Two weeks later, a dry and happy Robert headed back to Arizona for some well-deserved leave, in preparation for the next chapter in my life. I would soon become a submarine sailor.

6 – "IT'S A BIG, BLACK TUBE"

The first two years of my Navy career did little to develop my skills as a future trans activist, but did hamper my progress towards self-awareness of my gender difference. I did however get to travel, meet interesting people and learn discipline in the Navy.

The women I encountered during these years did nothing to bolster my manhood, but that manhood really existed in a world of smoke and mirrors. I clung to it only because I didn't know of any alternative. 1972 didn't go down in history as being a banner year for information pertaining to the transgender experience.

Much of this and the next few chapters appear in my book *Blue and Gold*. That book is a fictionalized version of my time on the *USS Francis Scott Key* (SSBN 657), along with stories of other people and other submarines. This autobiography gives my real-life experiences.

I left Phoenix, bouncing around in the driver's seat of my van and gyrating to the beat of my favorite rock music on the stereo. While the rest of the country deeply immersed itself in the 1972 presidential election – being held the day I started my road trip – I made my way to Bremerton, Washington and my ultimate destination, the submarine *Francis Scott Key*.

Driving west on I-10, I decided to pull off for gas and a break in Indio, California. Little did I know, but my van decided to take a break of its own. When I finished my rest stop, I placed the transmission in first gear to drive away. Instead of moving, I heard a loud 'clunk' sound under the van. The engine instantly died and refused to start again. A sick feeling formed in my stomach.

One of the gas station's mechanics heard the loud noise and ran out to investigate the problem. "Don't try to start it," he ordered. The man then slid underneath to look around and, after 30 seconds, stood back up. "Your motor mount broke clean off," he announced calmly. He smiled, probably knowing that my problem would make him extra money.

"What? You've got to be kidding me! I just had this new engine installed a month ago in Idaho Falls! What the hell happened?"

"It broke." The mechanic almost sounded sadistic. "Take a look for yourself."

After jumping out, I crawled under the van to confirm the mechanic's diagnosis. The left motor mount appeared to have sheared off. A horrible feeling in my gut grew. "Do you think you can repair it for me?" I asked, after crawling out from under the van.

"The welder won't be here until the morning, so we can't get started on it until then."

"How much will it cost?"

"You're looking at about one-hundred and fifty dollars." The mechanic smiled again.

"I guess I'll sleep in the back of the van tonight."

I spent a long, cold night in the back of my broken-down van, sleeping next to my dirt bike. Luckily, I had a sleeping bag and several blankets.

The next morning, the welder attached another motor mount to the van's engine, but unfortunately the mechanic who installed the new engine in Idaho Falls had mounted it crooked into the housing. This meant the welder could only fix the motor mount. He couldn't correct the crooked engine. Three hours and $150 later, I continued on my journey, singing along to my favorite tunes once again. Meanwhile, the evil engine waited, hatching a new and more sinister problem for me down the road.

That new problem began shortly after I reached Sacramento. A strange pulsing sound started vibrating the engine housing between the seats. As I drove on, the reverberations became louder and louder until it drowned out the music. Apparently, the motor had blown a head gasket, but I couldn't afford the time or the money to stop and have it repaired. So, an unbearable noise became my constant companion for the next 600 miles.

At first, the exhaust leak hadn't affected the engine power, so I opened up the throttle on the lonely Northern California roads to try and gain back the time I lost in Indio. The flawless plan would have worked in most states, but in this case the ever-vigilant California Highway Patrol intervened. The speeding ticket I received became just another unfortunate event that slowed me down on my way to Bremerton.

My orders said for me to check into the ship's office in less than 24 hours or they would consider me UA – an unauthorized absence. Since my daddy didn't head the CIA or serve as a Texas Congressman, I couldn't get away with that. After a long drive, I pulled into the next rest stop, where I once again spent a cold night in the back of the van.

The next day, the engine noise became impossible to stand. Additionally, so much of the exhaust now escaped through the head gasket that the power level of the engine dropped below what I needed to climb some hills. I began making horrible time, reaching the Bremerton city limits just after midnight. On the last downhill, I managed to pick up some speed, only to get caught once again on police radar.

When the policeman arrived at the van window, I quickly blurted out, "Officer, I know I was speeding and I'm really sorry, but I'm late checking into my new duty station at the shipyard. Here are my papers." I handed the policeman a copy of my orders, which he looked over quickly before handing them back.

"All right, but I want you to be more careful while you're here in town," he demanded. "I'm going to let you off with just a warning. The main gate to the shipyard is still a couple miles down the road. Please drive a little slower, will you?"

"Yes sir, I will."

Just after one o'clock in the morning, I handed the Petty Officer-In-Charge my orders.

"A little late, aren't you?"

"I had car problems like you wouldn't believe." Damn, I felt tired.

"Don't worry about it. It's no big deal. The barracks is that big building near the gate. Report to the barge next to the sub's dry dock first thing in the morning."

"Where's the dry dock?"

"Go out this door and walk between the two buildings across

the street. The *Key* is in the dry dock on your left. You'll see."

Walking across the street and between the buildings, I saw the pier and beyond that, the icy waters of Puget Sound. To my left, in the water next to the pier, I saw a huge concrete structure with hundreds of lights shining all around. People moved about inside, some carrying equipment and tools, as they crossed a walkway to a large black object in the middle. When I stepped close enough to see the interior of the dry dock, I could distinguish my new duty station – the *Francis Scott Key* – among the myriad of shipyard equipment.

So many hoses and cables, and so much scaffolding, surrounded the ship that very little of it appeared visible. The shipyard had cut huge holes into the hull, presumably to install large pieces of equipment inside. Attached to the back, I saw the enormous, seven-bladed, brass-alloy screw that would eventually propel the *Key* through the water. The recently polished screw, with its huge blades, shone brightly under the powerful dry dock lights.

People worked all around the *Key*, doing the jobs needed to complete all necessary repairs on time. Tremendous wooden blocks supported the ship, keeping the hull off the bottom of the dry dock. Even being one of the largest subs in the world at the time, the Key looked lost and tiny in a dry dock built to hold World War II aircraft carriers.

Seeing all the holes in the hull, I wondered if the *Key* would ever float again. "The welders better do their job carefully when it comes time for them to seal those openings," I thought. After staring at my new duty station for half an hour, I turned and made my way to the barracks for some much-deserved sleep.

The next day, I reported for orientation at the Barge, a pre-WWII, box-like vessel that served as office and on-duty bunking for the two crews of the *Francis Scott Key*. The crewmembers joked that the barge would never move again because of all the coffee grounds that anchored it to the pier.

The *Key* had the distinction of being one of the Navy's top-of-the-line, 1970s high-tech, Fleet Ballistic Missile (FBM) submarines, also called Boomers. The term Boomer comes from the tremendous explosive power carried by FBM submarines, with their 16 multi-warhead missiles. When fully loaded and ready for sea, she carried more destructive power than all the explosives released in World War II combined. From the North Atlantic, the warheads could cover all of the Soviet Bloc countries and half of the Soviet Union itself. From the North Pacific they could hit North Korea, all of China and the rest of the Soviet Union.

The next morning, for the first time in my life, I walked aboard a nuclear-powered submarine. The inside didn't look like anything I could have ever imagined and, with the yard work going on, it didn't look like it would when repaired and underway. In the Engineering Spaces, the place where I would soon stand my duty stations, it looked like a jumbled mess of wires, pipes, machinery, valves, pumps, steam turbines, huge gears, electrical panels and a maze of electronics. My job would be to learn what everything did, where to isolate it, the operating parameters of each unit, and how to fix most of it.

In the early days, I counted myself lucky if I could get from one place on board the sub to another without getting lost. How can someone get lost in a big, black steel tube? Leave it to me to figure out how. They gave me just a few duties in the beginning, including standing fire watch and guarding various access locations. Fire watch meant standing near a welder with a fire extinguisher. It was as boring as it sounds. Occasionally, they made me fix something the yard had no responsibility over. At least during those times, I felt useful.

Not too long after arriving, I bought all the parts I needed and, in one day, I sat in my vehicle in the cold Washington winter and tore apart the top of my van's engine. I enjoyed repairing the V8 and getting it running smoothly again. However, in spite of the overhaul, evil still lurked in the heart of my van.

During early December, the Engineer decided that reactor start-up would begin right after the first of the year. That meant preparations for the testing had to begin just before Christmas. The Engineering personnel – Nucs, for being nuclear-trained – could only go home on either Christmas or New Year's Day, while those people who worked forward of Engineering – affectionately called Forward Pukes – made plans to go home for both holidays. They needed enough Nucs to stay behind and perform the pre-critical testing; testing that could have waited two more weeks.

During those weeks, I got my first little taste of discrimination, but the Navy would never have called it that. Over the course of my service on submarines, there had been many times when the Forward

Pukes took liberty, while the Nucs stayed behind to keep the lights on.

To make things worse, I picked to go home for the New Year's holiday instead of Christmas. However, as soon as those who took Christmas off came back, the Engineer decided that we would do a reactor start-up two weeks early, canceling my trip home.

Over the next two weeks, we did an intense and slow start-up of the nuclear reactor, took it critical and tested our entire steam systems for integrity. During January and February, the Nucs spent long hours with little sleep, testing everything in the Engineering Spaces that we could. I had several 24-, 36-, and even 48-hour shifts during this time. If it didn't work, we would either fix it, or have the yard replace it.

At the time, the lack of sleep and intense demands on my time and energies made me have second thoughts about having picked submarines as my career. My experience back then saw the Engineer pushing us to the limit to get done early, just to impress the Big Boys in the Pentagon. The way I saw it, he needed to be sure that when his name came up for promotion, his hard-ass job of getting the sub out of the shipyards early would make him look good.

With the experience I have today, I now look back and see the bigger picture. I now understand why the Engineer did what he did. Saving taxpayers' money, along with national security issues, appeared to motivate the Commanding Officer and the Engineer to start testing early. Today, I would have done the same thing in the Engineer's position, had our roles been reversed.

I learned a lot from that period in the shipyards, but it took time and wisdom to realize what I had learned. My journey toward becoming a trans activist had finally begun and I didn't even know it. However, my journey toward living my true life as Monica still needed more time to develop.

7 – LUCK BE A LADY TONIGHT

When the intense reactor testing came to an end, so did the 48-hour shifts, which made my life a little easier. The test went so well that afterwards the Nucs even had an unheard-of two-days off in a row. Wow, I didn't know what to do with myself having that much time off.

In late February 1973, I had one of those rare consecutive two-days off, on a weekend no less. Being a curious young lad, I ventured into what I heard of as a "good bar to visit." Very quickly, I discovered that my intel on this bar had been flawed. I couldn't find the MME (Music of Mass Entertainment) that my sources had said existed there. Instead, I found a funky country band that would be considered poor even in a small town. And Bremerton was a very small town.

I'd sought out the bar because a shipmate had suggested it to me. Only a few people sat listening to the lousy band, but the bar at least had a pinball machine. It called out to me. "Robert! Get yer ass over here and put money in me!" Okay, okay!

Being a weak-minded person at the time, I reached into my pocket and pulled out a dime. Yes, a dime. Remember? 1973? The machine lit up, but before I could shoot my first ball onto the playing field, a lone woman sitting at a table nearby caught my eye. This lonely-looking woman didn't seem to have a companion with her. Even with that intuitive observation, I decided to still play the machine rather than going over to speak with her. It didn't last long. The machine easily kicked my ass. I blamed it on poor upkeep and not operator error.

Over the years, I've had to overcome my fear of meeting new people. Back then, I didn't have the social skills needed to walk over and say "Hello" to the lone woman in a bar, much less speak to a Senator or a Governor as I one day would. Such skills can't be learned in an instant, but one must overcome such innate fear if a person plans on becoming a trans activist. Or even if one simply plans on picking up women or men in a bar.

Since the pinball machine had beaten me, I decided to try my luck with the woman. "Hello," I said. I felt afraid. "Would you like to dance?"

"Not really. You can join me though, if you like."

"O... okay. My name is Bob."

"Hello. I'm Midge."

"What do you think of this band?"

"They're lousy. I know of another place that has better music. Would you take me there?"

I felt a bit stunned. "I guess. Show me the way."

After 15 minutes of driving, we arrived at another place that had a full parking lot and plenty more people. The music sounded much better. We managed to find a table.

"So, I see you like good music," I remarked.

"Oh, yes!"

The loud music made it difficult to hear her. "Is there anything else you like to do?"

"I like to..."

"You like to read?"

"Yeah, that's it."

"So do I. Mostly science fiction."

We danced for a little while, before she asked, "Can you take me home?"

I heard that. "Sure."

"It's not far from here."

We drove to Midge's place. The only sound we heard the entire time came from the radio and the van's newly repaired engine. I had no idea what to expect.

Midge lived in an old house on the side of a hill, with no streetlights. As soon as I turned off the headlights, the only illumination came from the radio dial light. From past experience I knew the evening would end there. One kiss and she would head inside. "I had a wonderful time," I remarked.

"Would you like to come in?"

My jaw dropped. Oh, my god. Is this 'it'? "Ah... yes. I do."

The inside of Midge's house looked like the typical hippy abode. Even though the peak of the hippy era happened five years earlier and the lifestyle had become less in-vogue, many in 1973 still clung to the trappings of that time, especially in the Northwest.

We sat on the couch. She kissed me then said, "Remember in the club when you asked me what else I liked besides music?"

"Yes."

"And, you thought I said, 'Read'?"

"I remember."

"What I really said was, 'I like to fuck'."

"Oh..."

"Let's go to bed."

At that moment on the radio, I heard the Beach Boys singing, "Sail on, sail on, sailor." I thought to myself, "Forget it! This sailor ain't sailing nowhere!"

I won't go into the details, but when we had finished, she asked, "It's been several months for me. What about you?"

"Well," I paused. "Would you believe twenty-two years?"

"What? I'm your first? I love it." Midge gave me a big hug and a kiss, then we started up again.

That evening taught me a few things about women, especially how they interact with men during sex. Over time, I realized that, even though I had sexual intercourse like a man, how I related to the women I encountered seemed more like another woman would. Early on, I couldn't see that, but from the vantage point of 40-plus years later, all the signs were there.

Some people reading this may not fully understand that looking back at this shows signs of my future self. This and later encounters with women went a long way to helping me understand my sexual orientation of only being attracted to women. It did little to help me with my gender identity however.

Midge and I saw each other a few more times. One of the most amazing nights I had in the Sounds area happened when I took her to Seattle, by ferry, to see Emerson, Lake and Palmer, one of my favorite groups. They sounded fantastic. On the way back, Midge and

I made love in the back of my van as we rode the ferry back to Bremerton.

Trans people are good with trigonometry, so I will now go off on a tangent. My love for music started forming before I attended high school and has only grown since then. It has allowed me to see the beauty of the world through the lyrics and melodies of many great artists. In junior high, I danced to Beatles songs, I read *Lord of the Rings* on a submarine with Led Zeppelin playing in the background, fell asleep to Gordon Lightfoot ballads and cried to Eric Clapton's *My Father's Eyes*.

Music has always been the thread that kept the many parts of my life connected. I can't hear the Beach Boys' *Sail On, Sailor* without smiling and thinking of that night with Midge. Some songs remind me of lost loves, while others evoke feelings of adventure and discovery. The Masters, such as Beethoven, Bach, Mozart and Strauss float my soul to the clouds, then send it to the depths of Hell. Soundtracks send me "far, far away" and "long, long ago," to a 1920s speakeasy, to an ancient battlefield, or to a planet infested with Aliens. I can go wherever I want with music and pull up any emotion along the journey.

Over the years, I listened to music on whichever devices were popular at the time. In my car, I played AM radio, then FM radio, cassette players, CD players, MiniDisc players and finally iPods. I had cassette players for the longest time and recorded my favorite songs to create my own playlist. To make a tape, I had to select the songs from my vinyl record collection and record each song one by one in real time. It took hours to make each tape. CDs took far less time to burn on the computer, but I had to make many of them because they didn't hold as many songs. Today, it is so much easier. You can transfer 1200 songs on to an iPod in just a couple of minutes. I have all my favorite music on one tiny iPod and it's still only half full.

Some will have noticed I didn't mention 8-Tracks. I had friends who had 8-Tracks, but I hated them. I didn't like it when the song would cut in the middle to switch tracks. They also made it difficult to make your own mix tape. If you're nostalgic for 8-Tracks, my heart goes out to you.

Even though I love such a variety of music, spanning six decades and beyond, I have no musical talent. I have no hand/eye coordination, which prohibits me from playing a musical instrument.

I've tried to play the guitar and keyboards, but I just couldn't get very far. In order for me to type on this computer, I have to look at the keyboard directly, so I am very slow. I couldn't play the piano the same way I type on a keyboard.

The one musical instrument I can play is the kazoo. Okay, true musicians don't consider the kazoo a real musical instrument, but I can belt out a tune on a kazoo that sounds fantastic. The marches I've played would have made John Philip Sousa proud. It got to be popular on board the submarines I served on, especially after I played several tunes at Garbage Night.

Garbage Night, or what other subs call Halfway Night, served as a way for the crew to blow off steam and have a little fun, when reaching the halfway point in a patrol. On the *Key*, we had some men do skits, others sang or played musical instruments, and others still did comedy. We also had contests, races, gambling games, and lotteries.

One thing that took place on many ships in the Navy – submarines and surface ships alike – was that one man invariably performed his skit dressed as a woman. And, of course, "that guy" would have a set of women's clothes with him, just in case the occasion arose. Even though some men wanted to fool around in women's clothes, I always felt too scared to do that. I probably would have done too good of a job, making the other men start to wonder about me. Now that I know how prevalent cross-dressing is in the male population, I can see why some volunteered to dress as a woman for these skits.

Just before the *Key* left the Northwest on my first submarine deployment, we had to do sound testing on the equipment. We took the ship to a lonely place at the north end of Puget Sound to conduct the test. They hooked the ship up to shore power, then we sank the ship to 150 feet. While down there, we ran one piece of equipment at a time to get its sound signature and make sure it met the specifications. Once completed, the Navy had a unique sound signature for the *Francis Scott Key*.

While underwater, I got to call my parents from 150 feet below sea level. We also lost shore power for a time, during which the Nucs had to run around and complete a quick reactor start-up so we could get the power back. The Nucs came through that day.

Midge and I dated for about a month before she lost interest in me, but I had other encounters in Bremerton before the boat left the shipyards in May 1973. When I returned to Bremerton four years later, a new freeway cut through the area where Midge had previously lived. That small town on the west side of Puget Sound will always hold a special place in my heart.

8 – ON THE ROAD AGAIN

In May 1973, the Navy officially split the men on the *Francis Scott Key* into two separate crews, called the Blue Crew and the Gold Crew. This allowed for longer deployment of the sub and its missiles without any undue hardship on the men and their families. It looked good on paper, but a two-crew setup came with an all-new set of problems not found on any other Naval ship. Once the ship began its normal patrol schedule, each crew would be deployed for 105 days, with a five-day turnover period at each end. I ended up on the Gold Crew.

With a 105-day cycle, if a man wanted to be home for the birth of a child, he would have to get his wife pregnant within the first seven days of returning from patrol. Do the math. This didn't happen very often, so typically married men would get the news of a birth through a Family Gram while at sea. A Family Gram consisted of 14-word radio messages that the Navy allowed family members to send to their loved ones at sea. The family members would mail in the message and then, when a sub came to periscope depth to pick up any radio traffic, the messages would be received as well. The crew treated Family Grams like nuggets of gold. Getting one made you feel fantastic, though my family didn't send me very many over my five patrols.

The precise nature of our patrol's schedule also made for some interesting drama. Especially for those marriages experiencing difficulties. Wives knew to the day and hour when their husbands would return home, making it easy for those planning a quick getaway. I can't count how many times I witnessed a sailor arrive home to an empty house. The wife, the kids, the furniture, everything all gone. Sometimes I felt lucky not to have a spouse.

Of course, the cycle didn't help the single men either. Three months didn't provide enough time to establish a relationship that remained strong enough to endure a 105-day waiting period. I myself had more than one relationship end prematurely because of this. During each patrol cycle, we would be submerged for 70 days. To me this felt like being in suspended animation. The rest of the world went on without us interacting with it or the loved ones we had left behind. A single man would come back wanting to resume his relationship where he left off, but more often than not his love interest had moved on. The world had moved on.

One aspect of our routine scared the hell out of me. Once the ship dived at the beginning of the patrol, it would not break patrol cycle for almost anything. Rare situations did occur, but they wouldn't break patrol cycle to send someone home for a family emergency. I always feared that one of my parents would die while I sailed under the sea and I wouldn't know about it until we came back. The Executive Officer would hold on to news like that if it reached him. So, if it happened, my family member could die and be buried long before I would ever hear about it.

A 105-day patrol cycle also favored one crew over another when it came to holidays. One crew would be at sea for three to four major holidays in a row, while the other crew would be at home during all of those same holidays. I spent three Thanksgivings at sea but got to go home for three Christmas/New Year's holidays in a row. I missed just one family Christmas out of eight while in the Navy, the one that took place while in Bremerton. Ironically, when they found out about my decision to transition, my parents told me they never wanted to see me again, so after that I missed seven family Christmases in a row. That only changed in 2004 when my father passed away.

In May of 1973, the *Francis Scott Key* became officially seaworthy once more. The Navy ordered the Blue Crew to sail the ship south to Panama, then to our homeport of Charleston, South Carolina. While they had 'fun' at sea, the Goldies drove across the country to Charleston, taking extensive leave before arriving.

As I drove south through California, everything seemed to be going well, but once again fate had its own plan for me. At 65 miles per hour, I suddenly heard a loud clunking sound coming from under my van. I lost power and slowed to 55 miles per hour. Then, without warning, the rear wheels locked up, sending me skidding down the freeway, nearly out of control. My dirt-bike-riding instincts took over and thankfully I guided the van safely to a stop along the side of the interstate.

It took several minutes before my heart slowed to a normal pace. I still had a hard time catching my breath. The cassette in the car radio at the time happened to be playing a song by Emerson, Lake and Palmer called *Lucky Man*. When I regained my composure, I realized how appropriate that song had been.

When I inspected the underside of the van, I discovered what had gone wrong. Because the engine had been installed crooked, undue stress had been put on the universal joint, just behind the transmission. One pivot point on the universal joint had snapped, putting the stress directly on to the standard transmission, twisting its main shaft. It froze solid. The scariest part of the whole thing had been that if the universal had broken off completely, the front end of the drive shaft would have jammed into the interstate asphalt, likely flipping the van over and over at 55 miles per hour. Had that happened, my life probably would have ended at the age of 22.

Wonderful. I once again found myself stranded in the middle of a long trip, and once again in California. I waited for the longest time, but no California Highway Patrol passed by. It figured. They're never around when you need them.

Somehow, I had to get a tow truck. In desperation, I decided to gas-up the dirt bike with the aim of riding into the nearest town for help. Just before I could set off however, a California Highway Patrol officer finally showed up.

Eventually a tow truck took me to the nearest junkyard, but when I got there, I found that they didn't have the proper transmission. They told me that another junkyard could send one over the next morning. So, the next day I replaced the transmission all by myself without any mechanical lifting assistance.

The incident taught me a lot about the need to be cautious. Had I been more cautious in Idaho Falls, when I had a mechanic install the V-8 in a vehicle designed to handle only a straight 6, I likely wouldn't have had any problems with the van. Facing death for the first time also gives a person a new perspective on life: the realization that life is full of long periods of monotony broken up by unexpected events.

The rest of the trip, to Phoenix and then on to Charleston, ended up being uneventful by comparison and, after arriving in Charleston, I got rid of my 1966 Ford Van and bought a much better 1969 model.

In Charleston I visited a bar called The Flying Dutchman. I found it to be the best place for dancing, meeting women and playing pinball, but it also had an air of Southern redneck about it. During the Vietnam War, military personnel didn't receive much of a welcome in places like The Flying Dutchman. Short hair also didn't exactly appear in fashion back then. But, in spite of the unwelcoming atmosphere, I managed to enjoy myself there. My leave ended quickly however, so I didn't have much time to see the local area before it came time to do the job I'd been trained for.

After the Blue Crew handed over the boat to the Gold Crew, we sailed a short distance to the beautiful waters outside the island Grand Bahama. The Commanding Officer decided to give us a rare treat – swim call in the tropics. The azure-blue water of the Bahamas looked more beautiful than anything I could have ever imagined. The water was so clear we could see the hull of the *Key* to the point where it curved under.

One of my shipmates stupidly decided that he would dive down and try and swim under the ship to the other side. He had to go about 30 feet under and then back up again to make the swim. He made it, but he came up with his nose bleeding. A few years later, the same guy held his girlfriend hostage at gunpoint in their apartment. Not the brightest bulb in the pack.

The flat missile deck made a great place to lie out and catch a few rays, while the cooks rigged up a grill and cooked hamburgers and hotdogs for us. All the while, sharpshooters stood watch on the bridge at the top of the sail, looking out for sharks while the crew played in the ocean.

Some of the crew used the Fairwater Planes that jutted out from the sail as high-dive platforms. They stood about 20 feet above the water. I enjoyed jumping off of them because it reminded me of jumping off the cliffs at Canyon Lake, just outside of Phoenix.

While enjoying the activities on deck, a moment of creativity came over me. I hurried to Engineering and found all the necessary parts I needed to construct my vision. Using plastic rods, plastic sheeting, duct tape and string, I built a good-sized kite and flew it off the back of the sub. The crew loved it. I had to go on watch an hour later, so I gave the kite to one of my shipmates. I later found out that they flew the kite off the top of the sail until the sun went down.

One of the most interesting things I witnessed in the Navy took place after we left the Bahamas and sailed to Cape Canaveral. For about three weeks we worked our asses off preparing the ship to test-launch a real Poseidon missile. For the entire time leading up to the event, we sailed the sea each day to practice simulated launches. Our crew went through the whole drill, ending each time by blowing a cement plug out of the tube with high-pressure air. The plug weighed the same as the actual missile. Up until then, I had never seen the Forward people work harder than the Nucs. At night, the Nucs enjoyed some much-needed time off, visiting the same bars that astronauts once frequented. It felt good to be the lazy ones for once.

On the day of the actual launch, anxiety filled the air. The entire Poseidon program hinged on the success of our launch. We had all seen movies of failed launches and how they had to destroy the missile when it went off course. We had also seen examples of when the missile had failed to ignite, falling back into the sea and on top of the sub. Each of these possible scenarios gave the crew something scary to ponder.

As the moment arrived, you could feel the tension mount. The practice launches had little danger associated with them, but this would be for real. I sat in the Engine Room listening to the announcements over the intercom and then, finally, the countdown. In all the years of launching model rockets, I had never felt the excitement I felt that day. And I wouldn't even be the one pushing the button.

When the countdown hit "zero," I felt the ship rock, as high-pressure air blew the live bird out of the tube. We had a successful ejection, but would it fly? Moments later, we received the word that the missile ignited on time and flew a perfect course down the test range. A shipmate on a distant observation ship filmed the launch with my Super-8 movie camera. It looked great on film, even though the image looked small because of how far away my friend had been. Unfortunately, I lost the film a few years later, when my van got broken into.

After the successful launch, we headed back to Charleston where they loaded all 16 tubes with real Poseidon missiles containing real warheads. The Blue Crew then took the ship out on a full patrol. While they were gone, I explored more of Charleston. In January 1974, I would be heading to Spain with the rest of the Gold Crew to take over the ship once more.

9 – THE IRISH VIRGIN

While trying to discover my inner woman, I also tried my hand at long-term relationships. Throughout this self-discovery phase of my life, I grew in many ways. Importantly, I came to realize that my need to appear as a woman didn't replace my need to have sexual relationships with women. In later years, when I understood myself better, I realized that sexual attraction, gender identity and gender expression are three separate issues, none of which are dependent on each other.

Society's labeling of sexual orientation however, depends on a person's gender expression. As a man attracted to women, society considered me straight. When I started living my true self as a woman, but still liked women, society labeled me a lesbian even though the gender I found attractive hadn't changed.

While a young man in the Navy, I occasionally had some luck in my search for female companionship. I had a few experiences with women while stationed in Charleston. Some of these relationships turned out to be exciting and wonderful, but most didn't. Regardless of their outcome however, they all helped to peel away some of the naïveté that had previously coated my life.

Before my patrol, I got the chance to explore Rota, Spain, the port the *Francis Scott Key* operated out of. Rota had both a US Navy port and a US Air Force Base. The US military single-handedly supported the town, located on Spain's Atlantic coast. Being a typical 'military town', Rota had several bars catering to servicemen, some of which the Navy banned us from frequenting.

On my first night there, I decided to go into town. My Chief had suggested I try the Dutch Bar, located off Red Square. As I entered, I quickly realized the bar's attraction for military personnel. Each establishment hired women from all over the world to work there: women from the United Kingdom and the rest of Europe, the Americas, Africa and the Far East. In order to make ends meet while touring Europe, many traveling men and women would take jobs along the way and the southern shores of Spain had become one of the more popular locations for women to work, especially in the winter months.

I couldn't figure out why my Chief sent me to the Dutch Bar because it didn't look like anything special. It didn't appear very large and it only had one pinball machine and one pool table. The pinball machine looked familiar, but naturally all the words appeared in Spanish. It looked to me like a knock-off, cheaply constructed, and it had a different manufacturer's name from the one I expected. I lost interest in playing it very quickly.

One of my shipmates, who came to the bar with me, suggested I order some sangria. I liked wine, so I followed his suggestion, but I didn't expect them to serve it to me the way that they did. The barmaid pulled out a pitcher and began filling it with various wines and liquors, then added different citrus fruits to balance the sweetness. Each bar made their sangria differently, but they all tasted sweet. One could easily get wasted on a single pitcher and drinking two would require assistance getting back to the ship. I didn't even finish the first pitcher.

While at the bar, I spent most of my time speaking to two French women about their experiences traveling Europe. While talking to them however, I kept watching another barmaid who had caught my eye. I described her in my Journal on January 22, 1974:

> She was short, about 5 feet and small. I'd say 100 lbs. She had short, curly hair, wire-rimmed tinted glasses, and a fantastic smile, bubbling with personality.

Later, I noticed she had green eyes. To this very day, green eyes on a woman can easily melt my heart. Using the bar's large mirror, I subtly watched her going about her work. Finally, she served a man next to me, giving me the chance to talk with her. The bar had one rule however. To talk to the women working there, you had to buy them a drink. Since drinks in Spain cost much less than they did back in the States, this didn't stop anyone from having a good time.

I decided to break the ice. Again, from my journal:

"Hello. Where are you from?"
She smiled and said, "Would believe Japan?"
"It's possible."
"No. I'm from Dublin, Ireland."
"Oh! An Irish girl."
I watched her for a little bit until she came back around the bar.
"Hi, again."
"Hello." Her with a neat smile.
"Are you thirsty?"
"Yes."
"Okay."

I acted real slick back then. Not.

The evening went rather well. Here's what else I wrote in my journal from that night.

The rest of the night she sat there and talked to me. Her name was Pauline. We talked about many things. We even went over and played the pinball machine. Towards the end of the night, I reached out to hold her hand. She held mine and rubbed my fingers.

I asked her, "Would you like to get something to eat after you get off of work?"

"I'd love to, but I made a date for tonight. If he doesn't show up, then I'll go."

"I hope he doesn't show up."

Five minutes to 1:00 she got ready to leave. Still no sign of her date. Then he came. I don't think I was ever so pissed. He had a motorcycle helmet with him. She went over and talked with him. I think I overheard her say that she wouldn't go on a motorcycle. So, a motorcycle has been a friend to me again, but in a different way. If it wasn't for a motorcycle, I wouldn't have been able to take Pauline out and start a fantastic relationship.

Boy, was I still naïve? A 'relationship'? What the hell did I think back then? I had only had my first sexual experience 11 months earlier and I still didn't know squat about women and how they viewed men and relationships. Love makes people not only do goofy things but think goofy things. Now I know that not even age cures that.

That first night together, I discovered that Pauline had never had sex with a man. From my journal, here's how the night ended:

> We went to El Quoties. She wanted a steak sandwich, but they were out of steak, so we both had a hamburger. I swear I heard mine meow when I bit into it. It was beyond raunchy. We sat there after we ate. I felt that I have known her for a long time. Then, we kissed. It was a beautiful kiss.
>
> We left El Quoties and walked around. We couldn't go to her place because the owner did not allow military people in. So, we just stood by a new building and held each other. Around 4:00 she finally went in. I couldn't believe the whole night. I really met a fantastic girl and she even likes me. And, here I am about 8000 miles from home. I will be seeing her again on my next night off.

I found myself so infatuated with Pauline that I couldn't wait to tell my best friend on the *Key*, Bill. That turned out to be one of the stupidest moves I could have made. Bill let it be known that I had found an Irish Virgin in Rota. Throughout the patrol, the crew gave me one hell of a hard time about Pauline. This taught me to keep personal issues close to my chest, trusting few, if anyone.

I finally got to see Pauline again a few days later and discovered she had moved into a new apartment, one where I could visit her. After she finished work, we once again went to El Quoties. This time they had steak sandwiches. We ended up at her place and talked late into the night. I had fallen in love with her in a big way.

During that first visit to Rota, I got to see Pauline a total of eight times. On each occasion, we became more and more intimate, though our intimacy never progressed to oral sex or intercourse. I wanted her to come and visit me in the States, when I went back after my patrol. I hoped I would better understand how she felt about me then. My biggest fear involved the other man she had been seeing. He wouldn't be going to sea and so would have an uninterrupted chance to woo her for the next 70 days. This patrol would become the first time I experienced the kind of 'suspended animation' I described earlier.

My patrol started on Valentine's Day, 1974, and just before reporting on board, I saw Pauline one last time. She gave me a pen for my upcoming birthday and a card that said, "To Bob, with my fondest love. Pauline."

Rereading all of my journal entries about Pauline, I feel as if I have just read about a love affair between two women, rather than a man and a woman. My journal shows that I felt happy being with Pauline even though we didn't have sex. After that grueling first patrol on the *Francis Scott Key*, where I qualified in submarines, we pulled back into Rota on April 25, 1974. I couldn't wait to see Pauline again. Not only had I thought of her during what little spare time I had, but I had even dreamed about her. Unfortunately, I had spent all that energy on her in vain. This is from my journal on that first day back:

> Liberty! I should have taken death. Yes, I saw her and the odds were against me. She was engaged to the guy I knew was seeing her all this time.
>
> She has changed. She's not as flighty as she was when I left. She said she wrote me a letter telling me not to come and see her. I believe that by her choice of words and actions that she is not a virgin anymore either.
>
> So my dream was true.

That dream took place on March 15 and I called it, "Beware the Ides of March." In the dream, Pauline made love to another man.

> Thousands of miles away and a couple hundred feet under water and I still knew what was going on. It was all for the better. I did get emotionally involved enough to vent off – well "most" anyway – of my bottled-up love that I've been hanging onto. So, maybe I can take things on an "even keel" – her choice of words. This may turn out to be a profitable off-crew. It will be easier to have sex now without getting emotionally

involved, which I knew was a problem that existed.

Who was I kidding? All my life I've gotten emotionally involved when I've dated other women. I couldn't have been so far from the mark had I said I would one day travel in space. Love has the capacity to make fools of us all. I went on to prove that many times over, after my experience with the Irish Virgin.

I felt so heartbroken about my meeting with Pauline that I went to the NCO Club and proceeded to get drunk on wine. That became the one and only time in my life that I drank until I became sick, and the only time my shipmates ever had to help me back to my ship.

Rereading my journal, I remember now that Pauline said something to me the last time I saw her, which also missed the mark by light-years. As we parted for good, she said, "Submarines are going to be the death of you."

Wrong. So, so wrong. My service on submarines, and my subsequent life as a veteran, became the foundation upon which I built my activism as a trans woman. Being able to say, "I am a submarine veteran" has given me more pride and satisfaction than most other things in my life. More specifically, my activism started in 1998 because of being a submarine veteran and being denied membership of a national organization for sub vets. The strength I drew for my activism came directly from the intense training I received in the Navy, now over 40 years ago. I will always be proud of my time in the Silent Service.

10 – THE DAY OF THE DOLPHINS

My first patrol started in early January 1974. This began the qualification process for me to 'earn my Dolphins'. At the same time, I also started the process of qualifying to stand various Engineering watch stations. The combined workload severely taxed my sanity. We had 6 hours on-watch and 12 hours off, but because of the additional workload I had to stay awake for 24 hours more times than I can count.

Submarine life doesn't compare to serving on any other ship in the Navy. *The Francis Scott Key* had about 145 men stationed on it at any one time, living in a steel tube 33 feet in diameter and 425 feet long. Packed in with them it had a nuclear reactor, 16 ICBM solid-fuel missiles, each with up to ten nuclear warheads, 16 missile tubes, two steam turbines, a huge reduction gear, two turbine generators, a diesel generator, thousands of valves, dozens of pumps, hundreds of pieces of electronic equipment, two distilling units, air compressors, liquid storage tanks, O2 generators, CO2 scrubbers, AC units, torpedoes, torpedo tubes, a full galley, over 100 16mm movies, 120 racks, and thousands of miles of pipe from ¼ inch to 14 inches in diameter.

Every cubic millimeter within the submarine had a purpose. If it didn't exist as a place for equipment, or for a person to sleep, walk, eat, shit or take a shower, then it had a storage locker built into it. Submariners learned very quickly how to make efficient use of the limited space they have on the long patrols. This line of thinking has stuck with me all of my life and has come in useful when I'm getting ready for long trips, or even something as silly as packing the dishwasher.

Just thinking about living on a submarine would make most people tremble. A feeling of claustrophobia hits many people when a submariner talks about his or her experience at sea. I have had big, strong Army Rangers tell me about all of their rough and dangerous missions then ask, "So what did you do in the Navy?"

"I was on submarines."

"Man! People thought WE were crazy, but you guys were REALLY crazy."

Such comments always make me smile.

The crew had various divisions, each with their own specialty and their own duties. The Engineering Department consisted of four divisions, all trained in the Naval Nuclear Power Program, and 'A' Division, which consisted of non-nuclear trained Machinist's Mates. The A-Gangers and their counterparts at the forward end of the ship, the Torpedomen, would generally consist of the biggest, rough-and-tumble members of the crew. This seemed to be a tradition carried over from the early days of submarines, enhanced by the many submarine-themed movies Hollywood has made over the years. Other divisions had their share of the strong, macho types, but these two groups seemed to embody the spirit of the classic submariner.

The nuclear-trained members of the crew, the Nucs as I mentioned earlier, had to take care of the steam systems and all the equipment associated with the nuclear reactor. When in port, and in shutdown, I sometimes had to go inside the Reactor Compartment to do work in there. The procedure to enter an RC had several steps, including donning a yellow containment suit, affectionately known as a "canary suit." The temperature in the RC, even with the reactor shut down, could easily top 120° and the suit with its associated gasmask didn't help matters much. What the hell, I grew up in Arizona.

During our first patrol, those of us not qualified on submarines had to spend a lot of our sleep-time learning all the safety features and the location of the damage control equipment in each compartment. In Engineering, the Nucs had to learn these things and more as part of their qualifying for various watch stations. The Engineering Department required them to know how to operate every piece of equipment, how to isolate it, what each valve in that compartment did, the location of all of the electrical panels and what they controlled, what to do in a steam leak, a seawater leak, a freshwater leak, a fire, a flood, or a toxic gas leak.

When a Forward person came back to Engineering to get their submarine qualification card signed off for each compartment, they didn't need to know anywhere near as much as the Nucs needed to know, though obviously the Nucs didn't need to know everything about the forward end of the ship either. On balance however, Nucs had to learn more overall, since they spent a great deal of their off-time in the forward end of the ship.

Each sailor received a "sub qual card" and had to have a preset portion of it signed off each week. Those authorized to sign the qual card for each compartment would sometimes ask harder questions, unrelated to what a person really needed to know for emergencies. So, if crewmembers didn't like you, getting a signature could sometimes be difficult, slow down your qualifying or even become a roadblock. Thankfully, I didn't have an issue with this.

Getting behind in sub quals had a number of negative consequences. Qualified members of the crew referred to those who fell behind as "dinks", short for delinquents. Dinks got treated like shit by sub-qualified crewmembers. For dinks, sleep would become a distant memory. They would need to forgo sleep in order to study and obtain the missing signatures they needed for their card. They couldn't watch movies, read books, play cards, or even sit and rest. Occasionally, one would come across a sailor sleeping next to a piece of machinery with a training manual in his lap. The brutality toward dinks knew few boundaries, short of physical violence. Later in life however, I heard from some of my trans submarine friends that they had been sexually assaulted while trying to qualify on a submarine. To be clear, I never heard of it happening on the *Key*.

Nevertheless, the first, but not the last, time in my life I experienced institutionalized discrimination happened because of being delinquent on my sub quals. Verbal harassment would become the preferred way to intimidate us. Officers and Chief Petty Officers didn't have to resort to name-calling however, since they had a better way to motivate dinks. They would simply order us to stay up and work on our qualifications. On top of our normal duties we also needed time to qualify other watch stations, ship drills, Engineering drills, field days and planned maintenance. One can easily see that the

12 hours in between our six-hour watches got quickly used up. Luckily, they did sometimes give us time to eat.

Starting with this first patrol, I began keeping a journal, which I cleverly named *The Book*. I already included some of the entries in the last chapter. Using a military five-by-seven logbook, I wrote down my thoughts while at sea. I wrote the title *The Book* on the front cover in Elvish Tengwar runes, the writing from *The Lord of the Rings*. Here is an entry from March 2, 1974.

> FUCK! The best movie they brought on board was *A Clockwork Orange*. They showed it twice yesterday (Saturday.) Dinks can only watch movies on Sunday. I thought I was going to luck out and get to see it after midnight because they show the previous day's movie after midnight. Well, the mo-fugger started Casino Night at 10:00 Saturday Night and it lasted until the next morning, thus doing away with the only chance dinks had to see a movie. Fuck, I got screwed again. 51 days till Rota.

In the early part of my first patrol, I went through hell. Qualifying in submarines still remains one of the toughest things I have had to endure in my life, just behind starting my transition. I can't recall ever being as emotionally on the edge, physically exhausted and psychologically burned out all at the same time, as when I went through my sub quals. I felt angry and frustrated because I had no outlet through which I could let off steam.

Finally, after two grueling months at sea, I finished getting the last signature on my submarine qual card. That night, I celebrated by watching a movie in the Crew's Mess. While there, a Forward Puke, not knowing I had completed my quals, decided to give me a ration of shit for watching a movie.

I exploded and yelled, "Fuck off, asshole! I got my fucking quals done today!" Without meaning to, he had given me an outlet for all of my pent-up anger. It felt good. The others in the Crew's Mess clapped and congratulated me. I had become one of them, but for some reason it didn't make me feel good knowing this. Probably because of what I had to endure to join their 'fraternity.'

On April 9, 1974, I stood in the Officers' Mess with three other men who had also finished their sub quals. The Captain pinned a pair of Dolphins on each of us and congratulated us on a job well done. I had that original pair of Dolphins up to August 19, 2014, when I gave them to the Smithsonian, along with the original Transgender Pride Flag. I ended up completing five full patrols on the *Key*.

Writing became one of my most favorite pastimes while on patrol. I wrote a short story that I later turned into a novel, and even wrote a sequel to it. On my second patrol, the person who headed the ship's newspaper transferred off the ship, so we no longer had an editor or a paper. Since I had qualified submarines on the first patrol, I had a lot more time on my hands to take up the challenge of editing the ship's newspaper. I enlisted the aid of an excellent cartoonist and writer, a mess cook by the name of Dave, to draw cartoons and help with the paper. We later became good friends.

One of the early articles I wrote concerned a submarine phenomenon known as a "flapper." On submarines, in order to overcome sea pressure and dump water overboard, they either had to either pump it out with a high-pressure pump or pressurize a tank to blow it out. This included the sanitary tanks where the sinks, showers and toilets drained. The stainless-steel toilets on a sub had a large ball valve at the bottom attached to a long handle and, in order to flush the toilet, one would run water into the bowl and pull back the handle so the contents would flow into the sanitary tanks.

When the sanitary tanks became full, the Auxiliary Machinist's Mates would go to every toilet and place a sign on the door saying "Blowing Sanitary Tank" to make crewmembers aware. However, when a person woke up and wandered into the head half asleep wanting to relieve themselves, they didn't always notice the signs. They would finish their business, stand up, face the toilet and pull back the handle. High-pressure air and tank contents, as well as the contents in the bowl, would blow into their face and onto their body. The larger the pressure drops on the tank, the bigger we considered the flapper. The person getting the flapper would become the object of ridicule, at least until the next flapper occurred.

One of the funniest events that happened on my second patrol on the *Key* took place on the anniversary of Francis Scott Key writing *The Star-Spangled Banner*. Ten days after our patrol began, the Gold Crew celebrated the poem's 160th anniversary. The Captain asked me if I would play the National Anthem on the kazoo during the opening ceremony. That evening, the main event would be a Whimpie eating contest. From the ship's newspaper, here's what I wrote, word-for-word:

> After a rendition of *The Star-Spangled Banner*, the Captain stood in the back of Crew's Mess. "Welcome to the *F.S. Key's* First Annual Whimpie Eating Contest. Before we begin, I have prepared a few notes on the importance of Whimpies in history.
>
> "On the eve of this historic contest I think it would be appropriate to review the history of Whimpies, also known as "hamburgers." Legend has it that the Whimpie first began in the city of Hamburg, Germany around 1500. From there, the 'hamburger' had an immediate effect on history. Rumor has it that Martin Luther really began the Protestant movement in 1524 because the Pope wouldn't let him eat Whimpies on Fridays.
>
> "Following through history, we see that the early settlers on the American Continent coexisted with the savages – at least for a little while – by serving them Dimpies. They made these hamburgers from deer meat slapped between two pieces of hardtack.
>
> "During the American Revolution, we find that hamburgers played a very important, but a largely-unknown role. From personal research, I discovered the real reason George Washington defeated General Cornwallis in the Battle of Yorktown. It seems that Cornwallis visited his favorite cathouse the night before the battle and after satisfying one appetite, he indulged in several 'Tidewater Whimpies'. Unfortunately, he suffered an acute upset stomach and could not perform his duties in battle.
>
> "Strangely enough, hamburgers played an important role in the writing of *The Star-Spangled Banner*. You see, Francis Scott Key visited that British warship to arrange the release of a doctor friend, who in turn had been called out to treat the captain for an intestinal flare-up from eating a bum Baltimore Whimpie.
>
> "We next see the Whimpie in its history-making role during the Civil War. After Appomattox, a private overheard General Lee saying, 'If I had only had four wagon loads of Whimpies and a little more gunpowder, we would have

whooped them damn Yankees.'

"Whimpies have also left their mark on our illustrious submarine. LT Felton, after tasting a hamburger at a McDonalds, decided to leave Tennessee to experience the finer things in life, so he joined the Navy. On top of that, we have profited greatly from the amazing weight building properties of the Navy Whimpie. Because of them, we have the only human damage-control plug, capable of stopping up a twenty-one-inch hole or a twenty-five-inch hatch. Well done, Chappy."

The Captain finished to a rousing applause. When he sat, another officer stood up. "Okay. I have here the standard rules for the Whimpie Eating Contest, as written in the Uniform Code of Military Justice." He held up a copy of the UCMJ book. Opening the book, he pretended to read. "Each division on the ship must provide one contestant. Failure to do so will cause that division's members to be served last at all meals. All contestants must be amateurs, having no affiliation with the NWA... the National Whimpie Association.

"The Whimpies used in the contest must be of regulation size and weight, not including condiments. The meat patty must weigh between eight and ten ounces after cooking and has to contain at least twenty-five-percent beef." Evans paused. "This particular rule was the hardest for our cooks to comply with." The Chief Cook didn't find that funny.

"The contestants are given thirty minutes to wolf down as many Whimpies as they can. Liquids of any kind are allowed for washing down the food, but keep in mind, it will also take up room in your stomach. Vomiting is not permitted on the Mess Decks. Airsick bags are provided in the passageway.

"Now, let me introduce you to the contestants. For the Admin Division, we have Packin' Page. Pulverizing Patino for Sonar. Gobblin Gruber representing Radio. Chompin' Chappy for QMs. Vacuum Vanderhausen for the Nav Center. Snackin' Snatch for M-Division. E-Div. has Razorback Rathbun. Crunchin' Cox is representing RC-Division. Whistle Pig Sadler for A and IC-Division. Munchin' Mouse for Weapons. Oinker Addison for the Chiefs and Nine-Toed Privett for the Seaman. The winner will receive a generous kegger for him and his division. Gentlemen, start your Whimpies!"

One of the men stood to do the play-by-play announcement, while the Mess Cooks brought out the first tray of Whimpies.

"They're all at the starting gate. It looks like Number Three, Munchin' Mouse, is a bit jumpy. His owner and trainer went out to settle him down. Okay. They're set. There's the bell! They're off!

"Out of the gates, it's Munchin' Mouse out in front, followed by Oinker Addison, Packin' Page and Snackin' Snatch. On the back stretch, it's Packin' Page and Munchin' Mouse running Whimp-n-Whimp, followed by Snackin' Snatch, Oinker Addison and Crunchin' Cox."

For thirty burger-stuffing minutes, the men in the contest gobbled down the tasteless, odorless, colorless – but not greaseless – Whimpies. Several literally fell by the wayside, making it to the passageway just in time to utilize the plastic bags there. Toward the end, only three men remained - Cox, Gruber and Snackin' Snatch.

Snackin' Snatch and Gruber both finished nine Whimpies, while Cox lagged behind with eight. As the thirty-minute mark quickly approached, Gruber and Snackin' Snatch barely downed number ten. Cox had to make a hasty retreat to the passageway in order to take care of that "stuffy feeling."

"Come on, Snatch!" yelled 'M' Division. "Just one more! Gruber ain't going to make it. He's already turning green."

It took superhuman will power for Snackin' Snatch to reach for that eleventh burger. Gruber tried to do the same but couldn't muster the desire. Snackin' Snatch finished half of the Whimpie just as the time ran out. Everyone in 'M' Division cheered and made a path to the passageway for both men. The cooks served Whimpies to the rest of the crew for the evening meal, but none of the contestants joined them.

11 – WOMEN PROBLEMS

With my first patrol on the *Key* under my belt, and having qualified on submarines, I returned to shore for my first off-crew period. One of the Forward guys and I rented a two-bedroom apartment in North Charleston, in a nice complex with all the amenities. My roommate then decided to take a month off to go home and visit his family. This left me alone for the first time since I'd joined the Navy. It felt nice to go swimming in the pool, go out to nightclubs, and sleep every day until noon. Life couldn't be better, or so I thought.

About a week into my off-crew time, I found myself performing one of life's most mundane tasks: doing laundry. Obviously, I had done laundry before, but to my mind it always took too long to do. It felt like a waste of time. So, to ensure I wouldn't run into crowds that would slow me down further, I tried to do my laundry late at night. A few others had the same idea, but it generally made the process quicker.

That first night in the laundry room, I quickly got bored with the book I had brought to read, so instead I sat and watched the dryers toss clothes around and around. I felt mesmerized watching all the colors spinning this way and that. After a few minutes, the contents of one of the dryers caught my eye. A lace bra rolled around by the front of the glass door, disappearing for a few seconds, only to reappear again. I became transfixed.

A spark flashed through my brain, charging dormant synapses and connecting sleeping memories, all of which had been locked away in my mind, dulled by too much alcohol and marijuana. Images of the days when I tried on my mother's underwear came back to me, pulling primordial feelings with them. In addition to the chemical dulling, I now know what else had kept those memories tucked away: the obsession of losing my virginity had filled my every waking moment since joining the Navy. Up until this point, my sexual desire for a first encounter had pushed every other fantasy of mine onto the back burner.

Suddenly, all the gender-different psychological and physical elements of my life started coming together. Since I had already had a few sexual experiences with women, I no longer obsessed about losing my virginity. Instead I began to revisit those childhood feelings. As I stood watching the bra swirl around in the dryer, I sensed a growing desire to dress as a woman and to see the hidden woman within me.

Then the Woman in the Shadows spoke to me loudly and clearly,

"It looks so pretty."

I agreed. "It does."

"Don't take your eyes off of it."

"I won't"

"You should take it. Try it on."

"No!"

"Come on. One little bra won't hurt."

"I don't know."

"Please. For me?"

I walked up to the dryer, popped open the door, grabbed the bra and shoved it into my pocket. Then, I gathered my finished clothes, and rushed back to my apartment. When I got back, I pulled the bra out of my pocket, took off my shirt off in front of the mirror and put the bra on. I looked at my reflection and liked what I saw.

I had just stolen a bra from a dryer. More than that, I enjoyed wearing it. Was I a pervert? I didn't know. All I knew was that this felt exciting. It felt liberating and I wanted more. This time however, I would be sure to buy the clothes I wanted, rather than stealing them. I partially did this to ease my conscience. It would also ensure I could get the right sizes to fit me.

Over the next couple of days, I slowly began gathering all the items I needed to bring out my inner woman. I bought everything, including a wig. The thrill of buying the clothes became tempered by a fear that I was doing something society frowned upon. I am sure other gender-different males have had similar feelings when purchasing women's clothes for the first time.

That first off-crew did nothing to help me become a better activist, but it did become a turning point in my psychological development. My life would never be the same again.

Once I'd completed my shopping spree, I stood in front of my bedroom mirror dressed completely as a woman for the first time. I can barely describe what I felt. The best I can do is say that my first view of Monica, my true self, felt liberating to my very soul. Where had she been all my life? Why had it taken this long to discover her? Everything about what I saw and what I felt seemed so right. I had no doubt in my mind at all: this person was really me.

Despite the revelation I'd had, the thought of actually becoming a woman remained a foreign concept. Unlike today, in the year 1974 I had no easy access to information about gender identity. Only a few doctors in the world performed sex-change operations, they received limited publicity, and the Harry Benjamin International Gender Dysphoria Association Standards of Care wouldn't be written for another five years.

What had I become? The only thing I knew for sure was that I enjoyed the feeling of dressing and looking like a woman.

The feelings I had, dressed as a woman, ran the gamut of human emotions. Sexual excitement topped the list of what came over me while wearing woman's clothes. However, as time went on that feeling became less and less important, while the need to express my feminine side would grow exponentially. I once tried going out in Charleston dressed as a woman, but it frightened me so much that I never did it again until after the Navy had sent me to my next ship.

After my third patrol, Pat, the woman I had met previously in Idaho Falls, came back into my life in a strange way. Mike, the boyfriend she'd had in Idaho, showed up as a new crewmember of the Blue Crew. I ran into him as we were preparing to turn over the ship. He remembered me from the boarding house and told me that not only had he and Pat gotten married, but that they now also had a daughter. Mike went on to admit that he might not be the girl's biological father and also that he had filed for a divorce from Pat.

My first reaction upon hearing all of this was: *Wow. Now that I'm no longer a virgin, maybe Pat will have second thoughts about having sex with me?* I completely forgot about her other requirement.

"Mike, is it possible I can have her phone number so I can call her when I get back?"

Mike hesitated. "I don't know." He paused, then said, "Okay, why not? We're getting a divorce." He wrote it down for me. Looking back, this may have been one of the stupidest mistakes I've ever made concerning women. Had I known what fate had in store for me, I would never have asked for Pat's number, but of course hindsight is 20/20.

When I reread the ten pages in my journal where I talk about Pat and the summer of '75, I am amazed at all the crap I took from that woman. It hurts to relive those moments, but my conduct back then offers glimpses of the woman I would one day become. In fact, every woman I have ever interacted with helped me to define my sexual orientation. Throughout my life, and before and after my transition, whom I found attractive never really changed much and nor did the manner in which I treated them.

When the turnover ended, I decided to call Pat. Even after three years, she remembered me from Idaho Falls. This surprised me. More than that, she invited me to come and meet her at her place in Charleston.

When I arrived, I found her living in an apartment that looked like a tornado had just torn through it. Papers, toys, dirty Pampers, junk, dirty dishes and clothes lay everywhere. Housekeeping must not have been one of her strong suits. I would later come to the conclusion that she had few, if any, strong suits. We had a good time catching up though. She told me about her conquests and how proud it made her feel to be desired by men. Her life, and what she had done, meant everything to her, but she showed little interest in what I had to say about me and my life. I should have realized the kind of person I was dealing with, but I couldn't see the woods for the sexual trees.

Over the next few weeks I helped her financially, mostly because I felt sorry for her daughter. Pat needed money for bills and food and I didn't want to see her daughter go hungry. Because Mike had left her with nothing, I quickly became her sugar-daddy, though I got nothing in return for my time or money.

We would go out to nightclubs and she would ask me to buy her drinks and then proceed to ignore me. Sometimes, she would even ask me to sit elsewhere in the bar, so we wouldn't look like a couple. That gave her a better chance of snagging her next victim or sexual partner. Looking back, Pat had all the motives and methods of a black widow spider.

This went on all summer, with gullible me being there for her financially and nothing else. We did have a few minor sexual encounters, though these apparently did nothing for her. On one occasion however, she discovered that, even though I couldn't satisfy her during vaginal intercourse, I had another compensating talent – one that I gradually perfected and which prepared me well for my future life as a trans lesbian.

By the end of my off-crew, I had convinced myself not to waste any more time, money or emotional capital on Pat. At the time she owed me nearly $700. I knew I would never see a dime of that back. My dealings with her didn't end when I left Charleston for my fourth patrol on the *Key*. I would have considerably more contact with her between my fourth and fifth patrols, but she wouldn't receive any more money from me.

While on my fourth patrol, although I felt enthralled by her, I promised myself that I wouldn't let her get to me like she had on my last off-crew. She made that easy however, as she had found herself a new sugar-daddy while I'd been away. This meant I could go out to nightclubs and other places, enjoy myself, and try to meet other women. Taking leave, I decided to head back to Phoenix and have fun with my friends. I even dated a couple of women while there.

Three months later, when I returned to Charleston, I found Pat had not been looking after things for me as she had promised. She had watched my van for me while I went to sea, but had been involved in a minor accident while driving it. In addition, my dirt bike had been stolen. I also found she got me behind on my bills since Pat had no concept of responsibility in that regard.

When I eventually left Charleston for San Diego in July 1976, to drive across the country in my brand-new Dodge van, I brought Pat and her daughter with me so that I could drop them off in California with one of Pat's relatives. The idea had looked good to me on paper but turned out to be a disastrous decision.

Before we could leave Charleston, Pat wasted five days of my leave trying to cram as much of her stuff into my new van as she could. The movers had already come for her furniture and the few big things I owned.

Our cross-country trip gave me further insight into Pat's personality. I had known she always wanted things her own way, but the trip showed her to be nothing more than a big whiner. I felt relieved when we finally reached Phoenix because it gave me a chance to spend time with my friends instead of her. However, leaving Pat with my family turned out to be another horrible mistake.

First of all, Pat told my sister that my parents didn't really love each other. Where she got that piece of bullshit I will never know. Then she left her daughter with my sister, telling her that it would be for just a short time. She was gone for hours. She also borrowed my father's pickup, saying she would take my brother roller-skating. Instead, she drove 18 miles to Luke Air Force Base to see a guy. The next day, she had the gall to ask my father if she could borrow the truck once again. Needless to say, she didn't make a very good impression with my family.

After ten days in Phoenix, we drove to San Diego where we met up with the wife of my best friend, Dann. She and her sister put us up overnight. I had a long talk with Pat and told her how fed-up I felt about all her crap. I'd decided to pack her off to her parents in Northern California. She made all kinds of excuses about why she couldn't go, but I refused to hear it. The next day, I placed her and her daughter on a bus. I thought she'd be out of my hair forever, but once she'd gotten back on her feet, she came back to San Diego to find a job.

Over the next two years we became better friends, partly because she no longer asked me for money. Also, I no longer found her sexually interesting. The lessons I learned from my experience with Pat must have taken time to sink in, because I fell into a few more bad relationships in the years that followed. The next two women I fell in love with – one in Charleston and another in Vallejo – made my time with Pat look like a high-school lovers' spat.

12 – EVEN MORE WOMEN PROBLEMS

In the middle of February 1976, our ship's entertainment committee put together a wonderful party at a swanky country club. In spite of all of the crap Pat had given me on the last off-crew, I invited her to the party as my guest. In true Pat fashion, she cancelled on me at the last minute, so I ended up going alone. I almost didn't go and, looking back at all that has happened since, I now consider that night to be one of the biggest mistakes of my life.

During the party, I noticed that one of my shipmates had brought with him a tall, good-looking woman. I couldn't take my eyes off of her. My shipmate refused to introduce her to me, so I introduced myself, making him a little mad in the process. She told me her name was Ann and said, "I'm just a simple country girl." She may have been a country girl, but definitely not 'simple' as I would soon find out.

Toward the end of the evening, Ann and I danced several times together. She took a little convincing, but I got her to allow me to take her home once the party had ended. My shipmate didn't object too strongly because earlier that evening he and Ann had broken up. They wouldn't be leaving the party together.

Before I could take her home, Ann requested we stop at the Aqua Lounge so that I could meet her mother and mother's boyfriend. When we arrived, both of them appeared to have had way too much to drink. It took some time, but Ann and I finally got them in my van and I ended up driving them home instead. Once we had finally got them to go to bed, Ann and I fell asleep on the couch, holding each other closely.

For the week that followed, Ann stayed with me at my new place, one that I shared with a civilian friend of mine. It didn't take us long before we decided to move into a place of our own. I had fallen deeply and madly in love, yet again. As it had in the past, love blinded me to many things, once more giving my heart full authority to trump my brain. I asked Ann to marry me and she accepted. Then things started falling apart.

Over time, I began seeing Ann's true self: a drunk and a compulsive liar. She told me she had spent six years in the Marines, reaching the rank of E-9, despite being only twenty-eight years old. No one, no matter whether they had the most critical job in the military, could reach the rank of E-9 in that short a time, especially in the Marines. The Navy considered my job critical and the highest rank a person could hope for in the Nuclear Navy after six years would have been an E-7. Most Nucs reached E-5 or E-6 status in six years. She later changed her story to one of having been in the Marines for only two years, but even that turned out to be a lie. I later found out she was only twenty-one. She also told me she had leukemia and epilepsy, both of which would have kept her out of the military. Afterwards, her mother told me she didn't have either of those conditions. I quickly grew to not trust anything that came out of her mouth.

Her excessive drinking caused a number of problems for our relationship. She would go to the Aqua Lounge, get drunk, and then allow any man there to take her home. When drunk, she would stagger around, get mad, yell and sometimes fall over. I couldn't take it, but I wouldn't leave because of the amazing sex life we shared.

One day, Ann discovered the makeup and women's clothes that I had kept hidden in a suitcase in the closet. Up until that point, I had not revealed to anyone that I liked women's clothes, let alone my desire to dress as a woman. The fear I felt at her discovery made me feel sick. Adrenaline flowed through my body and my head pounded. I felt shame, but mainly I felt fear. Fear at what she would do with this information.

Despite my gut-wrenching dread, Ann took my revelation surprisingly well. Of course, she had been drinking earlier in the evening, but even so I wondered if maybe I had her figured out all wrong. If she accepted this part of me, then maybe I could overlook some of her bad habits. Her empathy and understanding proved to be short-lived however. Not long after, we got into an argument and, in a fit of drunken rage, Ann yelled at me and called me a faggot. That stung, not least because it felt wrong. Yes, I liked wearing women's clothes, but up until that point I was a man that felt exclusively attracted to women.

The *Francis Scott Key* didn't pull into Rota at the beginning of my fifth and final patrol. The Navy instead had her pull into Charleston to undergo repairs that simply couldn't be done in Spain. This meant that instead of spending a boring night on the ship, or getting drunk in the NCO Club or the Dutch Bar, I could go home on my days off. It also gave me more time to try and clear the air with Ann before the bulk of the patrol began.

However, the *Key* being based in Charleston brought with it problems as well. For example, Ann would borrow my van to go out and then not return the next morning in time for me to go to work. This occurred more than once and I got into trouble each time. I didn't know what to do. I felt trapped. If I broke up with her, would she share what she had learned about me? And who with? In my naïveté I also thought she had a chance to clean up her act. I was wrong.

Not long after we had pulled out for the patrol, I found out from Ann's mother that some of my stuff had been stolen. Ann had moved my things to a cheap sheet-metal shed at her mother's house. Her mother told me that someone had broken into it already and helped themselves to my belongings. Worse of all, I wouldn't be home again for more than two months. Would there be anything left by the time I returned? How could she be so careless?

I seemed to attract the most irresponsible women wherever I went during those times. I'm not sure what caused it. Maybe I had the word "sucker" tattooed on my forehead in letters only others could see. If I did, those letters must have faded over the years because my luck did eventually get better.

That last patrol on the *Key* didn't give me a lot of incentive to stay in the Navy. I looked forward to transferring off to go to the West Coast. I did however manage to finish my E-6 requirements during that patrol, which would mean I would get to take the test once I arrived on the *USS Flasher*, a *Permit*-class submarine which had the motto of "Best in The West."

While on that last patrol, the ship did something rare. One of the officers had been having a great deal of pain in his kidney area, leading the Corpsman to figure he had kidney stones. He displayed all the other requisite symptoms as well. This meant that we had to break patrol silence and come to the surface so that he could be medevaced off the ship.

Since I had already filmed several of the ship's functions with my Super 8 movie camera, I received permission to go topside and film the officer being taken away. After donning all of the appropriate safety gear, I climbed topside, connected the safety line into the track on the missile deck and made my way to the aft end of the sail.

Not long after, I saw the helicopter approaching in the distance and as it got closer, I filmed it circling the ship before hovering over the aft hatch. Then the Chief of the Boat came out and helped connect the officer to the helicopter's wench. Once everything looked good, the helicopter hauled him up. After securing the officer in the helicopter, they then lowered a big bag of mail.

When the patrol concluded and I arrived back in the States, my relationship with Ann ended in a whisper rather than a thunderous roar, as I feared it might. When I came back from that last patrol, she had found someone else. The idea of marrying her died while I patrolled the ocean, and the funeral for it took place while the rest of the country celebrated the Bicentennial. I returned ashore to find that some of my things had indeed been stolen, while others were ruined because the shed Ann had put them in didn't have a cement bottom. This meant the items sitting directly on the grass had soaked up a lot of water. I salvaged as much as I could, then I stayed at her mother's house until I had to leave to go to my next duty station.

My time on the *USS Francis Scott Key* had come to an end. I had had a few girlfriends over the time, made love to other women and had even gotten engaged. My time on the *Key* helped shape me in many ways. I lost some naïveté, had learned some lessons, and made a little progress in releasing the Woman in the Shadows. At the age of 25, I had just scratched the surface of what life held for me.

13 – WELCOME TO CALIFORNIA

My next set of orders had me stationed aboard a submarine called the *USS Flasher* (SSN 613). In case you're wondering how the ship's name came about, allow me to explain to you a bit of submarine history. You see, back when the Navy commissioned the *Flasher*, most fast attack boats were named after fish (e.g. the *USS Haddock*) while ballistic missile subs received the names of historic American men (e.g. the *USS Benjamin Franklin*).

Later, when the Navy decided to commission a new class of fast attack ships, they decided to name the new submarines after U.S. cities (e.g. the *USS Los Angeles*) while the new Trident missile boats were named after states (e.g. the *USS Ohio*).

When asked why the Navy had decided to update the naming convention, the late Admiral Rickover replied simply, "People vote. Fish don't."

So, by now, I'm sure some readers are asking, "Is there really a fish called a flasher?" Well, there is indeed: the flasher, or tripletail, belongs to the fish family Lobotidae. The flasher fish does however have one big problem. They have to special order those tiny trench coats.

In spite of the horrible time I had qualifying in submarines, my time stationed on them laid the groundwork for my future as a trans activist. The strong, independent thinking that I developed during both the training and everyday work became part of my personality and helped me forge my life philosophy.

Working around submarines also gave me some perspective on

life. While in the Engine Room of a submarine, had I made one little mistake, I could have sunk a billion dollars' worth of government property, killed 145 men, caused a major nuclear environmental disaster, and lost up to 160 nuclear warheads. These days, there is no accident I could be involved in that could possibly cause that much death and destruction. As such, I have tended to take the view that everything in my life that came after my submarine career is as a piece of cake. More or less.

After sending Pat and her daughter north, I got to spend some time with an old friend of mine, Scott, who lived in San Diego. Scott and I knew each other from high school, and we had even launched model rockets together. He said I could stay at his place for a few days before heading north to pick up the *Flasher* in Vallejo.

Fleetwood Mac would be playing in concert during the course of my stay, which gave me an added bonus to stay with him. Scott prepared something special for us to eat before we set off for the concert: brownies. I loved brownies, although these ones had been made with some special ingredients. Like an idiot, I pigged out on them.

Once we were inside the concert hall, the brownies started kicking in. I felt dizzy and disoriented. I couldn't speak well and I felt like I had no balance. I rushed off to the bathroom, but I didn't feel sick. I had no idea what was going on around me. I had never felt that way with weed before, so I guessed the brownies had been laced with something else. The feeling scared me.

Scott must have found me in my disoriented state and took me back to his place. I don't know what time we got home or how much of the concert he missed because of me. I missed all of it and I would have to wait another forty years to get the opportunity to see Fleetwood Mac again.

For the next three days, I couldn't function. I don't know if I ate any food or drank anything during that time. I survived, so I guess I must have. But I have little recollection of anything that happened during that time. I do remember one thing from those days however: I remember fantasizing about being a woman and having a man make love to me. This became the first time in my life that I had thought about having sex with a man. But as a woman? My brain must have been in overdrive.

Once I'd recovered, I said goodbye to Scott and headed north to

Vallejo. This time the roads of California were kinder to me, although the fact I now traversed them in a brand-new van probably made a big difference.

I arrived in Vallejo and checked in to the *Flasher's* office on time. The ship had just come out of the yards and was presently on sea trials, so I ended up with a lot of time on my hands.

Here's a little history on the *USS Flasher*. While the ship sat in the yards being built, the first boat in its class – the *USS Thresher* (SSN 593) – sank at sea with all hands lost. The loss of the *Thresher*, on April 10, 1963, sent a wave of fear and sadness through the Navy's submarine crews and sent the design engineers back to the drawing board in order to create safer seawater systems.

Up until then, all of the equipment in the Engineering Spaces received its cooling directly from seawater. In order to drastically cut down on the miles of seawater pipe in the ship, they redesigned the systems so that seawater cooled an enclosed freshwater system that would in turn cool most of the ship's equipment. They called the new designs "sub-safe systems." The *Flasher* initially remained in the shipyards an extra 18 months in order to become one of the first ships to incorporate these new systems.

Initially, I did a lot of relaxing and getting used to my new surroundings. They had me in a four-man room in an old barracks on the base. One day, I felt bored, so I reached under my rack to pull out the bag with my women's clothes inside. I quickly put on a bra and pantyhose and moved over to the mirror in order to look at myself.

Then I heard a knock at the door.

I lived in a four-man room. My three roommates were all at sea and I had the only key to the room.

Then I heard a key go into the lock. Fear gripped me. I quickly dashed under the covers of my rack. I hid the bra straps under the sheets, just as the door opened and in walked the Executive Officer and the Chief of the Boat (COB). The COB come over to my rack and whispered, "Helms? Helms?"

I slowly opened my eyes, "Yeah?" I said in my best sleepy voice.

"Just go back to sleep. We're doing room inspections." They looked around and then both walked out.

Holy fuck! My heart not only lodged in my throat, but also in the throat of the guy in the next building. I had dodged a big bullet, a cannonball in fact. How could I have been so stupid to take such a risk? I would have been kicked out for sure if they had caught me.

A few days later, I had another close call when I came through the base gate. The Marine stationed at the gate had decided that my van would be the next vehicle he'd inspect thoroughly. He opened the side door of my van and looked inside. He then grabbed the bag I kept all of my women's clothes in and tried to open it. Luckily for me, he had a hard time unfastening the zipper. It had a habit of sticking if you didn't know how to pull on it just right. I wasn't about to help him.

"What's in this?" he asked.

"Just some clothes my girlfriend left in my car."

The Marine felt the bag and decided it had nothing important in it. "Okay. You're good."

I'd dodged another bullet, but it became increasingly clear to me that I needed to find a place to store my stuff.

Older and much smaller than the *Francis Scott Key*, the *Flasher* was only 292 feet long, with a 31 feet, 8 inch beam. This compared to the *Key's* 425 feet length and 33 feet beam. The *Key* received priority attention by the Navy and the Department of Defense because the first Trident submarines wouldn't be commissioned until 1981. By contrast the *Flasher* didn't receive much priority as a fast attack submarine because the new the *Los Angeles*-class boats had been commissioned in 1974, making the older fast attacks second-class submarines.

This meant that, if an *LA*-class sub and the *Flasher* tied up next to each other for repairs, the *LA* sub would get the attention and the best treatment. If we needed something repaired, most of the time the crewmembers fixed it themselves instead of getting the sub tender people to do it. They also got the best food, like steak and lobster, whereas the *Flasher* would get hamburger and cold cuts.

Much of the equipment on the *Flasher* looked the same as it had on the *Key*, but in different locations. This meant I had to learn my watch stations and the ship's safety equipment locations again. It took a lot of time and effort that I really didn't feel like committing myself to. Since I had already earned my Dolphins, the *Flasher's* crew didn't push me around like they did the new non-quals, but they didn't exactly make my life easy.

I soon received my promotion to E-6, which on a surface ship would have greatly reduced my mechanical cleanup workload and increased my paperwork. However, since the lowest rank in the Nuclear Navy was an E-4, I had to do the same grunt work that the lower ranks did on surface ships. This, combined with some other issues I had, meant my attitude towards the Navy became increasingly negative.

The biggest difference between going to sea on the *Key* and going to sea on the *Flasher* had to do with storage space. The *Key* had that big Missile Compartment, which allowed for plenty of storage in between the missile tubes. When the *Flasher* went to sea, we had to stack dry goods boxes from the deck to the overhead, in a center passageway between Crew's Mess and the Wardroom, as well as in many other cubbyholes throughout the ship. With the middle passageway blocked, any movement forward and aft through the ship had to go through the Crew's Mess, even during mealtime.

Mess Cooks even used some of the racks for storage, meaning more of the lower-ranking sailors had to 'hot bunk'. Hot bunking meant that when one person stood watch another person could sleep in their shared rack. Sometimes three people on three different shifts shared a rack. Hot bunking has been a way of life on submarines since before WWI, and isn't a great attribute of submarine life.

Because the *Flasher* didn't have a strict patrol schedule like the *Key*, she could go places and do things the *Key* could never do. On one trip, we went to Santa Catalina Island, just off the coast of California, and anchored in Avalon Bay. This gave the crew a chance to visit the town and view the island's beautiful scenery.

While anchored in Avalon Bay a large sea lion decided to sunbathe on the aft end of our ship's deck. He looked content, even when one of the Mess Cooks approached him to get a picture taken next to him. Some of the crewmembers took a hint from the sea lion and laid out on the deck to catch some rays themselves.

In May 1977, while stationed on the *Flasher*, a historic event took place. Well, for some of us it was historic. The first *Star Wars* movie came out that month. I went to see it the very first week they released it and I went back to see it again and again. I even tried to see it in as many different cities as I could. I mention seeing this film because of the long-lasting effect *Star Wars* and its two sequels, *The Empire Strikes Back* and *Return of The Jedi*, had on my film, video-making and writing.

14 – MY TIME ON THE FLASHER

I got to go to some cool places while stationed on the *Flasher*. On one trip we went up to the Puget Sound area, stopping first at the Canadian naval port in Victoria, British Columbia. The *Flasher* became the first nuclear submarine ever to anchor there, and to celebrate this event a Canadian destroyer crew invited us aboard their ship for beer. The Canadians still allowed beer on their ships, a tradition carried over from the British Navy.

While in Victoria, a few of us visited their version of a Veterans of Foreign Wars (VFW) hall to socialize with some Canadian sailors. The locals all treated us with respect, and a good number wanted to buy us drinks. The year was 1977, two years after the Vietnam War had ended. Had we been in an American establishment we would have been treated like shit. Americans had such a prevalent attitude toward the military at that point. The Canadians thought differently, probably because Canada didn't participate in the Vietnam War.

An interesting thing happened to me while in Victoria. As I drank with my shipmates at their VFW hall, one of the Canadian men introduced me to his girlfriend and she started coming on to me. It surprised the hell out of me, while he didn't seem to mind. Later, I discovered from the woman that they had an open relationship. I'd heard of that before but never met anyone who practiced it. My education on this kind of relationship went much further when the woman took me back to her place so the two of us could get better acquainted.

After a day in Victoria, we cruised into the Sound to the location of a new Navy base north of Bremerton, situated in an out-of-the-way place called Bangor. The base was so new that it didn't even have permanent personnel stationed there. This would one day become the West Coast home of the new Trident fleet of ballistic submarines that would replace the *Francis Scott Key* and her sister ships. The *Flasher* docked there to prepare for special operations later in the year. Owing to its brand-new status, the crew got to stay in squeaky-clean, two-person dorms built for housing the Trident crews and support people.

While we were there, I rented a cheap car to see the local sites and visit some familiar places. I drove south to see if I could find the house Midge lived in four years earlier. As I stated previously, when I arrived in the area, I discovered a new freeway had replaced the houses in her neighborhood. I didn't expect to find Midge, but it would have been nice to see the house where I had my first romance. I felt sad as I drove back to the ship.

One night, my shipmates and I traveled into Bremerton to do some drinking in a local bar recommended to us by some of the other Navy men who helped with the preparations on the *Flasher*. It seemed like any small, local bar with music and a small dance floor. One of the women there appeared to be very popular, but she didn't take the crap the others on the *Flasher* tried to use on her. Being a very experienced and tough woman, she could easily see through their bullshit. None of them could get anywhere with her. I didn't even want to try if the others had failed so easily, but I did approach her just to talk. She seemed to warm up to me after a short time and a few dances.

Her name was Linda, and she lived in a house north of Bremerton, and north of the new base in Bangor. She had me take her home that night, which surprised me. This woman, with a tough exterior, had a beautiful soul and a soft, gentle heart. I seemed to have the ability to bring out the softness in her that she hid so well from the others at the bar. She told me she had to put a wall around her heart in places like that so she wouldn't be hurt by anyone. My shipmates at the bar had all acted like typical guys. I guess she felt safer around me. We spent a few wonderful nights together and became so close that we kept in touch and wrote to each other up until the time I got out of the Navy. I would have liked to go back to see her, but over the years neither the money nor time materialized.

Before leaving the Puget Sound area, we made one final stop, tying up at a pier in Seattle so we could participate in their annual Sea Fair. People from all over the Northwest traveled to Seattle to take part in the fair's events and celebrations. I spent one afternoon watching speedboat races in Lake Washington and touring the city. The last time I'd visited the area it had snowed and rained from the day I arrived until the day I left. This time, the weather was gorgeous.

That first night in Seattle, I went to a popular nightclub built on a pier. It had a dance floor on the ground level and balconied floors above it, each of which had tables, all of which had great views of the people dancing. Popular disco music filled the air and all of the women wore sexy, silky cocktail dresses. Seeing how beautiful each of them looked in their outfits made me green with envy.

Sitting at a table on the upper floor, I could see almost everyone below me. At another table sat a group of women, one of whom caught my eye. She wore a beautiful light-blue dress, had short blonde hair and a cute smile. This combination compelled me to take a chance and ask her to dance. When I arrived at the crowded table, I felt fairly nervous, but I held my nerve and asked the blonde to dance. She clearly sensed my nervousness, but accepted my invitation and walked to the dance floor with me.

The woman, Patty, happened to be five years older than me, shy of just one day. Our age difference didn't seem to bother her, because we danced, talked and smiled together the whole evening. We found that we had several things in common and I, of course, found her extremely attractive. I sensed she felt the same about me. When the evening ended, I walked her to her friend's car. She leaned in toward me and gave me a soft kiss on the lips, sending a tingling sensation down my spine. I asked if she would come to the *Flasher's* pier in the morning so we could spend the day together. She said she would try, but it would be closer to noon before she could make it. Even with all that happened that night, and the kiss, I still doubted she might show up.

The next day I sat around in the Crew's Mess, watching a movie and snacking on cold cuts and bread, hoping Patty would turn up. Others in the crew took people on tours of the ship, or at least as much as we could let them see. I had different plans for Patty. Of course, many pieces of equipment in the Control Room had covers over them to keep spies from finding out about our technology and capabilities, including how fast and how deep we could go. No one but crewmembers could go into Engineering, the part of the ship I worked in. Years later I came across Tom Clancy's novels about espionage and the Cold War, which are reckoned to be written with detailed precision. He wrote a number of wonderful books about submarines and what they can do, and even had a chance to ride on some. Yet, with all the subs he has been on, he would never have been allowed in the Engineering Spaces.

After what seemed like an eternity, I received a message that someone waited for me topside. When I climbed out of the hatch, I saw Patty standing on the pier waving. My heart raced. We left the pier in her friend's station wagon to explore the city together. The weather looked gorgeous.

Patty and I had a great time that day, riding all over the city, feeling closer and closer with each passing minute. If it takes chemistry to make attraction stronger, then there was an explosive reaction happening between us. We knew we had to find a motel room and fast. Yet, because the Sea Fair took place all weekend no hotel or motel, no matter how small, had a vacancy. We drove further and further out of the city and still found nothing. The frustration became maddening.

Finally, we found a deserted road, pulled off into the trees and made love in the back of the station wagon. We had a magical experience, but unlike Linda at the other side of the Sound, Patty didn't wish to stay in touch. It seemed she only cared about a quick fling.

I did meet some interesting women in San Diego, when we came back to our home port in between trips at sea. Pat eventually moved to San Diego and found not only a job, but a car and apartment as well. All by herself. Her cleanliness also improved greatly, turning her into a person I could almost tolerate. We saw each other now and then, but it wasn't what you could consider a relationship. To be honest, I cared more for her daughter's wellbeing than I did for Pat.

I met another woman, Cathy, at a science-fiction convention. She served in the Navy as a Wave, or female Naval personnel. Not only did she work on the submarine base at Point Loma, but she lived in the same dorm building that I lived in. I found her very attractive, but cold when it came to showing affection. Now that I think about it, her actions and responses to some of the things we talked about seemed more like those of a lesbian. I couldn't see it then, because of my lack of experience with lesbians, but looking back today all the signs seem to point in that direction. When I acted like a typical guy, she responded negatively. When I did little things that showed sensitivity, she responded in a positive way. Of course, I could be completely wrong in my assumption.

Cathy showed me early on that I could trust her with anything, so I felt comfortable leaving her my van when I went to sea. But, one time when I came back, I discovered that she had moved out of the dorm rooms and into a house with other Waves. It took some extensive detective work, but I finally located her. Her move turned out to be fortuitous for both of us. The house she now shared had an extra bedroom and the women there needed a fourth person to bear the expenses. As an E-6 I could afford the rent, and this gave me a room off-base in which to store my women's clothes. The other two women didn't mind having a guy moving into the house. Saving money seemed more important to them and I'm sure I appeared harmless. Ironically, that year the sitcom *Three's Company* had become a big hit on television. The comedy revolved around two women sharing a house and renting out their third bedroom to a man.

This move turned out to be a valuable learning experience for me. For the first time in my life as an adult, I shared a living space with women with which I had no romantic ties. The previous closest experience had been the boarding house in Idaho, but other men also lived there and I had not become acutely aware of my feminine side. This new situation gave me a unique insight into the world of women that I would not otherwise have gotten.

In the house, I had to be very aware of what I did so as not to offend my female roommates, a challenge for any submariner. On the boat, using foul language and walking around near-naked occurred all the time. I personally never felt comfortable being nude or semi-nude in front of my crewmembers, but I sure as hell knew how to use really foul language.

As Cathy and I became closer friends, another woman in the house caught my interest. Her name was Bobby Joe, a woman who lived her life in a polar opposite way to Cathy. BJ, as she liked to be called, loved going out with men, having a new date, and a new love practically every weekend. These various encounters with men didn't always turn out the way she hoped, causing her some pain at times.

She frequently opened her heart only to have a man break it in two. Looking back at BJ's love life and how she wore her feelings on her sleeve, I see that she and I had a lot of things in common. She and I had several serious conversations about her feelings and how men treated her, which seemed to help her cope. At the same time, I got more in touch with my feminine side in order to help her with her man problems.

One weekend, when all four of us were enjoying some quiet time in the house, Pat came over for a visit. She and BJ hit it off right away when the both of them discovered how much they enjoyed making fun of me. As the ribbing continued, Pat mentioned my small "attachment," which seemed to amuse BJ. The two women began tickling me, then cornered me in my room, on my bed. At that point, it got a bit sensual, or at least it did for them. They convinced me to take off my clothes, while they kept most of theirs on. I felt so embarrassed and emasculated that even seeing their partially nude bodies on my bed did nothing for me. That made their taunting even worse. I had always dreamt about making love to two women at once, but this experience burned my self-esteem deeply. I moved back into the dorm not too long after that.

15 – MY WORST TIME AT SEA

Just before my last birthday in the Navy, March 8, 1978, the *Flasher* pulled out for an extended patrol called a WESPAC run. WESPAC stood for 'Western Pacific' and included Southeast Asia, Korea, Japan, Guam, The Philippines and even the coasts of China and Russia. A WESPAC patrol could encompass many things, but it all boiled down to one inescapable truth: you would be gone for up to six months or more. Of course, during that time the ship would make stops in various ports along the way.

This WESPAC started off badly. The entry in my journal from March 9, 1978, the day after my 27th birthday, tells the whole story:

> Yesterday was a suck-ass day, the worst birthday in my life, and thank God, my LAST in the Navy. I now have 99 days left on board and approximately 129 left in the navy.
>
> Yesterday was a 25-hour day because we went through a time zone. During that time, there was an hour for training, 4 hours for Field day, 6 hrs of watch and 4 hrs of training watch. The day went shitty…
>
> I'll be damned if I'm ever forced to work under these conditions again in my lifetime.

True to my word, since leaving the Navy, I have never worked under similar conditions.

The entire patrol became a continuous recurrence of the most intense bullshit I have ever encountered in the Navy. If they didn't have us up doing drills, then they had us doing cleaning. Because I had less than a year left in the Navy, my Chief and Division Officer focused on trying to get me qualified on all of my watch stations, while the Chief of Boat focused on getting me qualified on the *Flasher*. Since every ship is different, a person had to qualify on each ship, even if they had already earned their Dolphins on another.

The workload became so extreme that one time I came within a frayed nerve of punching my Chief on the nose. The thought certainly crossed my mind, while we stood having heated words with one another. Of course, I never did hit him, and he kept the details of our argument to himself.

Eventually, I qualified on both the *Flasher* and my required watch stations, while the Chief I had argued with appeared on the dink list the day after I qualified.

My last patrol had its highlights however. The biggest and most memorable one was when we pulled into Pearl Harbor and the crew had the chance to take liberty on Oahu. I got to go topside as we approached the *USS Arizona*, a battleship sunk by the Japanese with the loss of 1,177 officers and crewmen. I saluted as we passed by. After pulling in, I visited the *USS Arizona* Memorial and cried as I read the names of the dead on the wall. As I type this and remember that day, a tear has formed in my eye.

With three buddies, I rented a Ford Fiesta and we drove all around Oahu in a single day, seeing as many sights as we could. On the north shore we watched surfers ride big waves, cutting and slicing the water with the skills of master surgeons. At another location we found a beautiful waterfall crashing into a pristine pool. They allowed swimming in the pool, so I climbed to the top of the cliff next to the waterfall, about 20 feet up, and jumped into the water. Later, we drove through miles of pineapple fields.

The fun continued into the night as we sampled Honolulu's nightlife. An old English pub by the name of The Rose and Crown was the best place we visited. A pianist kept us entertained all night and the beer flowed. Ted Lange, who played Isaac in *The Love Boat*, sat alongside us in the bar with his girlfriend, making a classy ending to a great day.

One day while back on patrol, cruising at periscope depth, I asked the Captain if I could look through the scope before we submerged and he said, "Yes." When I looked out, I could see that dusk had arrived. Turning the scope, one of the most gorgeous sunsets I have ever seen in my life came into view, rivaling the ones I'd seen in the Arizona desert. A few minutes later, the Commanding Officer gave the order to take the ship to 150 feet. The water quickly flooded my view and as I turned the scope's mirror to look upward instead, I saw the calm ocean surface from underneath the shimmering water.

We had picked up some special passengers in Hawaii and they came with equipment that only they knew how to use. Officially they were called Communications Technicians, but the crew knew them by their more colorful name, Spooks. Spooks received special training in the use of high-tech equipment to spy on the Soviets. A great book to read that gives more details of how submarines were used in spy missions is called *Blind Man's Bluff: The Untold Story of American Submarine Espionage*, by Sherry Sontag, Christopher Drew and Annette Lawrence Drew

The crew didn't really need to know the specifics of the Spooks' mission. Their presence on our ship in this part of the world told us all we needed to know. Later in the patrol however, we began seeing evidence that the Spooks had begun their work. Field days and drills became less and less frequent as the Spooks' need for silence came first. Back in Engineering, the seawater temperature had dropped drastically, becoming so cold that you could place a soda can next to a seawater pipe and within 90 minutes it would freeze. Eventually, the Commanding Officer showed us a videotape, shot from our periscope, of the Soviets test-launching a new kind of missile from one of their submarines.

For my last patrol I had brought with me eight cases of Pepsi. The idea had been to drink them all myself, but the cans also became my own special trading currency, allowing me to trade for things that other crewmembers had brought with them, like candy. Unexpectedly, I lost several cans due to the changing pressure in the sub, which would make them leak through the can. I would take a can with me on watch and cool it next to a seawater pipe. I timed my consumption perfectly because I drank the last can on watch, on my last day at sea on the *Flasher*.

The incident that sealed my decision to leave the Navy occurred when we were required to do an extensive field day to prepare for a big inspection. I stood watch in the Engine Room, Lower Level, when the Chief wanted me to clean the bilges by climbing down into them and wiping them down with paper towels. To speed up the process, my Chief also climbed down, between the pipes to help. While we cleaned the oily and grungy pipes, I realized something profound: "I'm a Machinist's Mate First Class, an E-6, doing the same grunt work that an E-3 seaman would do on a surface ship. And in the bilges with me is my E-8 Chief with over twenty years of experience. Is that what I have to look forward to if I stay in?" I made my decision that very moment to leave the Navy.

I found out later from a friend who stayed in for 12 years and made Chief, that I made the right decision that day. He said that the Navy started decommissioning subs left and right and that they became so top-heavy with Chiefs that they couldn't find billets for them. In other words, they had too many Chiefs and not enough grunts. To get the required work done, some of the Chiefs had to double as grunts now and then.

One of my personal goals for my last patrol concerned the number of books I planned on reading before we returned to port. I brought a great selection of science fiction and fantasy novels to keep me occupied. On the second half of the patrol, after I'd finished my qualifications, I read J.R.R. Tolkien's *The Silmarillion*, then *The Hobbit*, followed by the *Lord of the Rings* trilogy. This was the third time in my life that I'd read Tolkien's *Ring* trilogy. After that, I tackled Frank Herbert's *Dune* trilogy (Herbert would, of course, go on to write three more Dune books) and I even completed Isaac Asimov's *Foundation* trilogy, finishing the last book, *Second Foundation*, on the day we pulled into Guam, May 15, 1978.

The *Flasher* spent two weeks in Guam undergoing repairs. I remained a crewmember the entire time, but didn't spend many days on the actual ship. My time aboard the *Flasher* had ended. On the day she pulled out again from the Naval base, I stood on the rocks overlooking the entrance to the port and waved her and the crew goodbye as they passed by. I figured I would never see the ship again, but fate, as it always does, had other plans.

In the summer of 1991, my wife, two sons and I spent our vacation in San Diego. On a whim, I called the security at Point Loma to see if the *Flasher* still existed. Not only did she still exist, 13 years later, but they had her tied up next to the tender. Base security put me through to the Ward Room and I convinced the Officer of the Day that I had served on her over a decade earlier. I told him I wanted to show my sons the last submarine I served on and they gave me permission to do so. My boys enjoyed seeing where their dad lived, slept, ate and worked for the better part of two years. They even got to look through the periscope. They were both young on that trip however, and sadly neither one of them today remembers that tour.

In May of 1992, the Navy decommissioned the *USS Flasher*. Sixteen months later they decommissioned the *USS Francis Scott Key*. I cried each time I heard about the decommissioning of one of my ships. Six years of my life would become nothing more than memories and mementos when they were cut up. I may have had some tough times on those ships, but they helped shape my character as much as any person had. I will always be proud of serving on both ships.

From Guam, I flew back to Hawaii on a Marine propeller transport that had no heat and no sound insulation. They had us sit on a tiny foldout seat with hydraulic pipes running across our backs. After taking the torture for over an hour, I wandered back to the cargo bay and discovered a papasan chair being transported to the States. I curled up in the chair and spent the rest of the 17-hour flight cold, but comfortable.

When I arrived in San Diego, I had a lot of time on my hands before I began my last month in the Navy. In the evenings I would leave base, find a motel room and dress up in my women's clothes to go out to gay clubs. There I met other cross-dressers and even some transsexuals.

One night, I decided to go to a drag club, but I didn't dress up because I didn't have the money to pay for a motel room. Instead I enjoyed watching the drag queens while dressed as a man and tried to get the attention of one of the cute ones. She wouldn't pay attention to me. At the end of the various performances, I was sat drinking when one of the other drag queens came over to talk with me. She didn't seem very attractive or very slender.

"You a Navy man?"

"Yeah."

"Why don't you come back to my place and we can have some fun."

I thought for a moment, then said, "Sure. Why not."

I then followed her to her apartment. She had her place filled with dozens of dresses, and wigs and she had makeup literally everywhere.

She looked at me and said, "Would you like to try on something?" She could apparently tell I loved seeing all of her clothes.

"A corset?"

"I have just the thing for you."

She pulled out a corset from her dresser and helped me put it on. It gave me a wonderful hourglass figure. When I looked at my image in the mirror, I couldn't help but be turned on. Then she started kissing me and things escalated from there.

That night, I had oral sex with a man for the first time, and although it fulfilled a fantasy, it didn't live up to what I thought it would be. I'd imagined having sex with a man, as a woman, but somehow thought it would be different. I didn't find it disgusting, but I never had sex with a man again while in the Navy.

For my last days in the Navy I spent my time handing out car bumper sticker passes to new military personnel in San Diego. As an E-6, they actually put me in charge. This was a new experience for me. After almost eight years in the Navy and with one month left to go, I finally got to be in charge for the first time! Partly I stuck around because the Navy doctors had to decide whether to discharge me or operate on my left ear. I had a genetic condition called otosclerosis, which had caused the three tiny bones in my left ear to deteriorate. I inherited the condition from my mother, but she also passed on many good things too, so I didn't hold it against her.

After a month of consulting with experts, the Navy doctors decided not to operate, and they gave me an Honorable Discharge on June 28, 1978. I packed my things in my van and drove back to Phoenix, ready for the next chapter in my life. The Navy had made a man out of me. Now, I had to tear that down to rebuild myself in my own image: as a woman.

16 – PAGING MISS MONICA

For eight years in the Navy, I'd had a guaranteed income regardless of whether I worked 24-hour days or spent a month on leave. Now back in the civilian world, I needed to find a job to keep the money coming in. Staying with my parents when I got back didn't quite cut it, so I moved into a house with other friends as soon as I could afford it.

Finding a good job proved a daunting task. The first job I found allowed me to use the mechanical training I had received in the Navy, working in the pipefitting area of a company that dug wells for large farms and rural houses. They had me cleaning the threads on old pipes from reclaimed wells and threading new pipes for future wells. Unfortunately, this meant working outdoors in the diverse Arizona weather, which I didn't find fun.

Not too long after settling back in my hometown, I tried to acclimate myself to the Phoenix nightlife, such as it was. The places I went to didn't do much for me, and I had zero luck meeting women. I also didn't have a lot of spare cash, which meant I couldn't rent a motel room and bring Monica back out. So, she stayed hidden for a while. That all changed however when I met Lorraine.

One day in the early fall of 1978, I was driving along a major street in Phoenix when I saw this tall slender woman hitchhiking. I decided to pull over and give her a ride. She looked cute, but I sensed something different about her. I couldn't pinpoint it at first, but I could feel it. When I thought I knew what it was, I didn't want to verbalize it because I would look ridiculous if I was wrong.

Lorraine only lived a few miles away. When we arrived at her place, she admitted she hitchhiked to have men pick her up and pay her for sex, but that she didn't want to have sex with me. She had sensed something different about me as well. I felt very nervous about the subject of my cross-dressing, but Lorraine didn't feel nervous at all. She knew I had something to ask her and tell her, so she waited patiently for me to bring it up.

Finally, I asked the question, "Are you... a... you know... a... transsexual?"

"Yes, I am. Is there anything about YOU that you want to tell me?"

"Well, I don't know how to say it."

"You want to change your sex."

"Not exactly. I don't know. I do like wearing women's clothes."

"I guessed that."

Apparently, trans-radar existed, and it had worked for the both of us. In spite of this, I still had no understanding of transsexualism or myself for that matter. Lorraine and I talked long into the night about everything. She told me when she started taking drugs to aid her transition and what they were. She told me she couldn't find work because employers wouldn't hire a transsexual and she couldn't get her ID changed from male to female. To her, prostitution seemed like the only option. This not only made me feel sad, but it made me fearful of wanting to change my own sex.

At this point, I should probably say something about terminology. When I write about a conversation I had with someone, I'm going to use relevant terms from that time period. Some terms, like transsexual may not be used today, but if we used it at the time, I will use it in this book.

Let me return to Lorraine. I felt bad for her situation, but had no idea how to help her. Back then, not only did I have no concept about how to fight for equality, but Arizona's mindset and laws would have made the task impossible. Arizona later made it easy for trans people to change the sex marker on their driver's license and to change an Arizona birth certificate so no one would ever know. As I understand it however, Arizona has subsequently made the process harder again.

Lorraine and I became good friends. We would go shopping

together and go out to nightclubs as often as we could. She would go to the mall with me and help me pick out the right kind of clothes. I got to own some of the very dresses that I'd seen women wearing at discos less than a year earlier. On weekends she would meticulously help me get ready, giving me tips on how best to apply my makeup, for example.

After Lorraine and I had finished getting ready, we would go to a local gay nightclub called His Co Disco, where we danced and flirted with the straight men who went there. Occasionally a man would pick up Lorraine and we would go back to her place so that they could make love, while I tried to sleep on the couch. Men tried to pick me up too, which gave my feminine side a bit of an ego boost. I flirted with them, but always turned them down before things went too far.

I later found out that my sister, Carrie, and her best friend went to His Co Disco occasionally, a revelation that sent a chill down my spine. That would have been all I needed, for her and her friend to see me at the club dressed as a woman. However, somehow I lucked out. In all the times I went there, I never ran into my sister or her friend.

For the rest of 1978 and a little into 1979, Lorraine and I were inseparable. She blended in so well that I even invited her to Thanksgiving dinner at my parent's house and to a New Year's Eve party with my high-school friends.

I started feeling more and more uncomfortable with her picking up tricks however, though I knew society had left her with few other options. If the thought of having genital reconstructive surgery ever crossed my mind in the late 1970s, seeing her lifestyle soured the idea instantly. Besides, I still hadn't figured out the feelings running through my mind and how I should cope with them. After a time, Lorraine and I drifted apart. The disco age began dying and eventually His Co Disco closed its doors. I looked for other gay bars in Phoenix to visit, but couldn't find any.

In summer, the Arizona heat kept me from dressing in women's clothes. I couldn't stand wearing makeup and a wig in that kind of weather. I tried a couple of times, but when I did the sweat poured out of me.

In the fall, I decided to take advantage of my GI benefits and study for an AA degree at a local junior college. I enrolled in a drafting class because I had always found mechanical drawing a breeze, plus I figured that once I had my degree, I might use it to get a job in that field of work.

During that first drafting class I noticed a woman with beautiful red hair and an equally beautiful smile. During our break, I went over to introduce myself. This woman, Donna, said that she needed to complete the drafting course in order to get a promotion from her employer. She also revealed, after much questioning by me, that she didn't have a boyfriend or anyone she dated on a regular basis. Eventually, I asked her out and she agreed to go on a date with me. I found her funny, intelligent, fun and wonderful to hold close. I fell in love with her. In time, when my family met her, they fell in love with her as well.

Donna had all the things I looked for in a woman and none of the problems that came with Ann, Pat or Carolyn. She had a good job and seemed responsible. I had found my future wife. One last hurdle needed to be overcome before I could 'pop the question' however. I would have to tell her about my cross-dressing.

So, one evening, after a nice night out, she and I sat in her parents' house talking about this and that. I sensed that my chance had arrived. I told her I had something I wanted to tell her, but that I felt very nervous about it. Finally, I summed the courage to tell her. To my surprise, she didn't seem to mind. So, with that obstacle overcome, I proposed to her right afterwards.

Both of our families celebrated the news of our engagement and we set the date of our wedding for August 1980. Later in life, Donna would deny that I ever told her about my cross-dressing. For the time being however, I felt like the happiest man on earth.

I got to know Donna's family and I found her parents to be wonderful, loving people. Her father, Clifford, worked as a machinist at Goodyear and had a great sense of humor. We had a lot of fun together. Whenever I worked on a mechanical project that needed something special to be built, I could always count on Clifford to know how to make it work properly. Donna's strong and loving mother, Margaret, knew how to both cook and care for her family. Had I been given the chance to create the perfect in-laws from scratch, I couldn't have done better than Donna's parents.

Prior to our marriage, I worked as a commission-based salesperson for an appliance store. I believe this and subsequent sales jobs helped me to eventually become a successful trans activist. This is because a successful salesperson has to be likeable. They also need to be able to read a customer and understand what they really want and what they really mean when they say something. Salespeople aren't born, they're trained and developed, but to my mind people with outgoing personalities find it much easier to acquire the skill to sell.

I actually had a number of jobs prior to and after marrying Donna. I worked for a time as a carpenter making cabinets for big screen projection televisions and bed frames for waterbeds. I also worked laying the foundations for homes, making fiberglass drinking troughs for cattle, cutting cardboard for use in making boxes, making 3D-looking photos, selling video movies, and repairing go carts. I couldn't find anything I felt comfortable doing.

Donna and I got married on August 9, 1980, on a typically hot day in Phoenix. My Best Man, Dann, arrived at church on his Harley. Afterwards, Donna and I spent our honeymoon in Southern California, where we visited several towns and had a lot of fun. One place we visited has stuck in my mind all this time however.

One evening, Donna and I went to the Queen Mary drag bar, located in Studio City. It is one of the most famous drag bars in America and it more than lived up to its lively reputation. Donna had a great time that night. She found the drag queens hilarious. At one point, she turned to me and asked, "Is this what you meant when you told me you liked dressing as a woman?"

"Not exactly," I told her. "I don't use quite as much makeup and I don't dress as flamboyantly as they do. They're doing it to entertain the public."

She seemed to understand. Or so I thought.

Six months into the marriage, I found out just how Donna really felt about my cross-dressing. She came home one day and found me wearing a dress. She went ballistic and told me in no uncertain terms that I would never dress like that at home ever again.

I hadn't felt the kind of fear and embarrassment that I felt at that moment since Ann had called me a faggot five years earlier. Donna's comments hurt even more than Ann's, because I loved her more than anyone else in the world. Nothing I could do would quell her fears or ease her hurt. I still had no idea what I felt or how to talk about my feelings. Life doesn't always give you the right tools at the right time.

After taking a few drafting classes, I found a job as a draftsman. For the first time in my life I worked at a job I completely enjoyed and looked forward to going to. I got to use skills that I had used for personal projects since a young boy. Now someone paid me to use them.

The company I worked for built storage tanks for different kinds of liquids, specifically oil and water. They would give me exact requirements and dimensions for the tank, and I would draw all the plans for it, including the shapes for the sheets of steel that formed the top and bottom, and any platforms and structural items on the tank. I enjoyed the work because they left me alone while I did all the calculations and drawings. While I worked, I would listen to music and snack on goodies. Unfortunately, sitting on my ass and eating all day caused me to put on some weight.

That wonderful job lasted for only 15 months before the deteriorating financial climate under 'Reaganomics' caused the company to go under. I received the news that I had been laid off on the same day as my first son's birth.

17 – THE PATTER OF LITTLE FEET

Two days in my life will always remain very special to me – June 1, 1982 and June 7, 1984. These are, respectively, the days that each of my sons was born. No matter what I do with the rest of my life, I know I will never feel happier than I did on those two days. I felt especially proud of Donna for all she had to endure during childbirth, not to mention the fact that she delivered each of them without the aid of any pain medication. That being said, I have to say that, despite all the pain she went through, I felt strangely envious that she carried and gave birth to both of our boys and I didn't.

We named our first son Robert Clifford, after his two grandfathers. This made Donna's father proud because, even though he had other grandsons, none of them had been given his first name of Clifford. Donna and I used our son's middle name when we addressed or referred to him. For the longest time we wrote his name down as R. Clifford so that teachers would know what to call him. Today, as an adult, he wants to be called Robert, even though the rest of the family still refers to him as Clifford. Personally, I call him Robert. This is because I think I'm the last person in his life that should go against his wishes when it comes to how he wants to be referred to. In this book, I call him Clifford up to the point he decided he wanted to be known as Robert.

I have an interesting side note to Clifford's birthday. While in the Navy, I would frequently remember the dreams I had because of being so frequently woken up in the middle of them. In one dream, which I later turned into a short story, I dreamt that a young witch had to marry a specific mortal man because of his particular astrological sign. When I wrote the story on the *Francis Scott Key* in 1975, I picked the birth date and time of the man as June 1, 1:33 p.m., Arizona time. Well, Donna gave birth to Clifford on June 1 at 1:03 p.m., Arizona time. Not an exact match, but close enough for me to double-take when I reread the story many years later.

As Donna's first labor lasted through the morning, the television in the delivery room distracted us with game shows from the era. The labor pains would come and go, and I would feed her ice and cater to her needs. When the pains began increasing, *The Price is Right* came on. As the doctor told us that it wasn't yet time for Donna to start pushing, because she hadn't dilated enough, the game show host yelled, "Come on down!" in the background. We all had to laugh when we heard that.

Clifford finally did "come on down," and I got to hold him in my hands after the doctor had checked him out. I cried when I saw the beauty of this new life. This new person relied on Donna and me for everything he needed to grow up to be strong and healthy. The love he would give us in return however would be priceless.

Early on, Clifford seemed to have some medical problems that had us worried. He began hacking every so often, as if his lungs had become filled with fluid. The doctors were concerned he may have cystic fibrosis, a disease that could have meant he wouldn't live to see the age of two. Donna and I cried every day during the testing and waiting period, not knowing what to expect. I felt so helpless that I prayed to God for the results to be negative. When the results finally came back negative, the whole family celebrated. After that, for the longest time whenever Clifford began hacking, we had to lay him on his stomach and lightly tap his back and sides. He grew up to be healthy, though a little shorter than most other boys his age.

Our second son came into our lives shortly after midnight, in the early hours of June 7, 1984. We named him Bryan James, to honor our two brothers. Once again, I cried when the time finally came and I got to hold him in my hands. He looked so helpless and so beautiful. Bryan didn't have any medical issues like Clifford had, but being born on June 7 meant that he would always share his birthday with my mother. I'd hoped he wouldn't be born on the same day because I wanted him to have his own distinct birthday. In later years however, his sharing my mother's birthday turned out to be a blessing. Each year after Bryan turned five, he and my mother went out to lunch or dinner together to celebrate their birthdays, though when Bryan got older and had his own family that tradition came to an end.

As I mentioned previously, on the day of my first son's birth, I lost my dream job as a draftsman. Well, fate repeated itself two years later because two weeks after Bryan's birth I once again lost my job. Donna and I decided right then that we would not have any more kids. We couldn't afford for me to keep losing my job each time! More realistically though, Donna and I were too old to have any more children. We figured two children would be enough and also that we didn't want to be raising children at ages when most people become grandparents.

My two sons grew up to be typical boys. They both loved basketball and, from a young age, they wanted to play whenever they could. When we had houses of our own, I installed hoops for them. When we didn't live in our own house, they played wherever they could. Both of them later played on junior-high basketball teams. In 1993, when the Phoenix Suns made it to the NBA finals against the Chicago Bulls, both of my boys watched the games on television with me. As they got older, their age difference mattered less, and their skill levels became comparable. I'm sure each of them would disagree with that statement however.

Out of the two boys, Bryan took the most risks. At an early age, he would take his big yellow Tonka dump truck and push it down the sidewalk as fast as he could, not watching where he headed. More than once we had to take him to the emergency room for a bad cut somewhere. Because of this, Donna cringed whenever I let the boys use power tools before they turned ten.

Both of our sons had natural mechanical abilities and understood technology early on. They could use tools with the skill of those twice their age. I can honestly say they came by it through genetics. As I mentioned earlier, Donna's father earned his living as a machinist for decades, and my father worked as an aircraft mechanic while in the Air Force and for different companies after that until he retired. Of course, I worked in the Engine Rooms of nuclear-powered submarines. When they got older, I introduced them to my favorite hobby, model rockets, and they had enormous fun building and launching them. When we got our first computer, they quickly began operating it with uncanny proficiency. Both went on to learn how to program computers in high school.

In junior high, Clifford took woodshop and had to build a gravity racecar out of a block of wood. He built one so beautiful and so slick that he won all of his end-of-term races hands down. The instructor made him his student assistant the very next semester.

One of the things I'm most proud about when it comes to my sons is their acceptance of diversity in the people they meet and socialize with. Donna and I taught them early on to accept everyone equally and the friends they have made over the years reflect that openness to diversity. Clifford's first best friend was a Latino boy three months younger than him. Both of my sons had friends of various races, cultures and backgrounds. Both dated Latina girls and both ended up marrying one.

My two sons have grown up to be responsible young men. At age seventeen, Clifford went to work for Montgomery Wards as a commission-based salesman in their large electronics department. In a few short months he became the best salesman they had. He then went on to work for CompUSA and became their top salesman too, then their store's head of security. Bryan also went into sales, working first at Petco and then also at CompUSA. He even received an award from the company's president as one of the top four salesmen in the U.S.

Part of why my two sons grew up with such a strong sense of responsibility came from the good work ethic that Donna and I gave them, as well as the work ethic their grandparents gave them. As parents, we gave the boys more responsibilities and independence than most kids their ages. When they turned five, we let them decide what clothes they wanted us to buy for them. At age ten, we allowed them to ride the city bus so they could go to the mall or the movies. Yes, we took a chance, with the world full of nasty people, but the chance paid off. I'm not sure how we would handle that same situation in the 21st Century.

When they turned twelve, we gave each of them their own savings account and showed them how to put money in and take money out. The tellers looked surprised at first, but quickly realized that our boys knew all the proper procedures relating to their accounts. Not long after getting his first savings account, Bryan started earning money by cutting grass for people. One time, when he had finished mowing the lawn, one of the women he worked for told him, "All I got at this time is a ten."

"That's okay," Bryan responded. "You can write me a check. I know how to cash it."

Early in their lives, Donna and I tried to convey the complex concept of love to our boys in a way they would understand. Telling a three-year-old you love them can be confusing, even when you follow that with a hug. Instead we said, "I want you and I'm so happy you are in my life." In my opinion this statement conveys to the child that they are wanted and needed. This meant that when they were older, they truly understood the strength and meaning of the word love.

18 – DON WE NOW OUR GAY APPAREL

Right after I lost my drafting job on Clifford's birthday, Intel hired me to work in their video production department. I had started taking courses in video production at Glendale Community College, and the job with Intel had come about from that. Video production had always interested me even more than drafting. The filming I'd done in the Navy on Super 8 had jump-started my creative juices, a creativity that would carry over to my writing in later years. When I got my new job with Intel, it started a seven-year career in video production and tape duplication.

The man who taught the video courses at GCC, Bill Davis, later became one of my most trusted friends and my mentor in the video industry. It took a little time, but I proved to him that I had the talent to do anything and everything in the business, and to do it well by his standards. After a year of working at Intel, Bill hired me as his assistant at a new facility where we not only duplicated tapes for customers, but shot and edited original productions as well. The company was called Champion Video, a subsidiary of Tom Hopkins International. Our primary duplication customer would be Tom Hopkins, a motivational speaker, writer and sales guru who produced his own sales-training tapes, but we also got to work on any outside business that we generated.

Tom Hopkins lived in Arizona, so I got to know him and his family, which made his training tapes even more personal for me. For five years, I saw his videos over and over again, so I couldn't help but learn something from them. I later used several ideas from his training courses in the course of my trans activism. If I ever see him again, I plan on thanking him for all the help he gave me.

One of the many positive things he taught that stuck with me is that you may have to get through ten 'no's' before you get to one 'yes'. For a trans activist this means that, just because a politician will not support a piece of legislation today and gives you a 'no', doesn't mean the next politician won't give you a 'yes'. Often you have to get through many 'nos' to get a 'yes'. In other words, don't let rejection from politicians, or indeed anyone else, discourage you. They will not all support you, but someone somewhere will.

I learned another technique from him that became a useful tool in getting appointments: "Senator Doe, since you seem interested in hearing more, I would like to discuss this new bill with you in detail. Would Tuesday at 1p.m. or 3p.m. be better for you?" A person can use this technique when they have received an indication that a politician wouldn't mind discussing an issue, but seems reluctant to commit to a time. By picking the date and two times, you have narrowed down the options to an either/or choice. Most people will pick one of the two times you have offered, although politicians are a bit harder to pin down this way. It typically works well with their aides or staff members however.

For most people, closing a sale is the most difficult part of selling to master. It's hard because certain closing techniques work better for some people than others and have to be further adjusted depending on who the potential buyer is. Salespeople typically enjoy talking about the product they want to sell, but that alone isn't enough unless you actually ask your would-be buyer to buy it. The same applies when asking for support for a bill from a politician. A trans activist has to take that final step and actually ask for the politician's support. There is nothing wrong with educating a politician on our issues, because it could help us in the future, but in activism just as in sales, one must always try to get that all-important close: make the sale and get them to commit to supporting the bill.

"I'll think about it," is the most common blow-off line a salesperson receives and that goes for trans activists, too. My response to that line is "What is there to think about, may I ask? You have the figures in front of you now on how many trans people have been murdered in the U.S. over the last year. It hasn't stopped for decades and it will not stop tomorrow. The figures prove we're vulnerable, so why not add us to your bill today? Can we count on your support?" You have to close the sale! I may not always get a person's support, but I never give up when I hear those dreadful words, "I'll think about it."

During the summer of 1983, Bill and I built from scratch not only the editing and audio suites necessary for doing original productions, but also the banks of racks for the video-duplicating machines. We spent weeks cutting wood for the racks and tables, bolting and nailing pieces together, gluing padding on to the editing console, mounting equipment and monitors, and connecting miles and miles of video and audio cables, as well as connecting all the necessary switches. When we had finished, the backs of the racks looked like something I remember seeing on submarines.

While Bill and I worked on putting the facility together, I kept a television on in the background. One day, Phil Donahue had on his show members of the Chicago chapter of Tri-Ess (The Society for the Second Self) a national organization for heterosexual cross-dressers. The show caught my attention. It fascinated me to see individuals who considered themselves to be heterosexual, who also happened to be cross-dressers. "That has to be what I am," I thought. I watched the show, transfixed, and wrote down the contact information for the organization that appeared at the end. Hopefully, there would be a chapter in Arizona that I could find out about.

I wrote to Tri-Ess and a couple of weeks later I received a letter from an Arizona person calling herself Andrea. When I called the number, Andrea had given me I heard a distinctly male voice answer the phone. In spite of being nervous, I told her my name and agreed to meet for lunch the next afternoon. It felt good to talk to someone who had the same feelings that I had.

I had no idea what to expect when I showed up at the restaurant the next day. I also didn't know what Andrea looked like. Luckily, trans-radar helped us make the connection, even though both of us dressed in our men's clothes. We talked for a long time about our past and our feelings, both admitting that we were heterosexual cross-dressers based on what we knew about ourselves. Andrea, like me, had children, but had a much more accepting wife. She told me that others had contacted her after the Phil Donahue Show appearance and that they planned on having an informal meeting on

Saturday at a nearby hotel.

After my meeting with Andrea ended, I went back to work feeling incredibly excited about all I had learned and the upcoming meeting. I came home that evening wanting to tell Donna all about it, hoping that hearing about others like me would help to ease her fears. Sadly, it did not. As such, I knew that if I attended the meeting that Saturday she would be hurt. In spite of her feelings though, I knew I had to attend. When Saturday came and I told her my plans, she at first became angry and then stopped talking to me.

We had arranged to meet in a room at the hotel. When I arrived, Andrea had already dressed. She looked great. I could tell she had been doing this for a quite a while. After an hour of preparation, I stepped out of the bathroom wearing a dress, makeup and a wig. Two others by the names of Tina and Paula had arrived by then and the four of us talked all night about our experiences and our road to self-discovery. The stories we shared all sounded familiar in part.

During the evening we discussed forming a chapter of Tri-Ess and decided to have a second meeting two weeks later to formalize it. By the time that meeting took place, two others had joined us. Out of that meeting came the new Tri-Ess chapter, Alpha Zeta, so-called for the 'AZ' in Arizona. Alpha Zeta still meets today on a regular basis and is considered one of the strongest Tri-Ess chapters in the country.

Now let me point out an interesting fact about the six people who formed Alpha Zeta that Saturday in 1983. Four of the others ended up having genital reconstructive surgery before 1992 while the fifth, who hadn't considered herself a transsexual at first, began transitioning shortly after I started in 1997. It's not uncommon for many trans women to begin their coming out process as members of their local Tri-Ess chapter, with many even becoming organizing officers. Others however, never go through a cross-dressing phase.

When we formed Alpha Zeta, I couldn't run for the position of officer because my wife wouldn't allow me to spend sufficient time with the group. They did however nominate me for First Lady on more than one occasion.

By 1984 the hearing problem in my left ear had gotten so bad that I had to turn up the volume on the television just to be able to hear it. This didn't make Donna very happy since at the time she had perfect hearing. I decided to have my ear repaired by a specialist, who would replace the little bones inside it with tiny metal replacements. My mother had the same operation in the 1960s, so I figured I would likely have an even better outcome than hers given the likely technological improvements that had taken place in the meantime.

Having been prepped for the operation, the doctor put me under. I hoped to wake up hearing much better, but that's not what happened. Not only did I not wake up to better hearing, but I had also lost control of the left side of my face. When the doctor went in to fix my ear, the nerve controlling my left facial muscles had been exposed. He had bumped the nerve, which in turn caused me to lose muscle control. It felt and looked terrible. Moreover, when the signals came back a month later, they now went to different muscles, giving me an asymmetrical appearance to my face and my smile. Worse, the damage was permanent. I used to be able to whistle with a lot of control, but now I can't whistle at all. I have to say that I miss that. I wish doctors had a way to correct the problem with my face, but they don't, and I now have to wear in-the-ear hearing aids for both of my ears.

As I mentioned before, two weeks after my second son's birth, I lost my job at the video production and duplication company. However, the owners of Champion Video eventually hired me back a month later, though they didn't rehire Bill. So, I became the manager, overseeing one employee – me. To be fair, the facility really only required one person to work it.

The video production business tended to attract people who had big ideas but lacked the means to back those ideas up. They would come into the office and talk a good game, promising all kinds of work for me, while expecting me to do a bunch of free work for them. These con artists would try to take advantage of me, but the lessons I'd learned from Bill saved me more than once.

A con artist did reel me in one time however, shortly after I became manager. A person I met through a mutual friend wanted to make a video movie called *Bikers vs. the Undead*. He had all the costume and makeup support in place, but still needed the video equipment and expertise to tape and edit the movie. He promised to pay for my time, use of equipment and editing.

I actually had fun taping the movie and I contributed a lot of ideas used by Jim, the producer/director. But the final product looked horrible because Jim wouldn't listen to me when it came to editing. Also, the plot sucked, the quality reeked and the audio tanked. My camera angles looked great, but the old camera I used didn't make the footage look crisp.

When Jim held a premier for the film at a good-sized local bar, he attracted a pretty good crowd. Unfortunately, he wouldn't pay me a share of the door fees and later decided he didn't want to pay me at all. It left me with no choice other than to file a civil suit in court. Jim professed he didn't have the money to pay me, but showed up at court with a lawyer. Meanwhile, I represented myself and, after hearing the facts, the judge ruled in my favor.

In truth however, Jim really didn't have any money or other assets, so initially I didn't see a dime of what he owed me. Two years later however, he came into a healthy inheritance so, when I found out, I served him with papers for what he owed me. Not long after, the lawyer I had hired to serve him called and told me to come and pick up my check. I learned a lot from the whole experience.

One of the best experiences I had in the video business came when one of my friends got me a side-job working as a cameraman and cable puller for the new Diamond Vision screen at the Phoenix Suns' basketball stadium. I had a wonderful time and even got to bring my son Clifford to a few of the games, though my other son, Bryan, couldn't come along because of being too young. When I recount working those two losing seasons for the Suns, I tell people that, since I sat on the floor at the edge of the court, I got stepped on by some of the best players in the league at the time, including some future Hall-of-Famers. The job definitely solidified my appreciation for basketball.

By 1987 all my hard work at the Glendale Community College paid off when I graduated with two AA degrees. Around that time, I'd also started writing in a serious way. That year is principally memorable for me for something else however.

In October, Tri-Ess held their annual Holiday En Femme in San Francisco and four of us from Alpha Zeta decided to attend. Donna and I had made some extra money that year, so she begrudgingly allowed me to go. I felt thrilled by the prospect of being dressed as a woman for three days in a row, something I had never had the chance to do before. So, on the Thursday afternoon before the event weekend, I closed the doors to Champion Video and drove to the airport.

When I arrived at the hotel in San Francisco, I was as giddy as a schoolgirl. Then disaster struck. When I opened up my makeup case, I discovered that, to my horror, one of my nail polish bottles had opened up on the way and spilled everywhere. Several of my items were ruined including some of my jewelry. It took me a while to compose myself after that, but fortunately the rest of the weekend went well.

The Holiday En Femme event is a great way for Tri-Ess members from all over the country to get together and connect. They still hold it every year. For our trip in 1987, they scheduled a visit to a wig shop, training sessions on how to talk and walk like a woman, a trip to the wine country, dinner with a local trans group and another dinner at a restaurant on Fisherman's Wharf. We even had a tour of Alcatraz Island. The lessons on how to walk and talk like a woman didn't appeal to me because I had already taught myself and reached the point where I felt I could act like a woman without having to think about it much. The rest of what they had on the schedule sounded like fun though, especially since I would be dressed as a woman the entire time.

As we rode on the chartered bus through the wine country and into Napa, I couldn't help but remember Carolyn. Some of the streets we passed through looked strangely familiar, but for the most part, a lot had changed in 11 years.

We spent the rest of the day visiting different wineries. Some bystanders looked at us and laughed, while others would stop and ask some of us questions. Later, we stopped for lunch and one of the Arizona members videotaped each of us. When I watched the tape 12 years later, I made a surprising discovery. In the footage I introduce myself by saying, "Hello, my name is Monica Helms." I hadn't realized I'd begun using that name as early as 1987. I remember starting off as Barbara, but my sister-in-law had that name, so I decided to change it. Exactly when, I don't know. Also, I never used the last name I received at birth when dressing as a woman, though why I settled on Helms still remains a mystery to me. It sounded simple, so that must be why I picked it.

Over the course of the long weekend, I found myself spending more and more time with Tina, my close friend from Phoenix, than I did with the rest of the group. A month younger than me, Tina seemed to look very relaxed and natural when dressed as a woman.

She and I had become very close over the previous year. Both of us felt like we didn't have a lot in common with the other attendees, though I had difficulty at first verbalizing why.

Then, on our last full day in San Francisco, we waited on the pier together for the first ferry to Alcatraz Island. While sipping coffee at the cafeteria, Tina looked across the table at me and said, "I've decided that when I get back to Phoenix, I'm going to begin my transition."

I can't say I felt very surprised, but I still asked her, "Why?"
Tina began going over all the things that happened in her life that pointed to this decision, telling me all the feelings she'd had over the years. Strangely, she remembered praying to God to change her from a little boy into a little girl, just like I had at the age of five. As she spoke, something wonderful happened in my brain. All the pieces of my gender identity puzzle finally began to fall into place. I felt as if a fog had been lifted and suddenly a whole new, beautiful and scary world opened up before me. When Tina told me the reasons why she needed to get surgery, I realized that her reasons were also my reasons. Without knowing it she spoke for me as well. At that moment I became a transsexual. "Now what?"

19 – DESPERATELY SEEKING MONICA

Thirty-six years into my life, I had finally figured out I had been born a transsexual. This should have been a wonderful revelation for me, and it felt like that for one brief moment, until I realized that now I had to tell Donna.

My life had taken an interesting turn onto a pathway that would be full of both beauty and ugliness. A billion questions crossed my mind and each one of them raised a corresponding concern. Submarine training had prepared me for the unexpected, but nothing in life had prepared me for this. Previously, I had thought that being a heterosexual cross-dresser caused enough complications in my life. Being a transsexual would make that look like a walk in the men's aisle at a local thrift store.

How would I ever break this devastating news to Donna? Over the years, my need to dress as a woman had already caused her a lot of pain and bad feeling between us. I could only imagine how this news would escalate the problem and cause her yet more grief.

I also had the boys to worry about. They were only three and five in 1987, far too young to understand. The revelation would also likely devastate my parents. So, faced with all of these very real concerns, I did the only thing I could do to remain safe and keep everyone around me from pain. I did nothing. At least in the short run.

A year later, I took Donna to a concert of 1950s and 60s groups at the Celebrity Theater and, while there, she and I had a couple of drinks. We had such a great evening that I felt the time may have come for me to tell her about me. So, on the drive home I decided to tell her. I can remember the conversation that took place perfectly.

"Donna, I have something serious to discuss with you."

"You want a divorce," she responded rather quickly.

"No, that's not it. It has to do with something else."

She remained silent.

I continued, "I have done some serious thinking about things and..." I paused, the words sticking in my throat. "I realize I need to change my sex. I have to become a woman."

She angrily snapped back, "If you do that, I will make sure you never see the boys again in your life!"

Her threat and the anger that came with it meant I would remain near-silent for the rest of the drive home. When Donna asked me questions, I answered with simple answers. All of a sudden, my life became miserable. Even more misfortune awaited me.

In 1988, the owners of Champion Video sold the facility to a man who knew nothing about the video business. Along with the sale, Tom Hopkins stopped using the facility to duplicate his tapes, so our business plummeted. I saw the writing on the wall for Champion Video and quickly found a job at a new facility. A year later however, they sold that business to another company and I lost my job there as well. I wouldn't work in the video business again for another 29 years.

From April 1989 to January 1990, I once more worked a number of unsatisfying jobs for very little money. Donna's pay kept us afloat for a short time, but eventually we fell behind on our bills. We ended up filing for bankruptcy in 1990 and lost our home shortly after that. Our fortunes then changed for the better because, in January 1990, I got a decent-paying job with Sprint as a long-distance operator.

About that time, my friend Tina began her transition and started changing, but I don't mean because of the hormones. I watched her become less and less sociable. She stopped answering my calls and those from her other friends. We all became worried for her. After she had sex reassignment surgery, she wanted nothing to do with anything or anyone connected with her past. I couldn't understand why. In later years, I saw that happen many more times with other trans women. They focused so much on their transition that they let their connections with friends and family dissolve like salt in water. I could never do that. My trans family and my blood relatives mean everything to me. Besides, too many wonderful things happened to me before I transitioned. I could never turn my back on those moments and the people I shared them with. I am the person I am today because of my past.

I found being a long-distance operator for a major telecommunications company suited me for a number of reasons. The job required very little brainpower, which gave me the chance to do a great deal of writing and plenty of thinking. Being on the phone also meant that customers couldn't see me. So, on the first Halloween at work, I came in dressed as a woman in high heels and a short skirt dress, to take the tolerance pulse of those I worked with. One male co-worker looked at me, stunned and asked, "How come you can walk so well in those high heels?"

"I practiced a little," I replied.

Another person noticed, "You shaved your legs?"

"Well, I had to make it look good." Needless to say, I had fun that day, but it didn't really tell me how any of them might react if I started transitioning.

By 1992, I felt the need to begin my transition. So, I contacted a therapist who had helped some of my friends begin. After a few visits, she gave me an extensive test of over 500 questions called an MMPI, which stands for the Minnesota Multiphasic Personality Inventory. The creators of this test designed it to give a therapist a fairly accurate breakdown of a person's personality. If questions are answered truthfully, it can tell a lot about a person, including their gender identity. However, the questions on the test relating to gender identity are so blatantly obvious that a person could easily manipulate their answers to show the identity they want the therapist to see. I have heard of that happening, so I don't personally hold much stock in the test's validity in that area. Each of the two times I took the test, I answered the questions truthfully.

Back in the 1990s, the MMPI had become one of the many hoops a transsexual had to jump through before a surgeon would put scalpel to genitalia. The subject of gatekeepers – doctors and therapists who decide whether a person is a transsexual and when they can start transitioning – had become one of the most controversial subjects within the trans community.

Some felt the rules the medical community imposed on

transsexuals placed undue restrictions on their lives. Others saw the necessity to have a process in place to ensure that people don't get their surgery on a whim. I am personally neutral on the subject, because I can see the logic on both sides. Like religion and politics, the subject of gatekeepers sparked heated discussions within the trans community for the longest time. When it came to my transition, I felt the need to follow the rules, also referred to by some as guidelines.

My MMPI showed that I indeed was a trans women, but it also showed I had a slight distrust of authority and I exhibited signs of anger. My distrust of authority came from my days in the Navy, but my new job had further enhanced that. My therapist concluded that my anger stemmed from not being able to transition, which came out of both my work and my family situation. I took the MMPI a second time, a year after living as Monica, and my level of anger dropped considerably.

I knew that Donna wouldn't want to hear about my results from the MMPI, but I also knew I had to move forward, so I didn't tell her. The next step for me would be to see an endocrinologist and start hormone treatments. It became difficult to hide these visits and co-payments from Donna, but if she ever saw my insurance forms, she never questioned them. Somehow, I knew she probably suspected. Donna was a smart woman.

The doctor I saw prescribed the same hormone dosage for me that he had prescribed to a few others I knew. He prescribed me one drug, spironolactone, to eliminate the hair on my legs, chest and arms, but I suffered a horrible side effect while on it. I woke up one night with my heart racing so fast that I felt as if it would pop out of my chest like the creature in *Alien*. To ensure I had guessed the cause correctly, I stopped taking the drug for a few days and slept much better. Then, I started taking it again and, sure enough, I woke up with my heart racing. I never touched it again after that. Very few others I've talked to had the same reaction to the drug.

To pay for my hormones, I would save my 'mad money' until I had enough to pay for my Premarin in full. I would also cash my paycheck and put some in a personal account before depositing the rest into the family account. Donna knew I did this and occasionally got upset with me, and rightly so. I exhibited the same selfish attitude that some other trans woman displayed at the beginning of their transitions. When I look back and think about the life I lived in 1992 and 1993, I feel ashamed at the way I treated Donna and the boys. I know I can never make it up to them.

With the high cost of hormones, I asked a friend of mine visiting Mexico to pick up as much Premarin as I could afford and she could carry back with her. This was incredibly irresponsible of me. Since Premarin is a controlled substance, she could have gotten in trouble if she had been caught with it without a prescription. She did it once and only once for me.

I took the hormones for about eight months before I had to stop because of the cost and the pressure it put on my family. During that time, I lost all erections and began forming breasts. Thankfully, I kept the breasts hidden by wearing t-shirts. This meant no one but Donna would know about them. But she noticed them alright.

In 1993 and 1994, Sprint began making my job a lot more stressful. They would scrutinize every little move my colleagues and I made and placed ridiculous restrictions on us. It became so unbearable that a few of us decided to talk with the Communications Workers of America (CWA), the union for telecommunication workers. I stepped forward to become a leader in this movement, making my very first venture into the world of activism.

Trying to form a union in a non-union facility is activism in its most basic and regulated form. The federal government established the rules for forming and operating unions over a hundred years ago. At the same time, they established rules that govern acceptable behavior for what companies can and cannot do. Unions try to follow the rules the best they can, while in my experience companies bend and even break the rules quite often. Sprint acted no differently in this regard. At one location in California they racked up 50 violations of federal labor laws and weren't held accountable for any of them. I had even witnessed them breaking labor laws at our facility in Phoenix.

As we got further into the process, we needed to pass out information on union activities. We did this by placing a flyer through the mail slot into each person's locker. According to the law, union materials cannot be distributed on the work floor, but can in places away from the work area. The lockers occupied a small room that had several offices between it and the work floor. We planned on having a person who worked the mid shift place the flyers in the lockers and he did exactly that.

However, when I arrived at work the next morning, I found supervisors opening lockers and removing the flyers, in direct violation of labor law. The CWA filed suit in federal court against Sprint and I ended up testifying. Sprint lost, but appealed, which delayed the final outcome and to all intents and purposes made the problem go away for them. They had done the same thing in California.

During the drawn-out process, we witnessed Sprint do all the typical things a company does to fight the formation of a union at their facility. They had employee appreciation days, which consisted of cheap gimmicks to make their employees think that Sprint actually cared for them. I told them that if they really wanted to show us they cared, they could give us a pay raise to bring us up to what people got at other companies for doing the same job we did.

They also brought in union-busters to tell us horror stories of the bad things unions do. They would talk about all the violence that surrounded certain past Teamsters' strikes, while I would counter by saying that the CWA had never had a violent strike and had actually had fewer strikes than any other union. The company's techniques worked on many of the employees who knew no better, but the seasoned employees never bought their line of bullshit.

In order to make me an effective representative for the union, the CWA sent me to an AFL-CIO three-day training session in Oakland, California. This intense training made all of us who attended prepared for anything and everything we might see from the company while trying to form a union at our facility. We even had the chance to walk a picket line at a strike taking place in Oakland.

At this training we found out that the term 'right-to-work' legally meant something totally different from what companies try to tell their employees it means. The term has become a phrase to scare employees into thinking they have no right to complain if they get fired in a right-to-work state. In reality it means that if a shop or facility has a union in it, employees don't have to join the union to work there, yet they nevertheless still receive all the benefits the union has to offer. In a non-right-to-work state, a person has to join the union in order to work at a shop or facility that has a union present.

Companies have long convinced their employees that they can fire any one of them for any reason if they are in a right-to-work state. They fail to tell you that a person can also be fired for any reason in a non-right-to-work state as well. Just ask any trans person fired in states like New York, California or Massachusetts, or any of the other 25 non-right-to-work states. A union in any state can provide you with a bit more protection than you would otherwise have without one. And, as far as gender identity and gender expression goes, more and more unions are adding provisions to their contracts to protect trans workers. The AFL-CIO now has a strong constituency group called Pride at Work, which can help in this area. They can be found on the Internet at www.prideatwork.org.

Looking back, the training I received from the AFL-CIO represented the final step on my journey to becoming a trans activist. The Navy had taken a young, wet-behind-the-ears boy and turned him into a 'man.' Submarines hardened the shell and infused me with a sense of independence and ability to think on my feet. My love life then peeled away several layers of naïveté. Becoming a parent had taught me how to care for and love other human beings unconditionally. Working in sales and the training I received from Tom Hopkins taught me how to convince people to support my issues. Then the video business showed me how to spot a con artist and analyze people's intentions. Finally, trying to form a union at Sprint taught me the basics of activism.

20 – THE BIRTH OF MONICA

In the mid-1990s, I began growing more and more frustrated with my self-image and self-worth. I had stopped taking hormones for several reasons and when I did all the positive effects they had on my body slowly receded. All except my breast growth, which remained. I stepped away from my union activities in order to focus more on myself. My self-centered attitude became stronger as I grew more and more desperate.

I also became less tolerant of the annoying things my sons would do, which meant I yelled at them more often. I had become a horrible person to live with and a terrible dad. My family suffered as a result. At one point, I even considered taking my own life, so they could collect my insurance policy and I would be out of their lives. No beam of light came down to fill my soul with the knowledge of what to do next, no birds sang outside my window, and no gypsy with a gold-capped tooth told my fortune and opened my mind. Unlike some trans people who experience spiritual intervention, I had to work out what to do next all by myself.

In late 1996, I started seeing a therapist again, but not one who had experience in gender identity issues. Eventually, I changed my insurance coverage so that I could see the therapist I had been meeting with previously. With my therapist, I at least figured out one important step that I had to take. Then in December, right after Christmas, I sat Clifford, Bryan and Donna down to tell them: "I will be moving out on the first of the new year."

Subsequently, there has never been another point in my life where I felt as low as I did at that moment. We all cried. They didn't want me to leave, which made me feel even worse. But I couldn't continue hiding my doctor visits and medical costs, not to mention receiving hateful comments from Donna about my shaved legs and breast growth.

I also shared with them that my horrible behavior stemmed from the frustration I felt from not being able to transition or even see if the doctors would allow me to transition. It wasn't fair to them. They shouldn't have to put up with such an awful father and husband. In spite of all this, they still didn't want me to move out.

I love my two sons more than life itself and at the time I carried deep feelings for Donna. As I write about this part of my life, tears fill my eyes. These three people did nothing to deserve the pain I put them through. If a pill existed that would have changed my gender identity to fit the body I had, I would have gladly taken it. Instead I faced a choice about the two paths that my life could take. I could live the often hard and dangerous life of a trans person, or I could live the rest of my life as a man and be miserable. I knew that if I chose the latter, I would eventually succumb to thoughts of suicide. Realistically, I had no choice. I wanted to live. I wanted to try and be happy.

I made a compromise with my two sons and Donna that day in December. They would allow me to see which direction the therapist pointed me to and in return I wouldn't move out in January. If the therapist concluded that I should transition, they would let me pursue that course. They also said they would stop making snide comment about my dressing as a woman, in return I wouldn't dress as a woman at home. To me, they seemed to compromise more than I did, but we made our agreement with a desire to keep our family together.

Shortly after the first of the year, we purchased our first computer. We paid for it using the money I had set aside to move out. The computer gave us all access to the Internet for the first time. Up until then, our home computers had more or less served as glorified word processors. But Internet access opened a whole new world to me for the exploration of my gender identity. It also introduced me to the United States Submarine Veterans, Inc.

The USSVI is a national organization that at the time had about 7,500 members. The organization, and the men I met online, filled me with an enormous sense of pride for my earlier career. I also figured out that my pride at serving my country was independent from my gender identity. That understanding became the core of my future activism with transgender veterans. I joined the USSVI in January 1997 and began attending as many of the local chapter's meetings as I could.

I remember feeling a little sad during the opening ceremony of my first meeting of the Phoenix chapter, called Perch Base. At the beginning of each meeting, submariners would honor lost shipmates by reading the names of the submarines lost during that month in previous years. They would also ring a bell for each lost ship. Most of the lost U.S. submarines and casualties happened during WWII. The bell-ringing originated from a centuries-old maritime tradition whereby coastal town churches would ring a bell for each man lost on a ship that sank at sea. I remember crying during the ceremony because it affected me.

On February 5, 1997, I went to a local doctor to start hormone treatments for the second time, this time with the intention of not stopping. Dr. Fisher, a general M.D. who had previously treated many of the HIV/AIDS cases in Arizona, helped trans people by prescribing hormones for them and monitoring their levels. He gave me a prescription that began my journey to life as a woman. There would be no turning back.

Shortly after beginning hormones for the second time, my breasts began growing again. Since I already had some growth from the previous regimen, their size soon became noticeable and hence harder to hide. I didn't realize it, but people at work started to talk about the changes they had seen in me, though none of them mentioned it to me directly. Then one day while talking to one of the supervisors she unexpectedly said, "You know, if you ever need someone to talk to, you can always count on me."

Her statement puzzled me, though I suspected her reason for saying it, so I asked, "What do you mean by that?"

"You know, about the changes you're making."

Oh, shit! She knew. I fumbled a reply, "So, you know. How?"

"Some of your co-workers have been asking us about the changes they see happening to you."

"Does all of management know?"

"Yes, but we figured you would tell us when you were ready."

"Then, I guess it's time for my supervisor and me to speak with HR."

"It looks like it."

The next day, I asked my supervisor to set up a meeting with HR. Then, she and I discussed what they should expect when I began my transition. My supervisor asked a lot of questions that at the time I found very hard to answer. So, for the meeting with HR, I went online and downloaded some helpful information. Today, of course, there are thousands of websites and sources for trans employees and employers of trans people.

At the HR meeting, I found out where Sprint stood on the issue of transitioning at work. First of all, they told me they had no company-wide policy on transsexual employees. Second however, and much to my relief, the HR representative told me that Sprint would not tolerate any harassment of me because of my transition. Third though, they had no intention of warning my co-workers or undertaking any employee training concerning my change. They reasoned that if they trained my co-workers on my particular situation, they would have to do so for other minorities as well. Of course, that excuse wouldn't fly today.

So, I ended up springing my transition on my co-workers with no chance of warning or educating them ahead of time. In my opinion, Sprint disrespected my co-workers and was the likely reason they ended up treating me the way they did. Because I soon found out that, while I wouldn't be receiving any overt harassment, I would instead be on the receiving end of a subtle bigotry that Sprint would find hard to stop.

Finally, the meeting with HR reached "the restroom issue". Sprint leased the entire second floor of a three-story building and the restrooms on its floor weren't accessible to the public. The restrooms on the first and third floors however were open to the public. So, in order to avoid unnecessary drama with my colleagues, we agreed that when I came to work as Monica, I would use the women's restrooms on either the first or third floor. Sprint would allow me a bit more time off the phones to compensate for me having to go up and down the stairs each time.

What Sprint expected from me was what companies expected from their transgender employees back in 1997. Today, this would not be acceptable. Back then I didn't know any better and that's why

I accepted their rules.

Around this time, a friend of mine asked if I wanted to make extra money and suggested I apply for a second job at a lingerie shop that also sold and rented adult videos. I then applied for and got the job. The store's owner didn't care that I came to work dressed as a woman, nor if I changed into or out of my woman's clothes while there. Another employee ran the lingerie half of the store while I ran the adult video side. The lingerie side closed in the early evening while the video store remained open until 11p.m.

I enjoyed the position because it became a good segue from work to home. I would get up in the morning after Donna had gone to work and the boys had gone to school. Then I could dress as my true self. I would then go to work at Sprint, then to the video store, and then home. I would sometimes change back before leaving the video store, because the boys would occasionally stay up late, particularly at weekends. On some Fridays and Saturdays, I would also go to my favorite drag club in central Phoenix.

I will always remember my first day at Sprint as Monica. Everyone looked either stunned or shocked at seeing me dressed as a woman for the first time, outside of Halloween. Many of my colleagues approached me with all the usual questions such as, "Do you plan on getting surgery?"

When I replied, "Yes," the men cringed and covered their genitals with their hands, as if they somehow might be next.

A number of them inquired, "Are your breasts real?"

I smiled back, "Yes, my breasts are real and so are the prostheses that give me extra size."

They asked endless questions. Along with curiosity however came the subtle bigotry. Some taped anonymous, nasty notes to my locker, others whispered terrible comments behind my back, and some would move to another terminal if I sat near them. One day, a female colleague held the door open for several other women to go through and, as I approached, let it close in my face. HR couldn't do anything to prevent these incidents.

For two weeks in April I flip-flopped, coming to work as Monica on some days and my old self on the others. Then in May, I began going to work solely as Monica. When that happened, the only time I didn't live as my true self was at home.

During May and June, I called all of my siblings and best friends to tell them about my impending change. All but one friend rejected me, some worse than others. The most terrible reaction came from Dann. He initially remained silent, then became angry with me, spewing out all kinds of bigoted language. His response seemed to come from a place of deep hate for people like me.

My brother and two sisters also didn't handle it well, but their reaction came from a place of concern and they at least told me they still loved me. Even so, they told me they would need time before they wanted to see me. I understood this felt new to all of us, but it still hurt to hear them say that. All I had left to do would be to tell my parents. I dreaded that conversation, but it was one I would need to have face-to-face.

I told my parents on Sunday, June 22, 1997. The day before, I moved out from Donna and the boys. Having spoken to my therapist for the last six months, I realized where my future lay and what I needed to do. I took all of my small things into a new apartment in preparation for beginning my transition. I felt immensely sad in moving away from the boys, but I knew I had no choice.

I had some big items I needed to move too, so on Sunday I went to my parents to borrow their truck. This meant the time had come to tell them about me.

I entered my parents' house and sat them down at the kitchen table. "Mom, Dad, I need to borrow your truck."

"What for?" asked my mother.

"I'm moving out, to live on my own."

"Oh, no!" my mother exclaimed. "Are you getting a divorce?"

"Well, yes, but not for any reason you could guess."

"What? Are you gay?"

"No," I told them. "I'm a transsexual. I'm changing my sex."

My father's face went pale and my mother couldn't find words to speak. I pulled out a picture of me dressed as Monica. My mother looked at it and said that I made an ugly woman. Then she said, "It would have been better if you were just gay."

Later in my life, once I had transitioned and after I realized I only wanted to date women, I called my mother and said, "Mom, you got your wish. I'm gay." She didn't find that very amusing.

During that kitchen-table conversation with my parents, I told my mother that I would soon be changing both my first and last name. At the time, I had a different last name from Helms. Mom asked why I wanted to change my last name. I told her, "It is out of respect for you and my sons."

"Well, I think changing it is disrespectful."

"Mom, I don't want someone coming up to you and Dad, or the boys, and asking you, 'Hey, do you know a Monica _____'?"

She didn't respond to that, but no matter what I did I couldn't win in her eyes. With hindsight, I am very glad of the decision I made. These days, if you Google "Monica Helms," you will see a couple of hundred entries for me and my activism. But by not keeping my old last name, I have protected my sons and mother from the bigotry I am fighting against, just as I intended to.

In the end, my father did let me borrow the truck. When I brought it back the next day, he told me my mother had suffered a mild heart attack overnight, but he hadn't taken her to the hospital. As I left their house again, I tried to give my mother a hug goodbye, but she wouldn't put her arms around me. Instead she told me, "We're taking you out of the will and we don't ever want to see you again."

So, I walked out of my parents' home, never to speak face-to-face with my mother for the next seven-and-a-half-years. I would never get the chance to look into my father's eyes ever again, because he would end up dying a few years later. Even though the rejection caused me enormous pain, I knew I had no other option than to continue with my transition. To the outside world my actions may have looked selfish, but I can truthfully say that I only did what I had to do to survive.

I finished moving into my new apartment that afternoon. I took off my male clothes and ended my male presentation for almost the last time. The only other times the world would see me dressed as a man would be on Halloween, when I went to a drag club dressed as Indiana Jones. The very last time I presented myself as a man happened on Father's Day in 1998. My sons told me they would go out to dinner with me if I came looking like their dad. Only they could have asked that of me. I wouldn't have done it for anyone else.

The next milestone in my life came on June 26, 1997, when I stood before a judge to get my name changed. He asked me one question under oath, "Do you swear that you are not changing your name to avoid debt?"

"No, Your Honor," I replied. "I am not."

Then I laughed quietly to myself. Transitioning would more than likely get me into debt than help me escape from it. At the time, I didn't know just how true that quip would be.

After I received a certified copy of my name change, I went to Social Security and changed my name there, then to my bank to change the name on my bank accounts, then to my auto insurer, and finally to the DMV to change the name on my driver's license.

Arizona's policy at the time allowed a person to change the sex marker on their driver's license by showing a letter from a therapist stating they had reached the point in their transition of no return. Nevertheless, I had heard stories that, even with the right paperwork, some DMV agents would harass a trans person, including to the point of refusing to change the sex marker. As such, I had all my paperwork in order when I walked in.

The female agent I walked up to looked at my name-change form and some of the other papers I had brought, but didn't ask to see the letter from my therapist. This surprised me. When she'd finished, she handed the paperwork to the photographer and he took my picture. I then turned to sit down when she said, "Wait a minute. I made a mistake."

Shit. "A mistake?"

"Yes, I put an 'M' on your license. It was 'Female' you wanted, right?"

"Why, yes! Yes!"

I stepped back and had my picture taken again, this time glowing with happiness. The photographer captured my likeness at that moment, and I have never had a better DMV photo than the one taken that day.

I shared my new apartment with another former submariner trans woman, a cook by the name of Cindy. She had also begun her transition, moving from California to Phoenix in order to do so. I had introduced her to my therapist and doctor, and she found a good job in no time and begun transitioning. Cindy dedicated her life to one goal and one goal only: to get sex reassignment surgery. Her strong personality meant that she and I didn't always see eye-to-eye, but she remains one of the most trustworthy and responsible trans people I have ever met.

For around six months, we also had another roommate. The lesbian couple who lived in the apartment below us introduced us to

Michelle, a friend of theirs from Massachusetts. Michelle wanted to transition and, after talking with her on the phone, I invited her out to Phoenix to stay with us. This proved to be a huge mistake.

Michelle joined us in Phoenix but, unlike Cindy, couldn't be trusted at all. She was loud, rude, lazy and a con artist. Cindy tried helping her get a job, but every time Michelle got fired in short order. She would then lie around the house watching television and eating the food that Cindy and I bought. Finally, we became tired of Michelle's bullshit and kicked her out. Her stay ended up costing me over $1300, while Cindy lost around $600. After Michelle left the apartment, I would occasionally run into her in clubs, but I never knew what finally became of her.

Cindy and Michelle represented two segments of the trans community that I would eventually come to recognize.

Michelle would lie and cheat to get the hormones, or anything else, she wanted. One time, I even caught her stealing hormones from me. She felt like the whole world owed her a living for being a trans woman.

Cindy, on the other hand, believed that a person changing from male-to-female isn't really a transsexual unless they have surgery. She held on to the notion that unless you "go stealth" and blend in, you're not a true transsexual. I hate that term and find this attitude nearly as repulsive as Michelle's.

My early days as Monica at Sprint didn't go as well as I'd hoped, and not because of the actions of my coworkers. At 46, I had entered my second puberty and acted the part. I would experiment with styles of clothing that weren't appropriate for a woman my age. More than once, a supervisor would call me into their office for wearing dresses cut too short. The supervisor who picked on me the most happened to be an out lesbian, who used to be my friend before I started transitioning. I now look back at my wardrobe choices and am disgusted at how I acted.

Another part of my self-discovery at the time concerned my sexual orientation. I could now freely date as a woman and I quickly found out how difficult that can be. The clubs I visited had a large number of trans fans, also called chasers. We referred to them back then as 'trannie-chasers'. Since then, the word 'trannie' has unfortunately become a slur word, so the phrase 'trannie-chasers' is now no longer used. I actually debated using it in this chapter, but I do so for historical reasons.

A large majority of these chasers went to bars with a fantasy of having sex with a pre-op transsexual, often with expectations that transcended reality. I had fun flirting with them by using all the same female charms that had worked on me years ago. That part I found to be fun and educational.

Many of these fans dreamt of making love to a mythical 'best-of-both-worlds' creature. That creature does exist, in the form of she-males, but these fantasies are typically derived from pornography. She-males alter their bodies by surgery only and don't take hormones, consequently their penis can still function properly. In reality, when a chaser encounters a pre-op trans woman, they often become disappointed at the lack of penile erection – one of the effects from the hormone treatments most trans women take. In truth, many trans women aren't keen on a fascination with a body part they see as alien and typically want to get rid of.

Over the years I've known of some trans fans who will stay with and date trans women up until they receive sex reassignment surgery. In one case, a trans woman lay in the recovery room after getting surgery, when her boyfriend walked in. He broke up with her there and then, saying that, "Since your penis is now gone, so am I."

The trans woman became suicidal.

At the beginning of my transition, I dated a few men, but nothing lasted very long. They only wanted to have sex with me and didn't want a long-term relationship. In truth, though men physically excited me, they never could stimulate me emotionally. Eventually I realized I'm a lesbian as well as a trans woman. That feels right for me.

21 – HATE REARS ITS UGLY HEAD

On a Friday in December 1997, I happened to be watching ABC when the television show 20/20 came on and I saw something wonderful. They did an amazing piece on transsexual police officers and firefighters that impressed me greatly. A firefighter captain in the Los Angeles Fire Department by the name of Michele Kämmerer left a big impression on me. Her story moved me so much that I knew I just had to talk with her.

So, on Monday morning I put in a call to the main headquarters of the LAFD and asked them to pass on a message to Captain Kämmerer. A few days later, I received a call from her. We had a great conversation that included, among a great deal of other things, how Sprint and my co-workers had treated me when I transitioned. Michele agreed that Sprint should have at least done some training on transgender issues before my co-workers found out. She informed me that she and her partner, Janis Walworth, had formed an organization called the Center for Gender Sanity, which dealt with helping trans people transition on the job. Talking with Michele lit the fuse on my future trans activism.

During our conversation, I mentioned being a former submariner and she gave me the name of another male-to-female trans woman who had reached the rank of Lieutenant Commander in the Navy and served on six different submarines. Her name was Wendy Keiser. My subsequent conversation with Wendy set my activism in motion.

Wendy told me a story that still impresses me to this day. After she got out of Active Duty, she went into Active Reserves, where she could be called up at any time, if needed. While in Active Reserves, she began and completed her transition. Wendy's status allowed her to attend Navy functions in women's Navy uniform, complete with her ribbons and her Dolphins. When people saw a woman wearing Dolphins (because women couldn't serve on submarines at the time) they would ask how she got them, but Wendy just smiled and walked away.

When the first Gulf War started, they called Wendy to Strategic Air Command Headquarters because of her knowledge of Middle East targets. After she arrived, the Commander looked at her then said, "Welcome back Lt Cdr Keiser. I see you've changed a little since we last saw you. Please make sure you get a new photo on your security badge." Wendy did so well during that war that she received a promotion to Commander.

The next month, I had to contact the local USSVI chapter president to renew my membership.

"Hello, Bill. This is Robert. I guess you've noticed I haven't been at any of the meetings recently."

"Yes, you've been conspicuous by your absence."

"I want to renew my membership, but I've gone through a few changes recently."

"Oh? And, what are they?"

"I've changed my name to Monica and I'm in the process of changing my sex. I'd like to renew under my new name, and I was hoping you could ask the members to vote on letting me attend the meetings."

Bill didn't seem too happy with my news. He told me he would have to consult with the National Board to see if I could still be a member. The organization had gender-neutral bylaws however, and a person only had to have an Honorable Discharge and be qualified on submarines in order to be a member. I had both.

For the next two months USSVI, the officers of Perch Base and I went back and forth, trying to settle the issue. They first wanted me to become an Auxiliary Member, a class of membership that they reserved for wives and those who had never served on submarines. I refused. Then they wanted me to renew my membership using my old name and again I refused. In the end they accepted me back with my new name only because they could have faced a court challenge otherwise. After I renewed my membership, the Perch Base chapter voted to let me attend their regular meetings. I became the first and only woman in a national organization that had 8,000 male members. Since then, several other trans submariners have joined USSVI.

The struggle to renew my USSVI membership led to my first appearance on the Gender Talk radio program and also saw the local LGBT publication, *Echo Magazine*, write a story on me. In the very same issue, *Echo* ran an article about a new chapter of the Gay, Lesbian and Bisexual Veterans of America (GLBVA) that had been formed in Phoenix, headed by Wally Straughn. When I contacted Wally, he told me he planned on putting together an Honor Guard to march in the Phoenix Pride Parade. He wanted me to become part of it. The whole thing sounded fantastic, so I joined the GLBVA.

Up until this point in my life, I had never been to a Pride Festival. Now, not only would I get to attend one, but I would march up front in the Honor Guard. When the day arrived, and having lived as Monica for less than a year, I marched down Central Avenue carrying the Arizona state flag at the head of the parade. I had called Phoenix my home since 1953 and there I was, marching down the city's main avenue as the person I always meant to be. I felt a sense of belonging that no one would ever be able to take away from me. I also resolved never again to let people push me around. Since that first Pride Parade in 1998, I marched every year in an Honor or Color Guard all the way up until 2011. In a couple of those years I marched in two different cities.

My participation in celebratory marches wasn't always well-received however. The Phoenix GLBVA Chapter later marched in the local Memorial Day Parade, only to receive a slew of negative comments in the local press.

That first Phoenix Pride also introduced me to another local chapter of a national organization, the Bisexual Network of Arizona or BiNet AZ. When I saw BiNet AZ's booth, it dawned on me that, at the time, I considered myself bisexual. So, I talked to the people working the booth. Ron Owen, the Co-Chair of BiNet AZ, told me I looked familiar to him. Then he realized that he'd seen me in the current issue of *Echo Magazine*. My experience with the USSVI intrigued him and he encouraged me to join BiNet AZ, which I did.

Because of all the encouragement and advice that I received

from Wally and Ron over the immediate years that followed, I consider them to be my original activism mentors. Three other people have helped me greatly since I moved to Atlanta, namely Jamison Green, Angela Brightfeather and Dallas Denny, but their time will come later in this book.

The Phoenix chapter of GLBVA later received an invitation to take part in a flag-raising ceremony at the Tucson Pride, held in September of 1998. This meant I got to meet people in the Tucson trans community for the first time, a community that seemed to be better organized than the equivalent community in Phoenix. I also met my first trans men at Tucson Pride, members of the Southern Arizona Gender Association (SAGA.)

One trans man stood out for me. His name was Alexander Goodrum, a local activist. I later discovered that Alexander's involvement in the LGBT community in Tucson resulted in the city's new non-discrimination policy having gender-identity-specific language written into it. This unassuming man had done so much for trans people in the state of Arizona. I found myself really admiring him.

Two weeks later, I went back to Tucson to hear Leslie Feinberg speak. To me, this charismatic individual embodied the true spirit of the transgender warrior, which also happens to be the title of one of Feinberg's books. He spoke for about two hours, telling the tale of his recent run-in with the law at a protest in New York City. He weaved images of his intense experience trying to dodge arrest, with the terrible things that went on in jail once he and other protest leaders had been detained.

I sat, spellbound by the words and the images of Leslie's story. He made me want to stand up for what I believed in. A calling and a purpose for why I had been made transsexual became apparent to me. Leslie's stories inspired me.

Some may notice that I have used male pronouns when discussing Leslie Feinberg, even though others might well use female pronouns. In one of his books, he talks about neutral pronouns that best describe him, but that Western society and the English language haven't yet embraced these neutral pronouns.

In a talk he later gave at Agnes Scott University, a person asked him which pronouns they should use to describe him. Leslie in effect said, when I'm with non-transgender people, I prefer the use of female pronouns because of my male presentation. It makes some wonder when they hear female pronouns used on me with this look. When I'm with other transgender people, I like male pronouns because they show respect for what I have accomplished. (This is not an exact quote, so I didn't use quotation marks.)

In January 1999, I became involved in several aspects of the Arizona LGBT community, putting a face on the 'T' part of the acronym. BiNet AZ elected me Co-Chair of the chapter and The Rose, a Phoenix-based local trans support group, elected me Vice President.

In February 1999, Ron Owen and I became part of the Equality Begins At Home steering committee. A nationwide initiative, EBAH had people in every state gather on the same day to lobby their local legislators about issues important to LGBT people. In Arizona, we wanted legislators to remove the archaic sodomy laws that affected everyone, including straight couples.

At a planning meeting some members of the committee produced a single-person petition that they wanted to get hundreds of people to sign so we could bring stacks of them to the legislators on lobby day. After reading over the petition, I noticed it had non-inclusive language. Rather than making a big fuss about it, I took one of the petitions home, created an exact duplicate using the same fonts and layout, but with inclusive language. I handed the new version to the head of the committee at our next meeting. I told him, "This is the version we should use. It's more inclusive."

He looked it over, "You're right. We'll use yours."
I realize not all gay and lesbian people wish to exclude bisexual and transgender people on purpose. It's just that they sometimes need a gentle reminder. One year later, we had a similar situation arise with a different petition and thankfully I once again came up with a compromise that everyone agreed on. That first year, one of our gay legislators read the petition on the Arizona House floor on lobby day.

22 – THE BIRTH OF "IT'S TIME ARIZONA"

In the early part of 1999, the Phoenix GLBVA Chapter took on an ambitious project. We wanted to put a memorial to LGBT veterans in the Phoenix National Cemetery. This would be the first ever memorial of its kind in the National Cemetery system, and it would require many hours of dealing with red tape in order to get the memorial approved. Wally did an awful lot of calling and talking with people to make it happen. Luck also played a role because the person in charge of the cemetery at the time didn't personally object to the idea of a memorial for LGBT veterans.

After the permission had been approved, we settled on the design. We quickly realized it would be more appropriate for us to dedicate the memorial to all Americans who died in wars, not just LGBT people. The memorial would instead say that it came from the Gay, Lesbian and Bisexual Veterans of America. I felt a bit sad that the word transgender wouldn't appear on the memorial, but I agreed with the idea of dedicating it to all veterans.

Initially, the members tossed around several good ideas. Then the group came up with an interesting design, but my graphic arts background told me that it lacked symmetry. With a few tweaks, I added a triangle on either side of the eagle, so that we ended up with the perfect design. We chose for the memorial to be mounted on rainbow granite, which seemed entirely appropriate.

Next, Wally had to get our design approved, which also took some time. Once everything was in place, we began a national fundraising drive to raise the $5,000 we needed to commission the memorial. I stayed in Arizona long enough to see the money raised but missed the dedication, which took place on Veterans Day, 2000. I still feel proud to have been part of that effort. My only regret is that I wish I'd pushed for the word transgender to be included on the memorial.

In early 1999, at our monthly meeting of The Rose, I brought up the idea of starting a statewide trans advocacy organization and I even came up with a name for it. I called it AZTEC, which stood for AriZona Transgender Equality Coalition. At the meeting was Amanda Schrader, who had been working on the very same idea, but had been approaching it from a different angle. Amanda had begun forming It's Time Arizona (ITAZ) by completing all the necessary paperwork but hadn't spent any time in the LGBT community making contacts. I had made a lot of contacts but hadn't started any of the formalities to create an official organization. Both of us realized that by combining our efforts and talents, a statewide trans advocacy organization could become a reality. So, that meeting in early 1999 gave birth to ITAZ.

Amanda and I set about making ITAZ more visible in the community. She became the Executive Director and took care of the behind-the-scenes issues, while I took on the job of Director of Operations and continued making more contacts for us. We made it a point to become involved in as many LGBT functions as we could, putting ITAZ's name out there so that the community knew we existed. This visibility made for a lot of work for Amanda and me, as people began asking us to attend more and more functions, representing the trans community. The LGB groups had wanted to include trans people, but up until then they hadn't had any official contacts within our community.

In late March/April of 1999, while ITAZ still struggled to find its place in the greater community, we found out that Gender Pac planned on holding Lobby Days in D.C. in May. Amanda and I vowed we would attend and began a fundraising effort so that we could afford to go. In the meantime, I began calling and faxing the offices of all of the Congressmen and Senators for Arizona, hoping to arrange a meeting with them or someone from their office. When done, we had a scheduled meeting with every office except Senator John McCain's.

We soon raised enough money to pay for our plane fares, hotel costs and food. All we had to do now was attend. This would be the first time I had ever been in our nation's capital, but it wouldn't be the last. While there, I planned on visiting two specific sites as well.

The Vietnam Veterans Memorial topped my list of D.C. sites I wanted to see. A member of the D.C. chapter of the GLBVA met Amanda and me at our hotel and took us to the places we wanted to visit. When we arrived at the Vietnam Memorial's famous wall, the sight of all those names on black marble overwhelmed me. I'm not ashamed to say that I broke down and cried. Amanda and my friend had to hold me up. I didn't know anyone on the wall personally, but the names represented people from my generation. The men and women named on the wall didn't have the chance to grow up, have children, contribute to society or grow old with a loved one. By joining the Navy and serving on submarines, I had avoided their fate, and as such I honor their memory. I suppose at least part of my emotional reaction had to do with survivor's guilt. After I regained my composure, we visited the Smithsonian Air and Space Museum before heading back to the hotel for our lobby training.

When I met Riki Wilchens for the first time, I felt in awe of her and, for a fleeting moment, I thought about how wonderful it would feel to be just as respected by the trans community. Looking back, I can laugh at all that has transpired since. I did eventually achieve 'trans fame', but all the headaches that came with it have torn my heart apart many times over. As the saying goes, "Be careful what you wish for because you just might get it."

Amanda must have sensed the desire in me to make my mark because, before we left D.C., she sat me down and gave me a 'facts of life' talk. She warned me not to talk constantly about what I had already done and that I should instead just focus on the advocacy. The issues we fought for were more important than either one of us. As she saw it, if I just kept doing the work, history would take care of itself. I didn't disagree with her.

Over the years I have tried to follow Amanda's advice. Nevertheless, I know I have fallen short more times than I can count. Along the way I have angered many people with my arrogance and insistence that things be done my way. At times I have acted like a spoiled child or a bully, upsetting many of those I have called friends. My desire to get things done sometimes seems to have hindered almost as much as it has helped. To any friends, colleagues or allies that I have inadvertently upset over the years, I apologize. Hurting you was never something I would deliberately do.

I have often referred to the fight for transgender rights as the last civil rights movement. We in the trans community are aware of the historical struggles for women's suffrage and for the civil rights of African Americans. We also fought alongside our gay brothers and lesbian sisters to win equality for them under the law. We know that our actions today could affect not only our own lives but those of future generations. I think it's therefore only human nature that some of us jostle not only for our place in society, but for our place with the trans movement itself, even though we know it's of secondary importance to our cause.

If I look at myself, I believe I can point to the origin of any attention-seeking tendencies I may have. As a child, back in the first and second grade, other kids would pick on me, not because I demonstrated feminine traits or weakness, but simply because of my last name. The last name I had been given at birth could easily be made fun of and as a child it bothered me greatly when someone did. I remember promising myself that one day my name would be important and mean something. Even though I no longer have my birth name, I think that feeling has always stayed with me.

Amanda may not have realized it, but she made a big difference to me that day when she took me aside and talked to me. Her words echo in my mind constantly, reminding me of my frailties and failings. They remind me to try and be humble. I can never thank her enough for that.

I came back from D.C. a changed woman. No longer did I see Arizona as the only place to concentrate my efforts. The trip made me feel part of a larger community, knowing that what Amanda and I did in Arizona could have an effect on other parts of the country. Staying in contact with those we had met in D.C. would help expand our resources for the trans community in Arizona.

Then, in July of 1999, a tragedy that made national news caught my attention. At Ft. Campbell, Kentucky, a solider by the name of PFC Barry Winchell was found beaten to death in the barracks. The soldier who beat him, and the one who encouraged the beating, believed that PFC Winchell was gay, but in fact he had been dating an attractive trans woman who performed at a drag club in Nashville. The media portrayed his surviving girlfriend as a man and a drag queen, but when I saw her on the news, I knew she looked like neither. "She's a woman!" I exclaimed.

I contacted Calpernia Addams, Winchell's girlfriend, to let her know how sorry I felt for her loss and ask if I could do anything for her. After leaving my name at the club where she worked, she finally called me back. We had a long conversation that confirmed everything I had suspected. Calpernia was indeed a woman and one who felt immense sadness and anger at losing the man she loved. Her story eventually became a movie and we have remained friends ever since.

PFC Winchell's brutal murder sent me to a website that changed my life. The site I found, called Remembering Our Dead, had the names of 168 trans people who had been murdered, including some who had died very violently. As I read the description of each person and how they had been killed, my heart became heavy with sorrow.

In early 2000, I decided to take the information on the Remembering Our Dead list, summarize the statistics and place them in chronological order. I felt that by doing so, trans activists could use the information to help in their lobbying efforts. After getting the okay from the site's creator, Gwen Smith, I kept the list updated for the next four years until eventually I felt so emotionally drained that I had to give it over to someone else to maintain. My friend Ethan St. Pierre took over managing the list for 14 years before he too passed it on to another person.

In the middle of 1999, Amanda began attending meetings of the Arizona Human Rights Fund (AHRF), Arizona's gay and lesbian rights organization. At the time, they didn't include trans people in their mission statement and ITAZ tried to convince them to add us. The head of AHRF told Amanda that the discussion about adding trans people to their mission statement wouldn't take place until the middle of 2001. But, with all the good work ITAZ did for the rest of the year and into 2000, they ended up adding trans people to their mission statement much earlier, in March of 2000.

In August 1999, BiNet USA held their annual meeting in Phoenix. I attended and finally met in person a large number of people I had previously only known by email.

Two important things came out of that BiNet USA meeting that I will always remember. The first and most serious issue had to do with BiNet's support for the federal Employment Non-

Discrimination Act (ENDA), a bill that had been introduced in Congress for the first time in 1994 and reintroduced every two years after that. At the time, two national organizations, the National Gay and Lesbian Task Force (NGLTF) and the Parents and Friends of Lesbians and Gays (PFLAG), publicly stated that they wouldn't support ENDA unless Congress added the words "gender identity and gender expression."

On the last day of the meeting, I submitted a proposal for BiNet USA to follow in the footsteps of NGLTF and PFLAG and not support ENDA unless it became fully inclusive. The discussion that preceded the consensus vote was intense at times. Some people wanted to continue supporting ENDA because it protected part of the LGBT community and BiNet had a policy not to oppose protection for anyone. Others said that, because of ENDA's flaws and the lack of coverage for trans people, BiNet USA shouldn't support it unless it covered everyone. When they took the final consensus, BiNet USA came out against supporting ENDA unless it became fully inclusive. I cried at that outcome.

The 1999 BiNet USA meeting in Phoenix also became meaningful for me for a second major reason.

23 – THE FLAG

The second important thing that took place during that BiNet USA meeting happened at one of the dinners. While we ate, Michael Page – the man who created the Bisexual Pride Flag – casually said to me, "You know, the trans community should have a Pride Flag."

Until he mentioned it, I hadn't really thought about it. Nevertheless, I agreed with him and, after a few moments of brainstorming, started to suggest some ideas. Michael said that any design needed to be simple because that would make it cheaper to make and easier for producers to sell. My mind couldn't come up with any simple designs at the time and so the evening finished without a resolution or any clear direction. I continued to think about the issue over the next few days however.

About a week later, on August 19, 1999 to be exact, I woke up earlier than usual. A simple design for a Transgender Pride Flag had literally come to me after I woke up and lay half asleep in bed. The flash of inspiration actually made me jump out of bed. The design I'd subconsciously come up with had five equal-sized stripes going horizontally across the flag. The top and bottom stripes would be light blue, the traditional color for baby boys. The two stripes inside of the blue stripes were pink, the traditional color for baby girls. The center stripe would be white for those either in transition, those who have a neutral or undefined gender, or those who identify as bigender or agender.

I drew a mock-up of the flag on a piece of paper and sat back to take it in. I liked what I saw. It had a beautiful simplicity and symmetry to it. The palindromic design also meant that no matter which way you flew the flag, it would always be correct, which to me signified the underlying correctness of trans peoples' true self, regardless of the road they take to get there.

Having come up with the design, I contacted the same company that made the Bisexual Pride Flag and they sent me some fabric swatches from which to choose. I picked the colors and, around a week later, received the first Transgender Pride Flag through the mail.

I ended up marching with that first flag in several Pride Parades, often at the head of the parade as part of the Color/Honor Guard. It also came with me to dozens of trans conferences and events, has been displayed at Trans Pride booths, and has traveled with me to D.C. for Lobby Days. I also used it in a number of Memorial Day parades, Martin Luther King Day parades, protests, Transgender Day of Remembrances, and it even appeared in a made-for-Lifetime movie. The Flag's simple design has caught on. Although at least half a dozen other trans Pride flags have been designed over the years, mine was not only the first, but the only one to become universally embraced.

These days, the Flag's palette is replicated in trans art and merchandise the world over. I don't receive any royalties from the flags, mugs, t-shirts, pins, fridge magnets or other paraphernalia, but that is because a flag cannot be copywritten. I'm humbled every time I see it though, most of all when I see the Flag in places I would never have expected to.

Slowly, the Flag made its way out of the U.S. and to other countries. During the 2013 Pride season, I began seeing the Flag, or the Flag's colors, in several countries around the world, including Britain, Finland, Serbia, Spain, Canada, Turkey, Argentina and Japan. Eventually it would be photographed on all seven continents, including Antarctica. One person, Erin Parisi, has taken a banner with the Trans Flag on it to the top of the highest peaks on four continents, and plans on taking it to the top of the other three. That means she will be taking it to the top of Mount Everest.

The speed with which the Flag's usage spread never fails to surprise me, and every time I see it, or a photo of it, flying above a historic town hall or building I am filled with pride.

With daily updates coming to me via social media about where the Flag had now been seen or used, I quickly realized that, since I had the original, I had to find a way to protect it. I figured the best way to do this meant I had to find a place that would appreciate its historical value. I thought at the time, "Why not start at the top?" So, I contacted the Smithsonian, in Washington, D.C., to see if they wanted it. I had uncanny timing. They put me in touch with a woman who had just begun a new project for the Smithsonian: starting an LGBT wing. She told me that having the first Transgender Pride Flag would be a wonderful addition to this project and so I agreed that I would hand it over to become part of their collection.

Now, the Smithsonian doesn't just take donated items like a thrift store. They wanted to verify I indeed had the first Trans Flag and, on top of that, learn everything about me. They record the history behind each item in their collection as well as the history of its creator or owner. Because of my experience in the U.S. Navy, they also passed me onto another woman who happened to be in charge of military items. I ended up telling the Smithsonian all about my Navy career, my trans life, and even my life before transition. They wanted pictures, articles, and to know as many things as I could tell them about the Flag.

Finally, they picked a date for me to go to Washington to hand over the Flag and a number of other related items. Mara Keisling and National Center for Transgender Equality (NCTE) helped get me to D.C. and put me up in a hotel while there. Mara even came with me to the ceremony.

On August 19, 2014, I arrived at the Smithsonian, 15 years to the day from when the design of the Flag had come to me. Other items being donated that day included a tennis racquet and some medical equipment from Renée Richards, as well as some *Will and Grace* scripts and items from David Kohan and Max Mutchnick.

In addition to the first Trans Flag I also handed over other items including a small Flag, trans-related buttons and a brass plaque I had received from the *Francis Scott Key*, which had my Navy ribbons, patrol pin and my original Dolphins mounted to it. Oddly, I felt more pain parting with my original Dolphins than I did parting with the Flag. That probably had something to do with how much pain I had gone through to get them.

Finally, in June 2016, the Obama Administration asked the

Smithsonian to display the Trans Flag in the White House during their Pride Month celebration. For whatever reason, I didn't get invited to any White House events that month, but in the photographs that I have seen the Flag looked beautiful.

My Troubles with Sprint

At the end of 1999, Sprint decided to take over the third floor of our building in order to add a training facility. As soon as they announced the plans, I went to the Head of HR and said, "You realize that I'm allowed to use the third-floor restroom, right? What will happen if one day, after training, several women go into the restroom and find me there?"

The Head of HR happened to be the same woman I had come out to two years earlier when I had started transitioning. She told me, "They'll have to realize that you're allowed to be in there. If they don't like it, then they can come back down to the second floor and use the restroom there."

"Okay. I just wanted to make sure you're prepared for any complaints."

Unfortunately, two months later Sprint transferred the Head of HR to another facility and replaced her with her less-than-capable former assistant. Then, about a month after the training facility opened, the scenario I had envisioned occurred.

Shortly after one of the training sessions had finished, I held back from leaving the training room and watched all the women make their way to the third-floor restroom. I had to pee too, so I went into the restroom I had become accustomed to using. The other women made it immediately clear they didn't want me there. Some gave me the evil eye while others rushed out when they saw me. I did my best to ignore them, stepped into a stall and did my thing. Then I went back to my desk to carry on with my work. Twenty minutes later, HR called me into their office.

The new head of HR told me, "Some of the women have complained that you went into the third-floor restroom after today's training session."

"Yes. I'm allowed to use the third-floor restroom as per our original agreement."

"Well, I wonder if we can come up with some kind of new

compromise?"

"No," I told her. "We agreed that I could use the third and first floor restrooms and I'm holding Sprint to that agreement."

I'd had plenty of experience as an activist since our original agreement. I didn't plan on giving in this time. With the issue unresolved, HR sent me back to my desk. A couple of hours later, they called me back into the HR office, this time with my supervisor present. To my surprise, the Head of HR told me that there wouldn't be any changes to our agreement and that the other women would just have to go down to the second floor if they had a problem with me being in the third-floor restroom. That seemed fair to me. After all, I had to go up or down to a different floor every day to use a restroom.

Then, as we left the office, my supervisor turned to me and let me in on a secret. "Before you came in, she wanted me to work out a compromise with you. I refused. I told her that if we tried to push for you to be excluded from the third-floor restroom, you would fight it and not only win the third floor, but access to the second floor as well. She decided not to press the issue after that."

My supervisor knew about my activism outside of the company and knew I would have pushed back if I wanted to. It felt good to register another win over Sprint. When I eventually transferred within Sprint to a location in Atlanta, I had no restroom restrictions at my new place of work. When the local HR representative informed me of this, the news made me smile from ear to ear.

I'm proud of one other major accomplishment from my time with Sprint. In 1999, I approached HR with a request to have gender identity and gender expression added to the company's Equal Employment Opportunities (EEO) policy. My request initially fell on deaf ears. Nevertheless, whenever representatives from our corporate headquarters paid a visit to Phoenix, I would always raise the issue, though every time they too would brush aside my concerns.

In Georgia, I made a little more progress. There, the HR representative felt more sympathetic and pursued the matter with head office on behalf of all of Sprint's trans employees. I then received a phone call from head office, during which an official told me that they had no plans to add trans-inclusive language to the EEO policy, but that I should rest assured that "Sprint will not discriminate against anyone for any reason." It seemed nice that they had taken the time to reach out to me personally, but the fact that they wouldn't do so in writing or by email made me question how valuable their reassurances would be.

In 2002, Sprint appointed a new CEO, who in turn added a Diversity Officer to Sprint's leadership team. The two of them visited Atlanta shortly after arriving at the company and I made a point of meeting them to make sure they understood the importance of adding trans-inclusive language to the EEO policy.

Unfortunately, it became obvious early on that the new Diversity Officer didn't feel comfortable talking about LGBT issues. They saw diversity more in terms of gender and race. Sprint actually pushed back when employees at their Kansas City Headquarters wanted to start an LGBT Affinity Group. Nevertheless, I continued to advocate for a change to the EEO policy whenever I could. Finally, in May 2004, and without any fanfare, Sprint added gender identity to their policy, bringing an end to my five-year campaign to have it changed. I don't know if they ever added gender expression as well.

Before the EEO policy changed, Sprint's insistence that they "will not discriminate against anyone for any reason," helped me to win another victory, this time with their medical insurance coverage.

When I arrived in Atlanta, I sought out a doctor who saw trans people on a regular basis, a specialist if you will. I found an endocrinologist I felt happy with, even though to me his staff seemed a bit standoffish. Then, after seeing this doctor for about two years, I received a bill from him for over $650 because my health insurance had declined to pay for his most recent services. I called Cigna, my health insurance provider, and they told me the reason they wouldn't pay was because the doctor had coded the lab work in question as being for 'Gender Identity Disorder.' Sprint hadn't authorized payments for GID-related issues.

For some reason, after two years of getting the same lab tests every three months, my doctor had decided to change the reimbursement code he used. I called the doctor's office and asked if they would change it back, but they refused and actually became pretty nasty about it. I told them that I wouldn't pay the bill. In response they handed my 'unpaid bill' over to a collection agency. Needless to say, this got me boiling mad.

Rather than deal further with my doctor or the insurance company, I decided to instead try and change the policy itself, within

Sprint. After all, Sprint had told me they wouldn't discriminate against anyone for any reason, but not covering GID-related medical issues certainly sounded like discrimination to me.

I called the Diversity Officer and he put me through to the Head of Benefits. After explaining the whole story, the Benefits Officer agreed to help and assigned a person to work on my case. In the meantime, however, the debt collection agency called me on a daily basis. Thank goodness for caller ID.

This situation went on for months. The collection agency would call me and leave threatening messages on my voicemail. I would then call Sprint's benefits office to ask if there had been any progress. Finally, after six months of this drama, I received a call saying that Cigna had paid the bill and that in future they would cover my medical expenses regardless of how they were coded – though for the time being not expenses related to sex reassignment surgery. Sprint also, reluctantly, extended the change of policy regarding coding to its other trans employees as well.

It's Time Arizona Made a Difference

ITAZ had a big impact on the Arizona LGBT community during 1999. In December of that year, a friend of mine who worked for *Echo Magazine* told me that a year earlier she had overheard one of the other *Echo* staff members staying, "Transgender people are amusing, but not very newsworthy."

She then told me that in a recent meeting they had almost selected a trans woman as Arizona's LGBT Woman of the Year for 1999, though in the end that trans woman lost out on the honor by one vote. The trans woman they almost selected was me. Even though they didn't crown me their Woman of the Year, Amanda and I believed these two anecdotes demonstrated just how far the trans community had come in one year. Apparently, we had proved to our gay, lesbian, and bisexual allies that not only could we be newsworthy, but we could be helpful in the battle for equal rights. In later years, another Arizona trans woman would finally receive the title of *Echo*'s Woman of the Year.

Then, in the fall of 1999, a big news story broke concerning a trans history teacher in Sacramento who had been fired for transitioning. We in Arizona followed the case closely, as the teacher,

Dana Rivers, fought back and won a financial settlement, though she didn't get her job back.

For our January 2000 meeting, we asked Dana Rivers if she would attend and address our members. She agreed to come and speak, and when she did a great number of trans people from all over Arizona showed up to meet and hear her. Dana did not disappoint and gave a very inspiring speech.

Then in February, Alpha Zeta put on its first 'Putting on the Glitz' event. When I heard about this event, I convinced Amanda that ITAZ should also be part of it and that we should try and get our trans friends from Tucson involved as well.

Alpha Zeta had an idea to sponsor a dinner and a dance during the event. I suggested to the people putting on this get-together that we should use this event to give an award to Alexander Goodrum, the African-American transgender civil rights activist, writer, and educator, for all of the great work he had done for the community. They agreed.

On the night of the event itself, we all had dinner and then they brought out Alexander's award, even though he couldn't be there that night to receive it. Having read his citation out loud, they then pulled out a second plaque, which they awarded to me! This came as a total surprise. They called it a Distinguished Service Award and they gave it to me as a thank you to me for all the work I had done over the years for Arizona's LGBT movement.

In later years the 'Putting on the Glitz' event increased to two days from one, and after Alexander Goodrum passed away, they changed the name of the Distinguished Service Award to the Alexander Goodrum Community Service Award. They created a great tribute to a man who did so much for the transgender community. Like too many of our trans brothers and sisters, Alexander took his life in late September 2002. I've said it before, and I'll say it again here: I miss him so much.

The last work I did for ITAZ concerned the Phoenix Police Department's LGBT Community Relations Board. In all the years that the Board had existed, there had never been a trans representative on it. Then, in March 2000, the gay representative for the Board asked me to join.

The first meeting I attended seemed to open the eyes of the police officers there. Previously, they hadn't had a clue what issues the trans community faced, nor the various categories of trans people that existed. Everyone agreed that Phoenix's police officers needed more training on the subject and that it would be covered at future board meetings. Unfortunately, I only got to attend one other meeting before I relocated from Arizona to Georgia. I felt happy however, to see not only several trans people at the next meeting, but also the Chief of Police.

In early 2000, Amanda Shaffer retired from ITAZ and activism more generally, to live a well-deserved quieter life. Today, Arizona has a new generation of LGBT community leaders and activists. I'm certainly very proud of all that we achieved during my time in the Grand Canyon State, and all the work that continues to be done there.

24 – GIRLS JUST WANT TO HAVE FUN

In the last chapter, I talked about all the work I did within the community, but I had a private life too, such as it was. In 1999, I started to tire of spending my time at a local drag club for entertainment. I also tired of men trying to pick me up, and of men more generally. They couldn't provide me with the emotional fulfillment I needed from a partner. So, I began checking out other places, with the help of some friends.

Phoenix had at least four women's bars, and which one I frequented depended on my mood. Bars typically closed in Phoenix at 1a.m., but a few stayed open after hours by not serving alcohol beyond that time. One place called Charlie's, a gay country bar, played modern music after hours, which made it a favorite of mine.

Phoenix also had a number of sex clubs, where they didn't serve alcohol at all. They charged men $35 admission but let women in for free. Trans women with an 'F' on their driver's license also got in for free. They played good music, offered free food and drink, and afforded patrons the chance to watch people have sex in windowed rooms.

I spent several months visiting these sex clubs. During that time, I had oral and anal sex with men on multiple occasions. I wanted to have sex with women too, but the opportunity never presented itself. That same year, Stanley Kubrick's last movie *Eyes Wide Shut* came out, in which Tom Cruise and Nicole Kidman also visit various sex clubs. In my experience the movie appeared somewhat tamer than real life. The months I spent frequenting these clubs enabled me to fulfill each and every fantasy I had concerning sex with men. This included orgies, hot tubs, you name it. But once I had gotten all of that out of my system, one thing became apparent to me. I realized I was a lesbian.

Following this realization, my favorite place to go became a popular lesbian nightclub called 'Ain't Nobody's Business,' which women casually referred to as 'The Biz.' I felt very comfortable there, as if I had found a home away from home. In late 1999 and 2000, I would go there three to four times a week to talk to and dance with other lesbians. In fact, I danced so much in 2000, and lost so much weight, that I got down to a size 12 dress size, something that hadn't happened to me for 20 years.

When I first started going to The Biz on a regular basis, I felt afraid to talk to the other women. During my lifetime, I'd learned how to interact with women as a man. So, after becoming a woman, I just took all I had learned and reversed it so that I could interact with men as a woman. But I had no experience interacting with women as a woman. I'm not talking about having friendly conversations with other women. I'm talking about flirting with another woman without coming off like a guy in their eyes.

Subsequently, I've heard and later seen that many lesbians don't want trans women encroaching on their space. If a lesbian suspected me of being a trans woman, or found out during our conversation, I always feared a reprisal. I didn't fear violence, only the cold, callous and instant rejection that sometimes took place.

Because I felt uncomfortable flirting with other lesbians, I would go to The Biz and either sit by myself, or dance by myself. No one ever asked me to dance. Occasionally, I would strike up a conversation with someone I sat next to, but usually nothing ever came of it. My confidence interacting with other lesbians in a social setting was a tiny fraction of the confidence I had as a trans activist. The imbalance and lack of companionship made me feel incomplete.

Then, in January 2000, an event took place that changed my life and gave me the confidence I needed. As I mentioned previously, Dana Rivers came to Phoenix to speak and she brought a friend with her, a post-op trans woman by the name of Connie. Connie had an air of grace and sophistication about her that I hadn't previously seen in very many trans women. The evening after Dana's speech to the

Arizona trans community, I arrived at their hotel to see if they wanted to go dancing and sample Phoenix's nightlife. Dana had done a lot of traveling earlier that day and felt too tired, but Connie accepted my offer and I took her to The Biz.

The Biz had a large crowd that Saturday night and I could tell Connie felt comfortable there. We talked for a little while and when a group of people moved to the dance floor, so did we. As we danced, Connie and I drew closer and closer together. I found her not only attractive, but sensual as well. I sensed she also found me somewhat attractive.

As the dance floor became more and more crowed, Connie and I moved even closer together. At the same time, the rhythm of our movements became so synchronized that I couldn't tell where I ended, and she began. I had experienced sensual dancing in the past, but nothing like this. We flowed as one and the rest of the world seemed to disappear. Then, she leaned in and kissed me. A tingle traveled up and then down my spine. For a moment, my legs felt weak and almost weightless.

Later, Connie suggested we leave. On the way back to West Phoenix she said, "I'm trying to decide whether to go back to your place or not." She paused. "I think not."

"Why?" I don't think I hid my disappointment very well.

She muttered something about it not being the best thing in the world for the 'post-op' when a 'pre-op' and a 'post-op' got together. She didn't want to go down that road. I tried to work around her logic, but to no avail. So, instead I drove her back to her hotel.

When we arrived, I parked the car thinking the evening had ended. We couldn't go up to her room because she shared it with Dana. So instead we talked in my car late into the cold January night. After a long conversation about our respective lives, Connie looked at me and said, "I have something to tell you. The Goddess has told me about you."

As an agnostic, I didn't really believe in any God or Goddess, but I felt so infatuated, Connie could have told me anything and I would have believed it.

"What would that be?" I asked her.

"She says you're doing fine, Monica. She said you made it."

"Made it?"

"You are a woman. You made it, but you still don't believe it."

I told her, "But, I can't see it. I can't."

"You are there, Monica. SRS will be nothing more than cosmetic for you. Your soul is female and that's what's important."

I fumbled a reply, "Okay." I felt lost, unable to grasp what she said.

"You don't see it, do you?"

"No," I told her honestly. "I don't."

"What you need to do is to go home, take off all your clothes, look into the mirror and say, 'I am a female!' You need to say it over and over until you feel it."

I felt skeptical, but I found Connie so attractive that it almost made me believe what she said. "Okay. I'll try, if you think it will work."

"It will." She then leaned over, gave me a kiss and got out the car.

On the way home, I heard Connie's advice on repeat in my head. I didn't have a lot of faith that her instructions would do me any good, but when I got home, I followed them to the letter.

I stood in front of the mirror totally naked. "I am female!" I paused. My voice became quieter, "I am female." Then almost silently, "I am female." I began to cry, but not because the chanting had worked. All that I had endured for the past 48 years became apparent. Praying to God to turn me into a girl at age five, putting on my mother's clothes at age twelve, the Navy, submarines, jobs, my problems at Sprint, Midge, Pat, Ann, Carolyn, BJ, Donna, Clifford, Bryan, my parents, my brother, my sisters, Amanda, It's Time Arizona, BiNet, Lobby Days, Connie, and not having undertaken sex reassignment surgery. Everything hit me all at once. I cried at what Connie had said about a post-op not wanting to be with a pre-op. I cried at what I saw in the mirror and what I didn't see in the mirror.

The hurt turned to energy within me and I cried out:

"I AM FEMALE!"

Then, something beautiful happened. I saw 'her.' I saw the woman I had become instead of all the things I still needed to change.

I saw the real me for the first time.

Readers may roll their eyes at what is written above, but it genuinely happened as I've described. Had I read it in another trans autobiography I might be skeptical too, but since this is my story, I can't tell it any other way than the way it happened. I probably wouldn't even have mentioned my time with Connie if a total change in my attitude hadn't manifested itself as a result.

Now, that attitude change didn't take place overnight, but I did feel different about myself from that moment onwards. The proof would be apparent the next Friday night when I went to The Biz. I didn't feel any different when I walked in, nor did I dress any differently from usual, but something happened to me that hadn't happened before. Shortly after the dance floor began filling up, a nice-looking woman came up to me and asked me to dance. I wouldn't have thought too much about it, because women had asked me to dance a few times in the past, however later that night two more women also asked me to dance. To say I felt surprised is an understatement. When I later analyzed the evening, I figured I must have been exhibiting more of an aura of self-confidence and self-assurance. Whatever happened, I saw a noticeable change in people's perception of me.

Before I left Arizona, another encounter gave me more hope that my love life would eventually get better. I spent a lot of time during 1999 and 2000 on different listserves (an early form of online message groups), talking with people from different parts of the country. On one list, sometime in November 1999, I struck up a conversation with a trans woman living in another part of Arizona. Her name was Michelle. We even spoke on the phone a few times. At the time, she lived with a man in her hometown. Then, one Saturday morning in May 2000, Michelle felt bored and asked if she could drive to Phoenix to go to a movie with me and hang out. I had nothing else going on, so I agreed.

Although Michelle and I had chatted, I didn't know that much about her. I knew she owned a successful business somewhere in Northern Arizona. She'd had SRS in the very early 1990s, considered herself heterosexual, and was a few years older than me. I didn't know much more than that.

When Michelle showed up at my house, I opened the door to find a tall, shapely and good-looking woman. Her beauty made me pause for a moment, until I remembered she only liked men. My mind quickly adjusted to act and react as I did with other straight women.

Together, we looked through the paper and found a new science fiction movie we both thought looked interesting and headed to the local mall to go see it. After the movie, we ate a late lunch and shopped a little, laughing and having a great time.

Michelle oozed charm, intelligence and had a keen sense of humor. It felt good to socialize with a friend, knowing we had no romantic connection. This kind of interaction with another woman didn't happen very often for me, so I enjoyed every moment of it when it did.

Then, after we returned to my house, Michelle and I began talking more intimately. She revealed that she had recently realized she didn't like men as much as she once thought, and now found women more attractive and desirable. She had suppressed this feeling for a very long time.

Today, what she said doesn't surprise me. Michelle started working toward her transition back in the middle to late 1970s. Back then, the psychologists had placed her on what they considered to be the most desirable path, even if it wasn't the right one for her. In those days, a man couldn't transition unless he exhibited sufficient feminine characteristics to pass as female without facial surgery. The doctors back then, predominantly male, took their role as gatekeepers to the most ridiculous extreme. As such, they imposed their chauvinist ideals of what really made a woman.

Some of the other requirements they placed on those wanting to transition were: 1) A person had to quit their job; 2) A person had to move to another part of the country; 3) A person had to make up a new and fictitious past; 4) A person had to come out of transition as a heterosexual and; 5) A man wanting to become a woman had to always wear makeup, heels and a short skirt.

Michelle spent so much time trying to convince the doctors that she only liked men, she ended up fooling herself. Even up to the time she had SRS, the surgeon required that she come out of the surgery as a heterosexual. Now, 30 years after starting her transition, and 10 years after SRS, she finally could admit to herself that she liked women.

I found Michelle's life experiences fascinating, but sad at the same time. It made me think back to what Lorraine had gone through, and I felt thankful that I hadn't started my transition back then.

After we'd talked about her past, the conversation took an even more intimate tone. She asked if I had ever been with a post-op. At that moment, I remembered what Connie had said to me.

"I was under the impression that post-ops don't want anything to do with pre-ops. So, to answer your question, 'No'."

"Not all post-ops think that way."

"Oh?" I mumbled.

Then Michelle leaned in and kissed me, and one thing led to another. Needless to say, over the next few weeks I became deeply infatuated with her. It became complicated after that.

25 – GEORGIA ON MY MIND

I never thought I would leave Arizona. Even though I can't claim to be a native, ever since I arrived in 1953, at the age of 18 months, I very much felt like one. The beauty of the architecture, the culture, the desert, the mountains, the lakes, rivers, streams and, of course, the Grand Canyon had an emotional hold on me that I couldn't find in any other place. My family lived there, all of my close friends lived there, and the majority of my childhood memories had been formed there. I couldn't leave Arizona any more than I could reverse my transition.

But things happened at the beginning of 2000 that changed all of that, and the roots I'd planted so long ago in the Sonoran Desert started to shatter. After observing my female-self emerge, other pieces of my life-puzzle began falling into place. In 1987, my friend's reasoning for starting her transition opened my eyes to why I should start mine. Now that Connie had told me I had already made it, another piece had been added to the picture, one concerning my future as a woman and a lesbian.

One day at work, a new and inescapable thought came to me: your destiny lies elsewhere. At that moment, I made the decision to leave Arizona and pursue my destiny in some other part of the country. There were a number of contributing factors that affected my decision.

First of all, I hated the job I'd been in for the last ten years. At first it had suited me, but it had subsequently become tedious. Sprint treated me well however, so I felt I should stay with them and keep my seniority.

I also wanted to leave Arizona because of my frustration with my family, specifically my parents. The pain of living just five miles from them but not being able to enter the house I grew up in became too much for me. If I moved a thousand miles away, it would make being apart from them more bearable.

I also had strong financial reasons for moving. Sprint didn't pay their long-distance operators as much as other companies, but those other companies weren't hiring new people. If I could find a better-paying job within Sprint, I might finally be able to get ahead. The child support I paid to Donna was bleeding me dry and I ended up owing the IRS at the end of every year because I had to increase the number of dependents on my W-2 just to survive.

One thing prevented me from being able to apply for other jobs at Sprint, however. I'd been placed on Corrective Action status after getting upset following a conversation with a particularly rude customer. After months of exemplary behavior on my part, the Corrective Action period ended in April, and I immediately started applying for jobs elsewhere within Sprint. I checked the HR website and made a list of the jobs I felt qualified to do. I focused my search on two cities: Sacramento and Atlanta. Sacramento had only one Sprint facility, like Phoenix, and the pay there looked no better than what I already made. Atlanta, on the other hand, had several Sprint facilities, any of which would likely mean a reasonable pay increase for me if I secured a position.

Sacramento still held some appeal. In Sacramento, I would only be a couple of hours away from several people I knew in the Bay Area and all the fun of San Francisco. Alternatively, Atlanta offered the chance to continue my trans activism and work with other important people in our community. Atlanta also hosted the Southern Comfort Conference each year, which I had always wanted to attend.

A further incentive to move to Atlanta arose when I discovered that the National Gay and Lesbian Task Force's Creative Change Conference would be held in Atlanta that November. Ron Owen highlighted it as the one conference I should attend each year. Everything seemed to favor Atlanta, so I concentrated my job search there and, after a month of applications and phone interviews,

Atlanta's Service Management Center hired me to start on June 12.

Sprint had a special program for their Phoenix staff. If one of their employees there found another job within the company, Sprint would pay their moving expenses. Had it not been for this program, I would not have been able to move. I wouldn't have been able to afford it. Elsewhere in Sprint, only top management qualified for relocation expenses, so I felt very lucky in this regard.

Now I had to tell everyone I would soon leave, including my family, my friends, my roommate and the LGBT community. Even though I had begun the process of moving to another state, my parents still refused to see me. My father's heath had gotten worse. He now suffered from both diabetes and Alzheimer's and my mother had become his care-giver and had shifted into an ultra-protective mode. In February, they had celebrated their 50th wedding anniversary. Mom figured Dad couldn't take seeing me as a woman, so she wouldn't allow me to see them before I left for Atlanta.

Leaving my Arizonan friends made me very sad. Some I had only known for a year, while others I had known for as long as three years. I had no friendships that lasted longer because everyone had disowned me when I started my transition.

The LGBT community felt disappointed that I had to leave, not least because of all the work I had taken on that would need to be redistributed in my absence. I felt more excited than sad. I knew there would probably be a lot of activism work waiting for me in Georgia, once I'd gotten to know the key people there.

I'd already done a little recon on the situation in Georgia by emailing Dallas Denny. She and I had never communicated before then, but I knew of her by the good reputation she'd established over the years. Dallas let me know whom I needed to contact, both in the community and at other activist organizations. In particular, she pointed me towards Georgia Gender Education and Advocacy (GGEA), which used to be called It's Time, Georgia.

I also asked Dallas about the local driver's license procedures. She told me that the only way to get the proper sex marker in Georgia was by a court order or proof of sex change. After reading that, I wrote back saying that I would make an attempt to change the status quo when I arrived. She replied saying that, before I tried to make changes, I should get there and work with others in the community before thinking I had all the answers. Her advice stuck with me and became advice that I have subsequently passed on to others moving to Georgia or starting work at the national level.

Everything seemed to fall into place. Everything but my new love, Michelle. We had just started our relationship when I got the news that I had a new job in Georgia. It put a damper on our time together, to say the least, but we made the best of what little time we had.

I found a place to stay in Atlanta by talking online to a person by the name of Rachael. When we later talked on the phone, I liked what I heard because I could tell Rachael had her life together. When the time came, Sprint had movers come and pick up my things and take them to Rachael's place. My roommate and I only had two months left on our lease, so the timing was perfect for both of us. Cindy had already made plans to move into a townhouse she planned on purchasing with her long-time boyfriend.

Before I left, Cindy told me, "You're making the biggest mistake of your life." Even though her warning came from a place of love, she could not have been more wrong. Although I left my family behind in Arizona, moving to Atlanta has been one of the best decisions of my life. Sprint shut down their Phoenix facility a couple of years after I left. Had I stayed I would likely have had to find another job with the economy in pretty bad shape. By moving, I kept a job throughout all that happened after 9/11.

I do have regrets about moving though. The poor state of my finances meant I couldn't fly back to Arizona to witness either of my two sons' graduations. I also missed sending my oldest off to the Marines and his subsequent boot camp graduation.

The saddest event I missed however was not being there when my father died. I talked to him on the phone the day before he passed, telling him that I loved him. My sister, who sat with him at the time, told me he made a sound when he heard me say that. She said it was the only reaction he had all day.

When I heard that he didn't have much time left, I decided to spend what little savings I had to make the journey to Phoenix. Also, my mother had finally said she wanted me to come home. Then, as I sat in the airport waiting for my flight home, my son called and said my father had passed away. So, I never got to tell him face-to-face that I loved him or look into his eyes one last time.

When I flew back to Phoenix for Dad's funeral, I found that his death unexpectedly led to a reconciliation with my family. I'm now closer to my mother than at any other time in my life. Leaving Arizona came with a price but staying would have carried one too. I don't wish that things could have been different, but I will always miss my Dad.

Returning to my cross-country move, after my furniture left with the movers for Atlanta, the time came for me to make the journey myself. I packed my little Nissan Sentra with some essentials, stopped in to give my two boys a hug goodbye, and headed north toward Flagstaff where I would take the I-40 across the U.S. Music blasted from my stereo as I made my first long road trip by myself in 22 years. All the other recent trips I'd taken had been with Donna and the boys.

On the way, I decided to visit my sister, Carrie, who happened to live in the same town as Michelle. Carrie is the closest sibling to me in age, being only four years younger. She hadn't seen me in the three years I'd lived as a woman, claiming she had difficulty adjusting to the idea.

After I'd arrived and found a motel room, Carrie and I met at the local Denny's for dinner. She had brought a camera with her and, after we'd finished eating, she handed it to the waitress and said, "Could you please take a picture of me and my sister? I haven't seen her in three years."

When I heard her calling me her sister, I nearly cried.

The next day, I tried to visit Michelle's office. I knew she had gone on a business trip, but I had an idea to leave something for her. I didn't know if it was a good idea however, so I called one of Michelle's closest friends, another trans woman by the name of Cheryl, to ask her opinion.

"Cheryl, I'm thinking of dropping into where Michelle works and leaving her a card, but I'm not sure if I should do it. What do you think?"

To which Cheryl replied, "All I can say is follow your heart."

So, I decided to pay her office a visit. While there, I spoke a little with the man Michelle lived with and also the receptionist. I used the restroom and, before leaving, placed a card I had written for Michelle on her desk. Soon after, I started back on the road and headed east.

My cell phone didn't have a signal throughout most of northern Arizona and New Mexico. When I reached Albuquerque, I decided to spend the night there. The next morning, I got gas outside of town and had a little breakfast. Since I knew I would likely lose signal again, I decided to call Michelle to make sure she'd received my card.

Michelle answered and as soon as she heard my voice, she tore into me with the fury of a hungry mountain lion. Some of her employees had been asking her questions about me. Michelle, who had mostly lived a stealth life, felt that by showing up I had somehow outed her, though in truth her employees had only made inquiries about me. How could I do that to her? What kind of game was I playing? How could I be so stupid?

I tried to reason with her. A person doesn't have to justify to others why they are friends with someone. There is no guilt by association. More than that, Michelle looked too good for anyone to speculate about her gender at birth.

Cheryl had made matters worse however, by telling Michelle that she had warned me against just showing up at her office. Cheryl and I would later cross paths and when we did, she would tell others that I intentionally went to Michelle's workplace to out her because that's what trans activists do. But why would I want to intentionally out the woman I loved?

The conversation with Michelle devastated me. I cried from Albuquerque all the way through the Texas Panhandle and into Oklahoma. The next day, I shifted into the subsequent stage of loss: anger. I thought about all the things that Cheryl had said and my blood boiled. Michelle struck me as an intelligent woman, why couldn't she just brush off the incident with her employees? Not long after feeling angry however, my mood once again returned to sadness.

Michelle and I later made up via phone, only to have an online falling out over a trans activism issue. I then saw Michelle at a convention a few years later and we hugged. Before the convention ended, I felt that we both had closure on all that had happened between us. We've since lost touch, but I wish her nothing but happiness in her life.

On June 9, 2000, I arrived at Rachael's house. Three days later, I started my new job within Sprint.

26 – A RAINY NIGHT IN GEORGIA

When I arrived in Georgia, I heard everyone talking about a drought taking place across the whole southeast. Yet, it seemed to rain practically every day after I got there. In Arizona they consider it a drought when it hasn't rained for over 150 days. In Georgia, a drought is when it rains every ten days instead of every other day. With green trees and growth everywhere, it didn't look much like a drought to me.

Two weeks after arriving, I attended Atlanta Pride and felt overwhelmed by the size of the event. A Phoenix Pride would consider itself successful if 30,000 people showed up. In Atlanta they regularly attracted crowds of around 300,000, with people coming in from all over the southeast U.S. I had already made some friends, so I hung out at the Atlanta Gender Explorations (AGE) booth and met some of the trans people from the area. One of the people I met that day was Karen Collins, head of Georgia Gender Equality Association, a sister organization of ITAZ.

Karen gave me a good overview on how things worked in Georgia. The trans community had come much further in Georgia than in Arizona, but still had a long way to go. They had already established a legitimate presence in the community and had the backing of the state LGB organizations. Karen also let me know that, even though the Democrats held the Governor's office and a majority in the state House and Senate, the politicians' views on LGBT issues weren't dissimilar from those in Arizona. She walked me to a few other booths so I could meet others involved in local LGBT activism, including people from the Georgia Equality Project (GEP) and the Georgia Stonewall Democrats (GSD.)

Later in the day, I got to meet the man in charge of the Pride Parade Color Guard, Danny Ingram. I told him about my experience in previous parades and with the Transgender Pride Flag, and he told me he'd make sure I would be part of the Color Guard the following year. When I stopped at the GSD booth, I discovered that they had been more involved in the politics of Georgia than the Arizona Stonewall Caucus had been, so I joined GSD that day. I also met a woman who would later become my girlfriend.

In early July, I contacted the NGLTF's Creative Change committee and volunteered to help. Being involved with the conference gave me the chance to meet some of Georgia's LGBT community leaders in a relatively short period of time. I volunteered for the Media Committee, to help get the word out about the event.

When the convention took place in November, I saw what Ron Owen had meant. Creative Change turned out to be everything Ron had said it was, and more. Coretta Scott King's speech inspired us all and, after the convention, I felt more empowered than at any time in my life.

Next, I contacted the people running the Southern Comfort Conference (SCC) to volunteer there and had an equally great time when that took place. I met several people I'd talked to online but never met before in person. SCC introduced me to many trans activists with whom I would work in the future, while Creative Change introduced me to many local and national LGBT activists.

In late July, Karen Collins called me to see if I could help a trans woman who had been harassed by her employer, Wal-Mart. The woman, Melissa White, had just begun her transition. The store she worked at insisted that she conform to its male dress code. She and I sat and talked one weekend and, as we did, I found her to be engaging and level-headed. She already had a Plan A formulated, but if it failed Plan B would be to protest the store.

On Monday, Melissa sat down with the store's management, having meticulously studied the employees' dress-code policy. Her managers insisted she follow the male dress code, until she pointed out to them that she already adhered to it. The male dress code consisted of a collared shirt, slacks and shoes with less than one-inch heels. For the meeting, Melissa wore a woman's collared shirt, women's slacks and women's shoes with less than one-inch heels. With the exception of not being allowed to wear earrings or make up, they had to admit she had followed the regulations to the letter. Plan A worked and Melissa and I became good friends.

Not long after Melissa's run-in with Wal-Mart, Karen and I helped a homeless trans woman find shelter. This became my first experience dealing with homelessness, an issue that would go on to monopolize my time for nearly a year. We tried various different shelters for her but got turned away from all of them. Finally, Karen used her own money to rent the person a motel room. The very next day, the woman in question found a job, which meant she would once again be able to take care of herself.

At my first Southern Comfort Conference (SCC), I finally got to meet Dallas Denny and discovered that she had a wonderfully skewed sense of humor, just like mine. Dallas had assumed the editorship of *Transgender Tapestry* and I shared with her my desire to write something for the publication. She asked me to submit ideas to see if I had enough material for a regular column. I did and my first column for *Transgender Tapestry* premiered just before SCC 2000. I received a lot of positive comments about my piece. Writing for *Tapestry* became a lot of fun. I would give Dallas a hard time about being a rich, corporate giant living in the penthouse of Tapestry Towers, and she would respond to me with wonderful comebacks to my jabs. We always had something to go back and forth about. I truly miss that. I ended up doing 19 columns for the magazine before eventually putting my pen down.

I also met Gwen Smith for the first time at that SCC and we discussed her idea of having a nationwide Day of Remembrance for trans murders that had taken place over the past year. San Francisco had held the first event in November 1999 and Gwen wanted to expand it to other cities for 2000. I promised her that Atlanta would be part of the expansion that coming November.

So, on November 28, 2000, Atlanta held its first Transgender Day of Remembrance in front of the State Capitol Building, also called the Gold Dome. Only 16 people showed up, but a handful of those that did would have a lasting impact on my life.

One of those people was Pastor Paul Turner, a man who would later become one of my closest and dearest friends. He led Gentle

Spirit Christian Church, an independent church in the LGBT community. The first TDOR impacted him greatly, turning him into one of Georgia's strongest advocates for the trans community.

Another person I met that day was a trans woman by the name of Dana Owings. Dana started her transition a couple of years after I did; she worked for IBM and had just come out to her workplace. She had never been to anything like the Transgender Day of Remembrance previously and the event moved her as much as it did Pastor Paul. It changed the direction of her life. She never thought she would be involved in trans activism, but the emotional TDOR opened her eyes. Over the next few months, I encouraged Dana to get more involved in activism, albeit at her own pace.

I also met a trans woman by the name of Gloria. We dated briefly, but she ended up breaking my heart with little explanation as to why. Later, Gloria tried to take advantage of several of my friends, including Dana and Pastor Paul. Over the years, a number of people tried to help her and came away feeling used. Like others I have met, Gloria felt the world owed her everything just for being a trans woman.

Around the time of Atlanta's first TDOR, Karen Collins decided to retire from activism and move to Kentucky. Before she left, she put me in charge of GGEA. Both of us agreed that the organization should probably be renamed after its activist wing, so one of my first acts would be to rebrand GGEA as Trans=Action.

Next, I set out to recruit more people to the organization. I'd been getting vibes from Dana that she wanted to get more involved. I felt she would be a good trans activist if she really put her mind to it. She approached problems in the same way I had seen from other good activists, but she still had one major factor to overcome: fear. Fear can keep a person from becoming a trans activist or stop one dead in their tracks even after years of work. Dana needed time to overcome her fear, which she eventually did, and in time she became one of the best activists I have ever had the pleasure to work with.

My new roommate, Rachael, had a trans friend in the Atlanta Police Department by the name of Denise. She seemed to be a nice person, but I heard that her supervisors had given her a hard time. They harassed her in many different ways, sometimes skirting the edge of the guidelines of Atlanta's non-discrimination policy covering city employees. I tried to see if anything could be done to intervene, but I either ran into a roadblock or else Denise didn't want me to take a particular course of action. At the time, Karen Collins sat on the City of Atlanta's Community Relations Board for the LGBT community, and even they couldn't help.

Denise had opted to fast-track her SRS, with her surgery scheduled for December, just one year after she started living full-time as a woman. She needed a little help financially, so she and Rachael convinced me to move in with Denise. I agreed, but it turned out to be a bad decision on my part. Since I had not finished training, I still worked the day shift. On top of now being twice as far from work as before, I had to travel in the worst direction traffic-wise. Nevertheless, I felt that by moving in with Denise, I could help her make it through her recovery.

Of the pains I had to endure in moving to Atlanta, the worst had to be the city's traffic and its streets. Being an old city, the layout of the streets resembled the spokes of a wheel, seemingly with little or no thought given to their design. Not only that, but the timing of the traffic lights made driving even worse. Combine all that with small one- and two-lane roads being used as main routes, poor visibility and a lack of road signs, constant road construction, and you soon have a nightmare on your hands. In fact, a recent study showed Atlanta to be one of the worst cities in the U.S. to drive in.

By comparison, Phoenix had been laid out in a grid pattern with major roads every mile, each with as many as four lanes in both directions. The lights are timed so well that if you traveled across town at a certain time of day, a distance of 20 miles, you might not hit a single red light. I've done it, but usually only at night. If a person moved to Phoenix, they could probably find their way around in five days. It took me two months to get my bearings in Atlanta and another six months to feel comfortable driving in the city. Today, I still have to use GPS if I'm going to someplace new.

After moving in with Denise, I quickly found she had a hidden mean streak that Rachael had never seen. In December, Denise had her surgery. Afterwards, I discovered she also had a hidden agenda. It started with her attitude. She thought that, now that she had a vagina, those at her workplace would no longer discriminate against her. I commented sarcastically that she acted as if her new vagina made her invincible, but she actually agreed with me. Unfortunately, Denise wasn't one of the most passable trans women around. She had a stocky build, stood over six-feet tall, walked like a lumberjack, and had a deep voice that seemed unconcerned by her new vagina. Granted, there are many trans women, both post-op and pre-op, who freely admit they don't pass well, and I don't see anything wrong with that. Many of them live happy and productive lives with partners who love them. The difference between them and Denise was that she thought her vagina instantly hid everything else and no one would ever know that she used to be a man. She needed a reality check.

While recovering, Denise began saying things like, "I'm no longer a transsexual," and "I don't want to have anything to do with anyone in the transgender or transsexual community." I really didn't care how she wanted to label herself, but the latter comment worried me because I could see our joint tenancy rapidly coming to an end. That happened in February 2001 when she got mad at me because I watched television in the living room with a friend. According to her, we made too much noise.

Denise told me she wanted me to move out in July, and it hit me why she wanted me to stay that long. She had to go back into surgery to have a labiaplasty and she needed me to keep paying my portion of the rent so she could afford it. I refused to be used like that and moved out on my own in March instead.

One of the biggest changes I experienced when I moved from Arizona to Georgia was cultural. Arizona has a very large Latino and Native American population and those cultures have helped shaped society there. By contrast, Georgia has a very large African American population and the culture of the state reflects that.

When I turned up for my first day of training at Sprint, I was one of only two white women in the training class. Everyone else was African American and, as a result, I instantly felt very comfortable. I have always received the most acceptance from African Americans, especially older African American women. They seem to understand the concept of accepting others more than any white non-trans people I've ever met.

As an activist, the civil rights history of Atlanta excited me. I now lived in the heart of the Civil Rights Movement and the lessons learned from that movement would go a long way in helping me understand my activism better. I remember the first time I stepped into the Ebenezer Baptist Church and heard a recording of Dr. Martin Luther King's voice coming over of the church's loudspeakers. I closed my eyes and I could see him standing at the pulpit, flailing his arms and empowering all who listened to him.

27 – AMERICA THE BEAUTIFUL

My involvement in national activism began in Arizona, in 1999, when I contacted Calpernia Addams and started working on the statistics for Remembering Our Dead. That same year, a discussion list I belonged to started talking about the formation of a national trans group to replace GenderPAC, after they expanded their scope to focus less on trans people.

Like me, many felt betrayed by GenderPAC and certain activities that subsequently came to light, such as allegedly conspiring with the Human Rights Campaign (HRC) to undercut the lobbying efforts of trans activists. I had my own issue with GenderPAC. If a person ever called their offices and said they had a trans-related problem and needed help, GenderPAC told them to go elsewhere. Yet at the same time GenderPAC traveled the country with the relatives of murdered trans people, raising money for their organization. To me, this lacked any sense of morality. A new organization needed to be created.

A group of trans activists formed a new Yahoo list and began working towards the creation of a new group that would eventually become the National Transgender Advocacy Coalition (NTAC). Alexander Goodrum and I both joined the list, as did many others. The initial discussions were heated. I had expected this, since the list included some of the best trans activists at the time, each with their own strong personality and each used to doing things his or her own way.

Alexander and I listened and participated for as long as we

could, but the discussions turned so bad that eventually both of us dropped off. A core group finally formed NTAC, but its tumultuous beginning followed the organization wherever it went. In the beginning, NTAC suffered from a poor reputation and many people stayed away from it because of that. This was sad, because NTAC did eventually develop into a good organization with respectable leaders.

In the beginning of 2001, I traveled down to Jacksonville, Florida to join the protest against Winn-Dixie, a supermarket chain. In 2000, the company's Louisiana division fired a truck driver when they found out he cross-dressed off duty. They claimed the employee's actions would give the company a "bad image." So, more than a dozen of us from various parts of the country drove or flew to Florida to stand in front of their corporate headquarters in the cold wind, carrying signs and chanting. The event organizer, a local trans activist from Jacksonville called Terrianne Summers, did a great job at putting the event together.

Sadly, in December of 2001, I received a call from a friend in Jacksonville that Terrianne had been shot to death on her driveway as she exited her car. Her purse hadn't been stolen and the police never found the killer. When we protested Winn-Dixie again three weeks later, more than twice as many people showed up. Eight of us made our way down from Georgia. Hopefully we made Terrianne very proud that day.

I began to get more and more involved with the Transgender Day of Remembrance in 2001. Principally this meant providing people from all over the country with updated murder statistics for trans men and women, a grim but necessary service. Atlanta once again held a TDOR ceremony, one of more than 30 such events that took place across the U.S. that year. City Councilwoman Cathy Woolard once again presented Atlanta with a proclamation for our event. Dana helped enormously with our second TDOR, and all the ones that followed, and I could not thank her enough.

In 2001, I decided to take another look at NTAC, because they had been doing good things under the leadership of their new Chair. After consulting with some friends, I joined the NTAC's Activism Committee, which gave me the chance to work with Angela Brightfeather for the first time. Angela lived in North Carolina and had heard of the work I'd been doing in Georgia. Not too long after joining the committee, they made me its Co-Chair.

In May 2001, NTAC held its Lobby Days in D.C., which meant I got to revisit the capital, this time to lobby members of Congress from Georgia. Later in August, I joined the board of NTAC and headed the newly-created VA Committee.

In the 18 months that I served on the board of NTAC, we accomplished a few good things, but we also ran into some snags. The board didn't always run smoothly because of the egos and personalities involved. Any one of the board members could have run the NTAC and done a good job of it, but together we seemed to hinder one another more than we helped.

I have to take my fair share of blame for the board's dysfunctionality. My own arrogance frequently got the best of me, and at times I acted like a spoiled child. Others did too, but I'm accountable only for my own actions. In time, Pastor Paul would bring me closer to my spiritual center. Writing this book has also done a lot to help exorcise a few of my own demons.

Oddly, one of the threads that has held national trans activists together has been their mutual dislike and distrust of the Human Rights Campaign. In 1994, with the help of HRC, Congress first introduced the Employment Non-Discrimination Act (ENDA). From day one, the bill never covered trans people and HRC didn't seem to care. At the time, HRC's mission statement didn't even mention us. When they eventually added us to HRC's mission statement in March 2001, many trans activists heaped praise on the organization. Our jubilation became short-lived however, when we realized they still didn't plan on including trans people in the ENDA or Hate Crimes bills they had lobbied Congress to pass.

Nevertheless, a handful of gullible trans people believed the change HRC made to its mission statement meant that they now fully supported us. Those people also pointed to some minor projects that HRC undertook on behalf of the trans community as being sufficient to earn our trust. I felt that, if an organization said they advocated for a group of people, then they should go all-out in that advocacy. An organization cannot throw crumbs to one part of its membership while saving the prime cuts for another. That is not advocacy to me. HRC had put us in their mission statement, so why wouldn't they insist on covering us in the federal legislation they had proposed?

Angela came up with a wonderful idea in response. She called her plan Educational Initiatives. She had trans people attend HRC dinners in various cities to educate the big gay and lesbian donors on how the organization left trans people behind. We found that a lot of gay men and women had no idea that HRC wouldn't insist on our inclusion in their proposed legislation. Many stopped giving to HRC because of what they learned from us.

We decided to hold an Educational Initiative in Atlanta at HRC's May 2002 dinner. By coincidence the SCC Planning Committee held their quarterly meeting in Atlanta that same weekend, which meant there would be plenty of trans people on hand to help us out. Some stood outside the hotel holding protest signs, while others handed out flyers to those attending the dinner.

We rented a suite in the hotel and invited attendees up to discuss trans issues with us after dinner. A few of us also attended the dinner to educate attendees from within the event. When the dinner ended, our people handed out flyers to members as they came out of the banquet hall. That night, over 200 attendees cycled through our suite. Many walked away having learned something new about trans people, about the discrimination we faced, and that HRC had excluded us from their legislative outreach.

When the crowd had thinned out, in walked Elizabeth Birch, the Executive Director of HRC at the time. She spent three hours talking with us, listening to us and trying to convince us that HRC really cared. Occasionally I would lift my left arm high into the air because Birch piled it on so deep, I felt I should save my watch. Yet, in spite of the rhetoric she served up that night, I felt we actually won Birch over a little. She did eventually become a stronger ally for us, just before she resigned as Executive Director. However, winning her over didn't mean the rest of the organization would follow. HRC's board called the shots and many on the board wouldn't budge when it came to trans issues.

28 – MORE PAIN FROM THE HRC

Shortly after Pride 2002, HRC came to Atlanta to hold a town hall meeting to get support for ENDA, which had just been reintroduced in the U.S Senate. A panel presided over the meeting, made up of local gay and lesbian activists, but excluded any representation from the trans community. Eight trans people attended the town hall, and I came ready for a fight.

At the meeting, each panel member spoke about the importance of writing to our Senators and asking them to support ENDA. The last person to speak came from HRC's national headquarters in D.C. Once they had finished, they asked for questions from the audience. I stood up and I did not hold back.

I actually can't remember another time during my career in activism that I sounded so angry in a public forum, but the words that flowed from my mouth did so clearly and precisely. I had been given the chance to publicly voice how the trans community felt at being left out of the ENDA bill, and I would make sure that the LGBs present knew how the Ts felt.

During my speech, I pointed out that, when the non-discrimination law had been written for the City of Atlanta, the local politicians had added gender identity and gender expression language without even needing to consult the trans community. Why did HRC, the lobbying organization that claimed to represent us, support less inclusion than a southern municipality?

Later, Dana got up and spoke in a calmer voice than I had,

though her message sounded principally the same. She decided to play the part of the good trans cop for the meeting, versus my turn as the bad trans cop. We did that often, though each of us agreed that we had more fun being the bad cop. One other trans person got up to speak, Sir Jesse McNulty. After the three of us had voiced our anger and concerns, the head of the local chapter of Log Cabin Republicans stood up and stated his support for trans-inclusion.

The panel's moderator claimed to be moved at the issues we had raised and invited me to be on the panel for the rest of the evening. It amounted to a token gesture however, because HRC's position on the deliberate exclusion of trans people from the ENDA bill they supported did not change.

Then, in late 2003 and early 2004, HRC changed their position, stating that they now supported fully inclusive federal legislation. Once again, trans people praised them, including me. Their change of heart made me finally want to work with them. But they had a hidden secret, uncovered by the NTAC's 2004 Lobby Days event. While HRC would go into legislators' offices and say that they supported a fully inclusive bill, they would also tell the legislator that if a non-inclusive bill happened to be introduced, they would support that as well. Of course, the legislators felt more comfortable throwing trans people under the bus, and with HRC giving them every reason to follow that line of thinking, that's what they did.

When news of HRC's tactics hit the Internet, the solid, darkish-colored human waste material made violent contact with the large, electromechanical, rotating, air-circulating device.

Trans people discovered they had been coddled once again by the doublespeak that HRC had become so famous for. "We did say we'd do that, but if you notice, we didn't say we wouldn't also do this." Their transphobic lawyers knew just how to structure a sentence or a statement to leave people believing one thing, while giving HRC enough wiggle room to have an out if they needed it.

The news of HRC's deception came out just before Pride season. In response, we mobilized a nationwide effort to protest their actions. This included handing out informational flyers to Pride-goers directly in front of HRC's booths. Trans=Action voted to do the same, but we approached it slightly differently from other protesters. Rather than ambush HRC during Pride, Pastor Paul, Dana and I instead sat down with Lawrie, Georgia's only HRC Board Member, and Betty, the Co-Chair of the local HRC Diversity Committee and a member of the local Pride Committee. We decided we would give them a heads-up on what we planned to do.

Trans=Action put together a flyer with ENDA on one side and the Hate Crimes Bill on the other, pointing out how HRC's proposed legislation left trans people behind. Like other protesters, we planned on passing out the flyers in front of HRC's booth. Our hope was that by letting the local branch know how angry we felt at their double-cross, they would then go to their August national board meeting arguing that HRC should support only fully-inclusive federal legislation. We hoped they wouldn't support anything that left trans people out, even if it meant slowing down the bill's progress. In our opinion, the days of incremental protection had ended. Betty agreed, but Lawrie acted very non-committal. Nevertheless, she said she would go along with what the rest of the local board agreed.

They then read the flyer we had produced and noticed that, on the Hate Crimes side, we had mentioned how HRC had ignored a recent trans murder that had taken place in Atlanta. They seemed surprised by this and asked why we felt the need to include it. We discussed the paragraph a little and defended why we'd put it in, before agreeing to remove it at their request. What they didn't know was that we had deliberately inserted that particular paragraph so that we could be seen to compromise and so they would feel like they had won a concession from us. It worked beautifully.

When Atlanta Pride began, a friend and I planted ourselves in front of the HRC booth and began handing out our flyers. After a few minutes, a young woman intern from HRC's D.C. headquarters approached me and asked what we had been handing out. When I showed her, she said, "But HRC includes transgender people."

"No, they don't." I told her.

"It says so in our Mission Statement."

I laughed and proceeded to tell her what HRC had been telling the legislators in their offices.

"Well, I can get you the name of someone you can talk to about this and they can explain it to you."

"I have all the contacts I need, thank you, including HRC's Executive Director, Cheryl Jacques. You and I are done talking."

"You can't be out here." She continued.

"Yes, we can. Lawrie and Betty gave us permission. If you'd like to confirm that, call Betty. She's on the Pride Committee."

The young woman walked away and called someone on her cell phone. I guessed she didn't talk to Betty because a few minutes later a security guard approached us.

"You can't be here," he told us. "You have to move on."

"We can be here. We have permission from Betty, which is what I told the young lady. Betty is a member of the Pride Committee."

The security guard walked over and talked to the intern and I overheard her telling him that the flyers we were handing out contained false information. I laughed at that. Finally, after some more tense moments, the intern got word that we could be there, but by then my friend and I had run out of flyers.

The next day, I tried to pass out more flyers, but the pouring rain made it impossible. Instead, Dana and I later spoke on the Pride's small stage about the importance of early trans activist Silvia Rivera's contribution to the Stonewall Riots, thirty-five years earlier. Betty had been the one who set that up for us.

Then in August, when HRC had their scheduled board meeting in D.C., a group of Transsexual Menace members gathered outside their building to protest. The day before, word had been leaked to magazine *The Advocate* that HRC's Board had already decided to support only a fully inclusive ENDA, but some trans people believed that HRC had leaked the news itself in order to discourage potential trans protestors. It didn't work.

Instead, the leak made the eight or so trans people that HRC had invited to the board meeting feel like they had been invited only for show. Nevertheless, even after hearing that the decision had been made ahead of time, one or two of them convinced themselves that their presence had actually changed HRC's mind. When the meeting ended and the HRC's Board officially voted on supporting only a fully inclusive ENDA, they invited the trans protestors outside to share lunch with them. By all accounts, most people treated the protestors with kindness and respect. That is, except for those who had been with HRC for several years and who had spearheaded the effort to keep trans people out of any federal legislation protecting gays and lesbians. According to one of the protestors present, not only would that clique not talk to the trans protestors, they wouldn't even look at them.

Later, in early 2005, when word came out that the U.S. House and Senate would introduce a Hate Crimes Bill, one of those very people who had refused to acknowledge the trans protestors said, "We didn't promise we would support a fully-inclusive Hate Crimes Bill." It showed that transphobia still lived in the HRC. Having said that, it felt refreshing to see that HRC's new President, Joe Solmonese, appeared to be far more supportive of trans-inclusiveness than any of his predecessors. Still, HRC had come out in support of a non-inclusive federal bill, which once again caused a lot of trans people to become angry with them.

I maintained a healthy skepticism as far as HRC was concerned. That way, no matter what they did, I wouldn't be disappointed. A good example of this happened when the new Hate Crimes Bill had been introduced in the House and the Senate. The House bill became the first-ever federal legislation that had language that included trans people. The Senate however, reintroduced the same old stale and non-inclusive bill it had introduced previously.

HRC made a point of saying publicly that they supported the House version but remained silent on the Senate version instead of stating publicly that they didn't support it. A friend of mine pointed out that HRC had always said more about how they truly felt when they stayed silent. I had to agree.

The Trinity Award

I first heard of the Trinity Award, given out by the International Foundation for Gender Education (IFGE), in 1999. Back then, I saw a list of all the wonderful people who had won it over the years. To me, they made up the best of the best from our community. I confess to thinking how nice it would be if one day I would be worthy enough to be included in that company, but I never expected it would actually happen. It didn't bother me because Amanda's words, spoken to me during Lobby Days back in 1999, still echoed in my mind.

Well, in late 2002, Dana decided to nominate me for the 2003 Trinity Award. That in itself felt wonderful, but when I heard about who else had received a nomination, I never gave it another thought. Then in February of 2003, Dana received word that I would be one of three people to receive the Trinity Award that year. When I found out, I couldn't believe it.

The organization presented the award to recipients at a luncheon during the annual IFGE convention. In my acceptance speech, I talked about the importance of humor in activism. For me, humor is the best defense against burnout and frustration. To demonstrate, I included the following comment about my family: "My family had a really hard time with me changing into a woman. Most of it had to do with their religious beliefs. My parents are Catholic, my brother is a born-again Christian, and I have one sister who is a Mormon. As such, I've been condemned to Hell in three different religions."

The following year, I nominated Angela Brightfeather for the Trinity Award, though at first she didn't want to be nominated. She told me, "Once anyone gets that award, they expect you to retire quietly and gracefully somewhere out of sight."

In reply I told her, "No, you're thinking of the Virginia Prince Award. When you receive the Trinity Award the community is saying, 'Hey, we like what you've done so far, so here's something nice for your mantle. Now, get your ass back out there and do more work!'"

Angela laughed.

29 – OLD SAILORS NEVER DIE

"Submarines will be the death of you." That's what Pauline, the Irish woman I met in Spain, had said to me the last time I saw her in 1974. In spite of her pronouncement, I stayed on submarines for another four years and ended up leaving the Navy with an honorable discharge. Moreover, being a submarine veteran allowed me to find my true calling in trans activism.

Even so, my interest in trans veterans' issues may not have ever surfaced if I hadn't been on a Yahoo Group list by the name of TSVeterans. Trans veterans formed this group specifically to discuss the various issues they faced, including dealing with VA medical facilities and other health-related issues. Specifically, people discussed their experiences dealing with different VA facilities across the country. Some on the list had great experiences, while others had been treated terribly.

Out of all the stories I'd read about, the one that lit a fire in my soul came from my friend, Alex Fox. Early in his transition, Alex went to the Washington D.C. VA facility to get help. When they discovered his trans status, they refused to treat him. So, he drove 60 miles north to the VA facility in Baltimore, where they treated him great.

I felt so moved by Alex's story that I told Angela Brightfeather, also a veteran, because I felt that this could be something the NTAC Activism Committee should work on. After Angela joined the TSVets list and saw for herself the problems facing other transsexual veterans, she felt that the scale of the problem necessitated it having a dedicated committee within NTAC to work on it. So, we formed the VA Committee to focus on the inconsistencies trans veterans faced at the VA's various facilities.

We later discovered that the inconsistency of service came from Public Law (PL) 104-262. Here is that Public Law, including later amendments. Please note the vague terminology at the end of paragraph two.

Public Law (PL) 104-262,
Veterans Health Care Eligibility Reform Act of 1996

Public Law (PL) 104-262, Veterans Health Care Eligibility Reform Act of 1996, "calls for VA to furnish hospital care and medical services that are defined as 'needed'. VA defines 'needed' as care or services that will promote, preserve, and restore health. This includes a treatment, procedure, supply or service." Some health care services "that will not normally be covered include abortion, membership in health clubs or spas for rehabilitation, special private duty nursing and gender alteration."

Department of Veterans Affairs M-2, Part XIV, Veterans Health Administration, Washington, DC 20420 November 17, 1993.

a. Chapter 11: Gender Reorientation (Sex Change). It is VA policy that transsexual surgery will not be performed in VA medical centers or under VA auspices. Veterans Health Administration (VHA) will not carry out any process or procedure involving genital identity revision.

Federal Register: November 1, 1996 (Volume 61, Number 213)] [Proposed Rules]
Sec. 17.270 General Provisions.

(a) CHAMPVA is the Civilian Health and Medical Program of the Department of Veterans Affairs. Pursuant to 38 U.S.C. 1713, VA is authorized to provide medical care in the same or similar manner and subject to the same or similar limitations as medical care furnished to certain dependents and survivors of active duty and retired members of the Armed Forces.

Federal Register / Vol. 64, No 193 / October 6, 1999
Paragraph 17.38 Medical Benefits Package (c) (4) was added to deny treatment for "Gender alterations."
Sec. 17.272 Benefits Limitations/Exclusions.

The following are specifically excluded from program (23) Services and supplies related to transsexualism or other similar conditions such as gender dysphoria (including, but not limited to, intersex surgery and psychotherapy, except for ambiguous genitalia which was documented to be present at birth).

What the Hell is "Genital Identity Revision"? It's not a term I've ever seen used anywhere else. You know what I think when I hear that terminology? Well, as many of us know, guys sometimes like to give their penis a name, or in other words, give it an identity. So, according to this Act, a veteran can name his penis, but the VA won't help him to change that name. Thus, he can't "revise" the "identity" of his "genitals." I mean, I don't have a problem with that.

However, the real problem for trans veterans resided not in that clumsy wording, but with the words "gender alteration". Some facilities looked at this law and thought, "This means we can't do the operation or pay for it, but we can do everything else for the trans veteran." Other facilities, like the one in D.C., used the law as a blanket excuse not to treat a trans veteran for anything. Most facilities fell somewhere in the middle, providing everything to pre-op trans people except psychotherapy and hormones, while most post-op trans veterans received everything they should.

Unfortunately, the typical trans veteran who needed VA assistance for their medical issues couldn't afford SRS nor pay the full price for the hormones they needed. So, what were they expected to do? When my wife and family wouldn't let me transition, it made me deeply depressed and bordering on suicidal. Is that what the VA wanted for trans veterans?

As we went about trying to help trans veterans, we had to be very careful when approaching the VA and asking for consistent medical treatment for all trans people. Knowing the VA and the federal government, they could have made the decision to be "consistent" and deny services to all trans veterans. This made advocating for trans veterans a very difficult task.

Angela and I felt we needed to support veterans, so we came up with the idea of forming a VA Committee, and we took the idea to the TSVets list. That proved to be a terrible mistake. Instead of support, we received a barrage of hateful emails. Many on the list told us in no uncertain terms to leave this issue alone. Oddly, the loudest complaints came from those who had received good service from the VA and didn't care if others received nothing. Even though a number acted selfishly with regard to their fellow veterans, the notion of not causing any trans veteran to lose good service became the centerpiece of our advocacy in this area.

In the military, we are taught to watch the backs of our shipmates or fellow soldiers and not to leave anyone behind. However, the selfish attitude trans veterans develop when they start to transition seemed to overshadow that training. Angela and I quickly learned that if we wanted to work on the issue, we couldn't go to the TSVets for help. Having said that, we did get supportive emails from a few people. One was Robyn Walters, the then moderator of the TSVets list.

One of those rare individuals in our community, Robyn had the right stuff when it came to activism. As an officer in the Navy, she worked on designing systems for submarines. She had a wonderful ability to look at a problem and see the steps needed to solve it. Like Dana, I saw the potential in her as a great trans activist, so I gently guided her in that direction. To this day, she blames me for getting her involved, but for the most part she says it with affection.

We formed a VA Committee at the 2001 NTAC board election. I had applied to become a board member and received enough votes to be elected. When we talked about the creation of an NTAC VA Committee, it started a very intense discussion. It appeared that for the most part, the veterans on the board supported the motion while the non-veterans didn't. Due to a number of abstentions, the formation of the VA Committee passed, but not without some very hurt feelings.

Some didn't see the need for the committee, nor the importance of supporting trans veterans. Angela and I pointed out that, as veterans, we had a unique position in the trans community. Americans find all kinds of hateful ways to vilify trans people and other minorities. But, when people in those minorities have served in the military, it becomes a useful tool with which to counter their hate.

"I served my country. Why didn't you?" Or, "I served my country and put my life on the line just like you did." Or, "I protected your freedoms. I guess I love this country more than you?" One can come up with so many responses for right-wing attacks if you have served in the military. If the person attacking the trans person is also a veteran, then you can establish a bridge that only veterans understand. These bridges become powerful tools in the fight for our rights.

Critically however, if NTAC helped trans veterans achieve equality within the VA, it would make NTAC look credible and win the organization a lot of support. In the end, the VA Committee existed for 18 months, with me as the Chair and Robyn as the Vice-Chair. We spent the time gathering information on all the issues facing trans veterans and the ways to combat this issue without affecting the good service some veterans received.

When HRC, Servicemembers Legal Defense Network (SLDN) and American Veterans for Equal Rights (AVER) – formally GLBVA – all got together to promote their Profiles in Courage program, designed to record the military experiences of LGBT veterans, we came out in support of it. But, being just a committee in an organization and not a fully-fledged organization ourselves, they wouldn't list us as a supporter.

As time went on, it became more and more apparent that the scope of the issues facing trans veterans would soon overwhelm a mere committee. Also, the restrictions and lack of support for our efforts from the rest of the NTAC board increased the level of tension and frustration that I felt. That frustration severely diminished my effectiveness and on January 12, 2003, I resigned from the NTAC board.

I felt that the issues facing trans veterans necessitated a national organization to solve them. I had formed a close friendship with Jamison Green, and I turned to him for his counsel. We talked about the deficiencies of NTAC's committee and I asked him if a national organization would do a better job of tackling these issues. He agreed it would, but also pointed out the perils and difficulties of starting a new organization. I weighed up the pros and cons and decided on a course of action.

So, on the day I resigned from NTAC, I went online and formed the Transgender American Veterans Association (TAVA). Like the NTAC, TAVA initially started off as a Yahoo Group. Eventually Angela and Robyn joined, as well as many of our community's leading activists. It felt exhilarating to form a dedicated group that could have a positive impact on trans veterans. Early on, we felt the need to include trans people still serving in the military so that, if any of them ran into trouble, they would have an organization to turn to and provide them with assistance. We may have had lofty goals, but we had honorable ones.

Less than one month after TAVA opened its doors, one of our members, Janice Josephine Carney, contacted the Library of Congress and set us up as a national supporter of their Veterans History Project. This project, on which HRC, SLDN and AVER based their Profiles in Courage project, recorded the military experiences of all veterans, but specifically WWII veterans. At the time, the Library of Congress said that 1,500 WWII veterans died each day and most had their contributions to our freedoms die with them. The Library of Congress had done a wonderful job of preserving many WWII veterans' stories. TAVA wanted to make sure that the stories of trans veterans would be preserved as well.

Over the next six months, TAVA set about establishing itself as a bona fide national organization. We wrote a mission statement, goals, vision statement, by-laws, and many other organizational documents. We created a website and designed logos and emblems. Finally, we elected TAVA's inaugural officers and board members. I felt humbled when the members elected me as TAVA's President. Now, we needed to get to work.

30 – TAVA'S FIRST MARCH TO THE WALL

In September 2003, Angela and I had a discussion over drinks at a bar in the hotel where SCC took place. Angela, the organization's Co-Founder, had been elected TAVA's Special Projects Director and she brought up an idea that she and I had kicked around for the preceding three years. In a sweat lodge in the mountains of North Carolina, she had a vision for a trans veterans gathering at the Vietnam Memorial in D.C. and all the healing that might take place there.

She proposed to a group of us at SCC that TAVA should sponsor the event. It subsequently became the first ever Transgender Veterans March to the Wall. During that initial discussion, we also decided to lay a wreath at the Tomb of the Unknown Soldier. We later settled on May 1, 2004 as the date for the march.

For the next three months, we discussed the proposed march only with TAVA board members, because we had witnessed a disastrous attempt by others who tried to plan a transgender march on Washington. A group of activists had the idea, but before settling on anything at all, they revealed their intentions to the entire trans community and proceeded to get torn to shreds. Trans people gave every reason for why it would fail and because the planners had nothing set in stone, they couldn't counter those complaints with solutions or counter-arguments. We knew that if we wanted to have a successful event, we had to have practically everything in place before we let the general public know about it. This included planning on how to respond to the various complaints that would undoubtedly surface.

When we finally made the announcement, we did indeed have the usual detractors that trans people get when they want to do something good in the community. Here are a few examples of what people said to try to rain on our parade:

Complaint: "Some people can't walk very far."
Our response: "We have already reserved a bus to take people to each location."

Complaint: "The cross-dressers will dress flamboyantly and make us all look bad."
Our response: "We are all veterans. Veterans know how to be respectful. Besides, we will not let anyone on the bus that is not dressed respectfully."

Complaint: "The marchers will be in danger."
Our response: "We have a security team and the Metro Police will be watching over us."

Complaint: "It won't be successful if not enough people show up."
Our response: "We don't care. If only two people show up it will be a success. This is not about having a crowd, but about helping our veterans heal."

Complaint: "It will be a media circus."
Our response: "We will have full control over this because of the security we are arranging and the presence of local police."

Through careful planning, we successfully shut down all of the detractors who might have otherwise derailed the event.

Over the next several months, we focused all our time and effort trying to make this historical event happen. We wrote to the appropriate authorities to get permission to lay the wreath at the time we requested, we raised funds to cover our expenses, and we made all the necessary arrangements with the hotel, bus service and flower shop. Angela left no stone unturned. She had shifted into her drill sergeant mode and it worked wonders.

Three things happened before the march that involved TAVA.

In the first week of October 2003, the Servicemembers Legal Defense Network held their annual End the Witch Hunts Dinner to raise funds to help LGBT veterans caught up in the Don't Ask, Don't Tell law. I decided to go, so that TAVA would be represented for the first time. This proved to be a wise move, because I made several new contacts and finally got to meet Calpernia Addams, as well as PFC Barry Winchell's mother.

A second important event took place in December 2003, when I went to D.C. to scout out the various locations we planned on visiting during our march. I stayed long enough to speak with a few people involved in the House VA Committee. This became the first time in TAVA's existence that its members engaged House Representatives on trans veterans' issues. In particular, we talked to a legislative aide to a high-ranking Congressman on the House VA Committee. I didn't go alone that day. Mara Keisling from the newly-formed National Center for Transgender Equality (NCTE) had set up the appointments that day and came with me.

Mara started NCTE around the same time TAVA began, with the purpose of providing the eyes, ears and voice of the trans community in D.C. She also helped individuals and organizations by arranging meetings and coordinating visits to Congressional offices. Over the years NCTE has proven very valuable to TAVA's work. As I stated before, Mara helped me when I donated the original Trans Flag to the Smithsonian.

When Mara and I sat down with the legislative aide, we gave her a lot of information on how devastating the current VA policy had been towards trans veterans. When she heard our stories, she looked surprised and appalled. She then told us that if any of our veterans needed help, to call her. She did help a few of our veterans, but sadly she left the post after a short period of time.

The third event I want to highlight had to do with an organizational issue. On March 9, 2004, TAVA became incorporated in the State of California, which was the first step toward acquiring a 501(c)3 tax-exempt status.

Then, on May 1, 2004, the Transgender American Veterans Association had its first scheduled event. The one we had been planning meticulously. Fifty people, most of them veterans, gathered in D.C. to attend our first March to the Wall. Angela took charge and had everything running smoothly. That morning, we filled a bus and headed to the Wall. In front of us drove Sgt. Brett Parsons, the D.C. Metro Police Department's LGBT Liaison, with the lights of his vehicle flashing. The police escort made us feel like VITPs – Very Important Trans People. He even stopped a couple of times to direct traffic. Through his actions that day, Brett became an instant hero to our community.

At the Wall, Angela's vision came true. We felt the cold, black marble on our fingertips, touching names with the gentlest of strokes. Each name on the Wall represented a lost son, daughter, father, husband, lover or partner. We cried and held others who cried close to us. Some had friends' names on the Wall. Others did not. It didn't matter because every name left a hole in our hearts. I had been to the Wall two other times, but this visit would remain forever etched in my memory. Fifty trans people and their loved ones came together to help a healing process unlike anything else in our community's history. The LGB people who observed us from a distance seemed to feel similarly moved.

That day, we not only made transgender history, but American history. The night before the march, we randomly drew the names of four people who would have the privilege of laying a wreath at the Tomb of the Unknown Soldier, doing what no other trans veterans had ever done before. Just before 3p.m., the team of four, led by Stephanie Heck, TAVA's Vice President, gathered at the Tomb's guardroom to prepare for the ceremony. While there, one of the guards initially said he couldn't find the wreath, which sent the team into a panic. The Master Sgt. of the Guard didn't appreciate the other guard's lack of respect to the TAVA members and ordered him to find the wreath. He had seen it earlier, so he knew the guard hadn't looked for it carefully. When the guard went back a second time, the wreath miraculously appeared.

Then, the Master Sgt. of the Guard asked if our organization should be announced as "TAVA," which is what appeared on the wreath, or the "Transgender American Veterans Association." Stephanie asked him to announce the entire name.

When the time came, our chosen four stepped out onto the top of the steps and the Master Sgt. of the Guard marched down the stairs and faced the crowd. "This wreath is being presented by the Transgender American Veterans Association." Every LGBT person in the crowd cried. I stood next to Phyllis Frye, one of our community's long-time activists, and she bawled like a baby.

In the crowd, a young girl asked one of our members, "Are you a veteran?"

"Yes I am."

"Are you with a group?"

"I'm with the Transgender American Veterans Association. We just laid that wreath today, the first time a transgender group has done that."

The little girl smiled. "You mean I got to see history being made?"

How amazing is that? A young girl, not part of our group, saw the historic nature of what we had just done. Moreover, did she say something that gave us a glimpse of a future world more accepting of trans men and women?

To hear the word "transgender" spoken on such hallowed ground couldn't have been more dramatic had Steven Spielberg scripted and directed the event himself. The pride I felt at that moment as a veteran, an activist, and a trans person couldn't have been higher. Had I stopped being an activist right there and then, I could have retired knowing I had been part of something big. Moreover, at just over one year old, TAVA had garnered respect not just for itself, but for the wider trans community as well.

With the exception of the wreath incident, the entire day went off without a hitch. Thanks to 'Drill Sgt.' Brightfeather we had staged one of the most well-organized events in the trans community's history. Several outsiders agreed with this assessment. We put on the same event in May 2005, but only half as many attended compared to the previous year.

In the months and years that followed, TAVA continued to grow, extending our influence and providing us with yet more exposure. Our board worked on creating a structure that would support chapters in various parts of the country, but that initiative sadly failed. We also worked on contacting trans veterans from other countries, but with limited success.

Finally, on July 20, 2005, TAVA received its 501(c)3 tax-exempt status from the IRS, allowing us to apply for grants and larger donations. Our goal of ensuring trans veterans received equal treatment in the VA still drove our efforts, and through this change in our status we secured more assets to help us in our work.

31 – POLITICS MAKES FOR STRANGE BEDFELLOWS

For most of my voting life, I registered as an Independent because I never liked being part of a party label. Instead, I voted for an issue or a person and never followed a specific party line. I remember voting for Barry Goldwater and John McCain, as well as Jimmy Carter and Bill Clinton. However, my loyalties became more focused after I started my transition because it became clear to me that most Republicans didn't have the best interests of LGBT people on their minds, while most Democrats did. So, in 1999 I became a registered Democrat.

The first person who made me question my Independent leaning has to have been my wife. Donna came from a family of long-time Democratic supporters, all of whom lived in the Midwest and had labor union backgrounds. Donna worked for the local phone company the entire time I knew her and had joined the Communication Workers of America, the same union I approached when trying to establish a union at Sprint. The reasons why Donna and her parents voted Democrat made a lot of sense to me.

Then, after living as a woman for a couple of years and seeing the direction in which politics was heading, my mind started leaning left. Ron Owens and Wally Straughn also influenced me, suggesting I join the Arizona Stonewall Caucus. The subsequent meetings that I attended finalized my decision, and I began engaging in partisan politics.

I hadn't had much of a chance to get involved in politics before I moved to Georgia. As I noted previously, I joined the Georgia Stonewall Democrats (GSD) at Pride in 2000 and began attending their meetings on a regular basis. Through GSD, I had the chance to meet several prominent state politicians. At various functions, I met the Lt. Governor, the Secretary of State, the Mayor of Atlanta, several State Representatives and Senators, Congressmembers and even former Senator Max Cleland. I came to know a number of them well enough that they recognized me at subsequent functions, and once I even got a hug from Atlanta's Mayor, Shirley Franklin. I also spent some time working on Congressman John Lewis's LGBTQ Community Advisory Group.

In 2001, the GSD membership elected me Secretary, giving me a chance to participate and contribute at a deeper level. My involvement with GSD allowed me to attend the State Democratic Party's annual Jefferson/Jackson fundraising dinner where Senator John Kerry spoke, long before he planned on running for President. I also attended the GSD's Partners In Equality Dinner, where they honored Maynard Jackson, a Civil Rights leader and former Mayor of Atlanta. When Jackson died in 2003, the City of Atlanta added his name to the airport, alongside the name of another former mayor, William Hartsfield.

Being involved with GSD introduced me to one of the most accomplished people I have ever met. I hesitate talking about her, because she has cautioned me about writing about living people. But I cannot talk about my life in Georgia without talking about Gareth Fenley.

Gareth served on the GSD Board and decided not to serve another term just as I became Secretary, the job that Gareth had previously held. She worked as an editor for a trade magazine, had been a reporter for *Southern Voice*, and worked for CNN. I found her to be highly intelligent and able to carry a conversation on any number of topics. She loved science fiction and read constantly on that and all kinds of other subjects. We had many things in common.

About two weeks after Gloria dumped me, I attended a GSD meeting where I told Gareth that my girlfriend had ended our relationship. She responded by saying, "So, does this mean I can ask you out?"

That surprised me. "I... guess... it does."

On my next night off, Gareth traveled from Alpharetta to Lithia Springs and we had dinner. Afterwards, we went back to my apartment to watch television and that was when Denise got mad at us for making too much noise. Shortly after that, Gareth and I began dating on a regular basis. To avoid any further allegations of unruliness, I would always go to her place. Gareth introduced me to Toastmasters, a nonprofit educational organization that operates clubs for the purpose of promoting communication. They helped me to improve my public-speaking skills.

Gareth did a lot to help me develop as an activist and as a woman. Her own activism had started in college when she worked on feminist and lesbian issues. She taught me things I might have otherwise never known, broadening my knowledge on several issues. At times, she seemed a little frustrated that I didn't understand things as well as she thought I should. The learning experience worked both ways however, because I helped her understand trans issues better than most.

I learned other wonderful things from her, such as how to cook certain dishes and how to properly prepare a variety of fresh vegetables. Gareth loved to eat healthily and I picked up a lot of what she had learned. I enjoyed trying out new recipes on her, as well as old favorites, as I attempted to expand my cooking skills. She really loved my eggplant Parmesan.

Gareth and I also enjoyed socializing together, going to parties, special events, lesbian social gatherings, fundraising events and, of course, Pride. She even liked attending the Friday night talent show at Southern Comfort. Together, we led a full and active life. But things changed when she decided to quit her job to get a master's degree in social work.

Gareth always tried to become a better version of herself and she had a dream of becoming a social worker. I felt proud of her for setting a wonderful goal, but we both expressed concern for the continuation of our relationship when she announced the best school for a master's degree in social work to be the University of Georgia, in Athens. Would our relationship survive a distance of over 70 miles? On top of that, the last time I visited Athens, Gloria treated me horribly, so going back there didn't sit too well with me. Nevertheless, I decided I could overlook that to spend time with Gareth.

When she started school, Gareth lived in digs that had no television reception. She didn't want to get cable because of her need to be frugal while completing her studies. So, during the week, I would record various television programs and bring the tapes with me when I came to spend the weekend with her. I would leave any that we didn't watch together for her to watch during the week.

Since Gareth's masters in social work program lasted two years, I ended up spending a lot of time in Athens. We got to know the town rather well and both felt comfortable there. We found all the good places to eat, venues that had live entertainment, and even a bar that had drag shows on a Saturday night.

One delightful bonus of being Gareth's girlfriend had to be her family. I came from a close family, one that shared many of the traditions of my mother's Italian heritage. Gareth's family had a lot of that same closeness. They had all long since accepted Gareth being a lesbian, and always welcomed her girlfriends as members of the family. For four years before dating Gareth, I had been shut out from my own family's functions. So, it felt amazing to once again be part of a loving family, especially during the holidays. Gareth's family got together several times a year, and each time we did I felt closer to them.

Over time, Gareth and I drifted apart for several reasons. Our love dwindled and our interests separated. With a new career to focus on, Gareth dropped a lot of outside activities and activism. I also felt a need to move on, but also felt afraid to be alone again after four fulfilling years with her. Our relationship formerly ended mere days before 2005, with sadness and a little pain. Today, Gareth and I remain in touch and she will always occupy a special place in my heart.

By 2004, partisan politics had become very intense across the country as the U.S. headed into a presidential election. The trans community acted no differently from other cross-sectional organizations, and on a number of occasions I had to warn people on the TAVA list to refrain from discussing politics, because of our work towards becoming a 501(c)3.

The presidential race heated up when the Democratic Party primaries began, whittling down the large field of hopefuls until finally a candidate emerged. I wanted to see how the field would play out, but I leaned toward Howard Dean before the primaries, because he was one of three candidates who supported trans rights. However, after the Iowa Caucus, Dean's candidacy fizzled, sending John Kerry into frontrunner status, with John Edwards close behind.

Kerry didn't openly support trans rights and, in a recent HRC survey, said he would support a non-inclusive ENDA like his good buddies from Massachusetts, Ted Kennedy and Barney Frank. By the time the Georgia primary rolled around – Super Tuesday in early March – Kerry had begun to dominate the pack. From my perspective, even though he didn't support trans rights, he was at least a decorated veteran. As far as trans rights went, I felt that we could get him to understand the issues far better than Bush ever could.

In February, John Kerry traveled to Atlanta to hold a town hall meeting in a downtown theater. I attended the event and sat in the bottom section, near the stage. Kerry came out amidst thunderous applause and gave a rousing, patriotic speech. Then he asked for questions. My hand went up and as luck would have it, he had been looking right in my direction. The red jacket I wore at the time helped give me more visibility. It must have worked because he picked me to ask the first question.

"Senator Kerry, my name is Monica Helms, I'm a Navy veteran and my son is currently serving in the Marines. Also, I'm a transsexual and the President of the Transgender American Veterans Association."

I heard people in the crowd hollering and clapping.

Kerry responded, "I thank you for your son's service."

He may not have heard me because he didn't thank me for my service.

"You recently took a survey by the Human Rights Campaign where you stated that you support the current, non-inclusive Employment Non-Discrimination Act. If elected President, would you consider supporting a fully-inclusive ENDA?"

I probably could have stated the question differently and more concisely, but that's the way it came out.

Kerry responded, "I support equality for everyone and will work with the Human Rights Campaign towards that goal."

His answer didn't make me feel particularly happy, because I knew the HRC would abandon trans rights at the first sign of a fight, but by the end of the evening I came away feeling that I wanted to support Kerry. Everything told me that he could be educated on the issue of trans equality.

Three news services later wrote about my questioning John Kerry and one, *The Washington Post*, actually interviewed me. A few days later, Tucker Carlson, on CNN *Crossfire*, blasted John Kerry and the Democrats for having a "man in a dress" ask John Kerry if the VA would pay for sex change operations. What an ass.

Because of my increased interest in state and national politics, I began attending meetings of the Cobb County Democrats. At one meeting, they passed out applications to become a delegate to the 2004 Democratic National Convention (DNC). I remembered hearing the stories about Jane Fee attending the 2000 DNC, becoming the first openly trans person in U.S. history to appear as a delegate at a national convention. Later, we found out that she didn't actually become the first, but she at least held the distinction of being the first trans person to be a Democratic delegate to a national convention. Having heard how people accepted Jane, the idea of going to a political convention fascinated me. So, I filled out the application and sent it in, thinking I likely wouldn't hear from them again.

To my surprise, in April, I received instructions from the Georgia Democratic Party on how to attend the district delegate elections, which I did. In our district, the state DNC allotted three delegates for John Kerry and two for John Edwards. As it happened, only three people showed up and applied to become delegates for John Kerry and two applied to become delegates for John Edwards. So, we all got in. We held an election anyway, as a formality, but that's how I became the first openly trans person elected as a delegate to any political party's convention from Georgia, or from the entire South, for that matter.

This meant that I would be one of eight trans people attending the DNC, and one of only five LGBT people from Georgia. But in order for me to go, I had to raise the money. That part sucked.

32 – THE DNC CONVENTION IN BOSTON

Becoming a delegate to the 2004 Democratic National Convention began an interesting journey that took me from Georgia to Boston. The eight trans people destined for the convention, in various capacities, started communicating with one another by email to ensure we worked together as a team. We became the first ever Transgender Caucus to any political convention.

Tucker Carlson showed himself to be an ass once again when he commented on us being at the convention, calling us names. He even tried to make light of us being there by having Jerry Springer on his show, but Springer, a Democrat, shut Tucker down by pointing out that the Republicans were nothing more than a party of rich, white men and the Democrats had true diversity.

Our group of eight also got grief from some trans people for all kinds of stupid reasons. We stood together through all the adversity because we wanted to present a united front both before and during the convention.

The biggest challenge facing the trans delegates came from the leaders of the convention's LGB"t" Caucus. They didn't quite understand how to properly speak for us and didn't ask any of us to be part of the Caucus leadership. Moreover, they never asked for our feedback on any proposed messaging for the convention. Of course, John Kerry, not really caring much about including trans people in anything, didn't give the LGB"t" Caucus leaders much incentive to include us. They thought the words "sexual orientation" somehow included us. Even after all of our efforts to educate people about the trans community, the gay and lesbian leaders in the DNC still couldn't grasp this simple concept. Sometimes I think straight people understand us better.

The issue of our exclusion hit hardest when the DNC Platform Committee drafted language for the party's platform. Since the LGB"t" Caucus left trans people out of their language, the Transgender Caucus proposed an amendment to the language via a trans-friendly gay delegate on the committee.

In a year when the religious-right vilified LGBT people more often than they changed their underwear, the Democratic Party wanted to play it safe and pander to the Republicans' hate-mongering. This meant down-playing their support of sexual orientation and ignoring trans issues altogether.

In the interest of party unity, but not in the interest of trans people, the Platform Committee told us that if we pushed our amendment, they wouldn't pass it and we would lose any access to the DNC's leaders. Reluctantly, the Transgender Caucus agreed to withdraw the amendment in order to preserve access to the upper echelons of the DNC and the Kerry Campaign Committee.

Scott Safier, a Platform Committee delegate from Pennsylvania, stood up and read the following emotional speech, withdrawing our amendment:

"Mr. Chairman and Members of the Committee, I rise today to give voice to a community with no member at today's meeting and invisible in our platform. I am speaking of the transgender community."

"Our platform touches on many issues important to the trans-community, from education to healthcare to hate crimes and workplace discrimination. This issue, important to us all, has particular resonance in a community that is misunderstood, often maligned, and whose members live in fear of violence and discrimination."

"Our platform says that hate crimes "demean good people." Gwen Araujo, Pvt. Barry Winchell, and Brandon Teena were not just "demeaned," they were murdered by individuals who saw no value in their humanity."

"Transgender people are good citizens who make valuable

contributions to their communities. Gender identity and gender expression are no basis to deny anyone a job, housing, an education or adequate medical care. These are mainstream issues, as Governor Vilsack's own executive order in his home state demonstrates."

"The transgender community understands that the Democratic Party's commitment to civil rights is "ironclad." Because of this party's outreach efforts, there will be at least 8 transgender delegates in Boston, an increase of 800% in 4 years, but more can be done. As a gay man, I can only be a surrogate for this distinct community, speaking second-hand in telling their stories and discussing their issues. We must do more to make certain that they themselves are included at the table."

"Mr. Chairman, I am instructed by the transgender delegates to tell this committee that the trans community stands united behind the Kerry/Edwards ticket and will work for a Democratic victory in November."

"At the request of the trans delegation, and in recognition of this solidarity, I have been asked to withdraw this amendment, and do so now. Thank you for your time."

Our stance on the platform language didn't win us many fans in the trans community. Had we pressed on with our amendment, we would likely have been heroes in their eyes. Instead we opted to risk pissing off a few perennial detractors, in order to gain some much-needed access to high-level people. We didn't want to see the trans delegation becoming the pariahs of the convention. In time, I think our strategy paid off. In 2008, the trans delegation didn't have any trouble getting trans-inclusive language into the Democratic Platform.

I had been to Boston only once previously, 32 years earlier. So, I considered this visit as being the equivalent of my first time there. Ethan and Karen St. Pierre had picked me up from the airport and taken me to their place in Haverhill, where I stayed a couple of nights. Ethan and Karen made me feel very welcome. I got to be live on Ethan's show TransFM on Sunday night. The following night, most of the Transgender Caucus joined me in the studio for GenderTalk. To get from Haverhill to Boston, I had to take a long train ride to the nearest Boston Mass Transit station and ride into the city from there.

On the first day of the convention, I saw Fred Phelps and his hate-mongering family protesting outside the fence of the Fleet Center, watched over by several police officers. Because of 9/11 and the threat of terrorism, the building, and Boston more generally, had a post-apocalyptic feeling to it, caused by the number of security and police officers in attendance. If a person screwed up and wandered into the wrong place, they could easily find themselves facing a dozen gigantic men with automatic weapons. If this would have happened to me, I'm sure I would have soiled a good pair of panties.

When I first stepped inside the Fleet Center and looked around. It too appeared surreal, but in a nice way. I had seen similar venues on television for years, even before color TV, but now got to see it in person. An American tradition that went back to the first convention in 1856 stared me in the face.

Tall poles, each with the name of a state on it, dotted the landscape of chairs, signs and other patriotic decorations. The names of all the world's news networks ringed the top of the stadium in bold lights. Balloons hung suspended from the ceiling, waiting for the right moment to drop. A huge stage dominated the floor at one side of the stadium, with three massive television screens hung above it.

Through the early part of the day, minor or past players in the party took to the stage to give speeches, cheered on by small groups of supporters. The heavy hitters got to deliver their speeches during prime time. On one of those evenings, a young Senate hopeful by the name of Barack Obama came out. He made a big impression on everyone.

In one section of the halls at the Fleet Center sat every right-wing radical talk-radio host. Each of them screamed their garbage to anyone who would listen, even if the only people who cared were the other right-wing radio people in attendance. To me, they seemed to be competing for who could sound the stupidest and in that respect they all won the prize.

A rather humorous incident took place just before Cheryl Jacques, Executive Director of the HRC, came to the podium to speak. Keep in mind that the convention took place at the end of July 2004, just a couple of months after trans activists discovered HRC's duplicitous Congressional office tactics and before HRC approved supporting a fully-inclusive ENDA. Just before Cheryl came out to speak, I received a call on my cell from Mara Keisling.

"Have you heard about the demonstration that's going to take place in front of the podium when Cheryl Jacques speaks?"

"No. I'm way at the top of the stands."

"Somehow a rumor got started that the trans delegates are going to protest in front of the podium when she speaks. They're even sending federal marshals to the floor around the podium."

From my vantage point, I could see the federal marshals taking their position around the podium. "I see them there."

"I wonder if any of the others know about this."

"Let me know what you find out."

I stood and watched as Cheryl Jacques arrived on stage and gave her speech. Nothing happened. I later found out that none of the other trans delegates had heard about this so-called demonstration either. I had to laugh at HRC's paranoia, though they truly deserved how stupid they ended up looking.

All kinds of people wandered the halls of the Fleet Center during the convention. I saw Ben Affleck, Al Franken, P. Diddy and several others. I also got to meet Al Sharpton, John Glenn and Howard Dean. Mariette Pathy Allen, our community's principal photographer for three decades, captured a picture of me turning the tables on Jerry Springer by interviewing him rather than vice versa.

When the Transgender Caucus initially discussed our participation in the convention, we came up with the idea of making special buttons for us to wear. I came up with the initial design and Babs Siperstein, from New Jersey, tweaked the design and had two hundred of them made. These buttons became instant collector's items, worth several other buttons in trade. We gave them to special people and later heard that one of the buttons made it into a Smithsonian display on the 2004 election.

We also decided to give Scott Safier a special award from the trans delegates for his help and the wonderful speech he had delivered on our behalf to the Platform Committee. We came up with the perfect name for the honor, The Jane Fee Award, in memory of the first openly trans delegate to attend a Democratic convention. Scott nearly cried when we presented it to him, as did I. We hoped the trans community would give the award to a deserving individual at every subsequent Democratic National Convention and from what I've heard that's what has happened.

In January 2005, Jane visited me at home as she traveled across the U.S. I gave her one of the 2004 convention buttons and read to her the wording on the award that now bears her name, the text of which I still had on my computer. She cried. She truly deserved the honor.

Every day of the convention started with each state's delegates enjoying a breakfast in their respective hotels. After receiving our passes, we then headed to the Fleet Center where various groups held rallies and caucus meetings. One such group was the LGB"t" Caucus. At one meeting, several of the speakers only said, "gay and lesbian." The Transgender Caucus became so frustrated that we created signs that said, "And Bisexual, and Transgender!", but we made them a little too late to use them effectively.

After the speakers finished, some of the gays and lesbians in the audience asked the leadership of the LGB"t" Caucus why they had left trans people out of the platform, embarrassing them in front of everyone. It felt nice to see others publicly stand up for us.

At the end of the meeting, I approached a lesbian former Army General who had used "gay and lesbian" interchangeably with LGBT in her speech. I gave her my TAVA business card and reminded her that trans people have also served proudly. She thanked me for my service.

One morning, reporters gathered in a meeting room to ask various VIPs questions. Only members of the press could go in, but through the exit door I saw Georgia's former Senator, Max Cleland. So, I walked in as if I belonged there and approached the Senator as he finished speaking to one of the reporters. I introduced myself.

"Hello, Senator. My name is Monica Helms and I'm from Georgia."

"Whereabouts?"

"Cobb County."

"Oh." The Senator knew that Newt Gingrich came from that county and sympathized with me.

"I campaigned for you in the last election."

"Thank you."

Then I showed him a picture of my son in his Marine uniform. "I just heard two days ago that he will be going over to Iraq next month."

A look of genuine sadness came across Senator Cleland's face. A veteran like him, who lost three limbs in Vietnam, knew the pain I felt at hearing this news.

At the Georgia morning breakfasts at our hotel, state politicians would speak, and delegates would get a chance to meet them. Out of all the people I wanted to meet at the convention, former President Jimmy Carter topped my list. My chance came one morning when he spoke to us over breakfast. As he finished, I positioned myself where he would have to walk past me to leave. I wore my Navy hat with my Dolphins. He approached me and we shook hands.

"It's an honor to meet you, Mr. President. You know, you and I have something in common."

"What's that?"

"We are both former submariners."

He flashed his famous smile and, at that exact moment, a person snapped a picture of us. I don't think it dawned on the President that women didn't serve on submarines back when I was enlisted. I would have loved to have seen the look on his face when he realized. I'm proud to have his name on my honorable discharge.

On the last day of the convention, the Transgender Caucus finally had a meeting with the top people in Kerry's Campaign Committee. It wasn't easy. We had to continually remind some of the LGB"t" Caucus leaders that they had promised us the meeting in return for dropping our amendment to the platform. We got a sense that they didn't want to honor their promise and hoped we would just fade away into the woodwork. But the eight individuals who made up the Trans Caucus had a history of not fading away for anyone.

The meeting itself seemed to go well. We brought up several issues affecting the trans community, including hate crimes and employment discrimination. They listened as if they really cared, but we walked away feeling a bit like children who had given their parents a wish list for Christmas. The one issue that seemed to most spark their interest concerned trans veterans not being treated fairly by the VA. It's too bad Kerry didn't get elected because, if he had, TAVA may have been able to achieve a number of major goals far sooner than it otherwise did.

On the last evening of the convention, John Kerry came out, saluted, and said the line the Republicans gave him so much crap for:

"John Kerry, reporting for duty." When he finished his speech, the balloons should have come down, but the release mechanism stuck. Instead, workers had to go into the rafters and release them by hand. Nevertheless, the convention ended with palpable excitement and energy throughout the Fleet Center.

I later tried to attend the 2008 Democratic National Convention, but that time I didn't make the cut. Nevertheless, the number of trans delegates increased at the DNCs in 2008, 2012 and 2016, and Babs Siperstein, who later became a Super Delegate, made buttons for each of those years. Sadly, Babs passed away in early 2019, so the trans community lost a real powerhouse in the DNC.

Our visibility at the DNCs can only be a good thing for the trans community. As I have said to my friends, "Visibility equals credibility." This is especially important for the trans community when it comes to our country's political process.

33 – TRANS=ACTION BY THE NUMBERS

Throughout my work with TAVA and other nationwide activism, I continued to work with Trans=Action. Much of what Trans=Action accomplished has already been covered in previous chapters, but a lot has not. This chapter details the previously unmentioned events that happened up to 2005.

2001

In January, Trans=Action became aware that a young man from Auburn, Georgia, Robert Martin, had been severely beaten with a blunt object and now lay comatose in a hospital. Martin identified as gay and liked to cross-dress on occasion. The local people liked Martin and he worked to support his mother and younger brother.

This became my and Dana's first experience dealing with law enforcement officials in Georgia, specifically the Georgia Bureau of Investigation. Robert eventually died from injuries to his brain on April 3, 2001. His murder mirrored that of Tracy Thompson's killing two years earlier in Cordele, just twenty miles north of Auburn.

In April, Trans=Action received a tip that there had been two other murders in Savannah, Georgia. One person, (Sissy) Charles Bolden, had been found murdered on October 15, 1999 and the other individual, Billy Jean Levette, was killed on November 20, 2000. Both had been arrested at one time or another for prostitution and both murdered in the same fashion. With Robert Martin's killing earlier in the year, and these two Savannah deaths brought to light, the Atlanta Transgender Day of Remembrance that year felt particularly disheartening and stressful.

In late June 2001, Dr. Erin Swenson and I performed diversity training at the Cobb County Detention Center. This initiative began when a friend informed me that the facility held a trans woman and had been denying her access to hormones. I also found out that the woman had silicone injections in her breasts and needed a bra to hold them in place. Otherwise, silicone can move to other parts of the body and can cause death. The facility refused to let her wear a bra, but before we could do anything to help her, the detention center released her on bail.

We held the diversity training on two different days. The attending officers and staff received our presentation very well. Sometime after, we found out that the training we administered later helped another incarcerated trans woman. We found out from her afterwards that she had been treated exactly as per the training they had received. They apparently kept this training up because I heard that in early 2019 another trans woman had been treated correctly and with respect.

In August 2001, the Transgender Mile came into existence. On behalf of the Transgender Community of Georgia, I had applied to have a section of Briercliff Road, between North Druid Hills and Lavista, designated the mile where the transgender community would clean up once a quarter for the Georgia Department of Transportation (GDOT). In return, in October, GDOT installed signs along the road that read "Transgender Community of GA". These signs became the first official state signs in the country with the word 'transgender' on them. Obtaining the mile had been easy, but maintaining it became increasingly difficult. After some initial enthusiasm, some in the community lost interest, so we eventually lost the mile and with it our credibility with GDOT. The signs came down in 2005.

On September 11, 2001, I had just got back from working a midday shift when I got a call from a friend.

"Someone just crashed a plane into the World Trade Center."

I turned on the news and for the rest of the day I sat, transfixed to the television. I finally got some sleep, shortly before I had to go back into work at midnight. Because of all the telecommunications cables that went through the Twin Towers, we quickly became slammed at work with tickets for circuits that had gone down. The issues lasted for more than a year.

The tragedy happened so close to Southern Comfort that many people felt that year's conference shouldn't take place in late September. Yet the Planning Committee for SCC decided the conference should continue as scheduled, because so much work had already been put in. However, many people who had planned on attending decided not to travel and as a result attendance dropped markedly. The 9/11 attacks caused Americans to fear many things, especially things they didn't fully understand. As a result, the effects of 9/11 went on to impact the trans community for years to come. Today, the TSA X-ray security checks and pat-downs have become a source of embarrassment and concern for thousands of trans people.

In 2001, Trans=Action initiated the 'Georgia Ultimate Transgender Service' Award, or 'GUTS' for short. The first two recipients of the GUTS Award were Dallas Denny and Dr. Erin Swenson, for all the good work they had performed for our community. Trans=Action presented the awards to them at Southern Comfort in September. In 2002, GUTS awards went to Dana Brown-Owings and Terry Murphy, while in 2003 the award went to Dr. Virginia Erhardt. No further awards were given out in subsequent years.

2002

During HRC's May 2002 dinner, I met Congresswoman Cynthia McKinney for the first time and began a long email conversation with her about trans issues. In August, a group of us met with the Congresswoman at her local office to discuss these issues in detail. Dawn Wilson, Monica Roberts and A.C. Casebeer came in from Louisville, Kentucky, and joined Dana and me to help educate Rep. McKinney. Sue and Bruce Nelson from the local chapter of PFLAG also joined us to add their support and input. The Congresswoman learned a lot in the 90 minutes we spent with her and carried it with her for the rest of her term. After losing in the mid-term election of 2002, she was re-elected again in 2004, but lost again in 2006.

In late September, the Mayor of Atlanta introduced the new Atlanta Chief of Police, Chief Richard Pennington. At that event, I presented the Chief with a welcome letter from Trans=Action and a list of our concerns. These included a long list of unsolved trans murders. Chief Pennington came from D.C. and New Orleans, where he had made inroads with the LGBT community. He promised that he would select an officer to become the community's first liaison to the Atlanta Police Department.

As promised, Sgt. Connie Locke later became the Atlanta Police Department's liaison to the LGBT community. Pastor Paul and I served on the committee that helped choose her. In early November 2002, at a meeting to shape the community relations group, we got our first chance to meet Sgt. Locke.

On December 16, 2002, one of the most tragic events in Georgia's trans community's history took place. Shortly after 9/11, Alice Johnston lost her job as a computer technician and for the next 15 months she tried hard to find work. However, she kept being turned down because of being trans. Alice, an Army veteran, had a degree in library science and broad experience as a programmer and computer technician. During her long unemployment period, she even spent time as a sex worker, but couldn't even get steady work there.

Finally, all of Alice's savings ran out and the people she stayed with couldn't help her any longer. Realizing she had only one option left, she called women's homeless shelters for help. Not wanting to lead any of the shelters on, she told them upfront about being a pre-op trans woman. They all rejected her, and she wouldn't degrade herself or put herself in danger by going to a men's shelter. Depressed and in despair, she went down to the Chattahoochee River, put a gun to her head and ended her life.

Alice was a friend of several people in the community, including myself, but she didn't ask any of us for help during those last days. She placed an automatic message on her Yahoo email address saying that she would soon be homeless and that she was "a goner." That appeared two days before her death. The sadness of her death hit the trans community like a ton of bricks. I vowed at her memorial that I would change how homeless shelters treated trans women. To add insult to her death, we later found out that her family buried her with a headstone that included her birth name.

2003

In early January, Trans=Action began making calls to various homeless shelters. Some put us in contact with United Way, where we found out about the Mayor's Commission on Homelessness and a public meeting being held at the end of the month.

We also talked with Anita Beatty, the Executive Director for the Taskforce for the Homeless, one of the largest men's shelters in the city. Jamison Green put me in contact with Marcus Arana of the San Francisco Human Rights Commission, because of his familiarity with his city's trans homeless issues and how they had addressed the problem.

On January 28, I attended the public hearing for the Mayor's Commission on Homelessness. When I got up to speak, I showed them a picture of Alice and told them her story. It drew a lot of attention, but became an issue that many talked about, yet did nothing to fix. We continued our outreach, but no one addressed the problem to our satisfaction.

As the homeless issue grew more complex, Trans=Action worked on other matters. We focused on lobbying for pre-op trans people to be able to get the sex marker on their driver's license changed once they had begun living full time as their true selves. At that time, the only way a trans person could get the sex marker on their driver's license changed in Georgia was with proof of sex reassignment surgery, or through a court order.

Dana and I made a series of phone calls to the Department of Motor Vehicles and Safety (DMVS) to try and find out whom we needed to contact. It became apparent that the founders of Trans=Action had made a similar attempt to change the process some five years earlier.

On April 10, we sent a letter to Neil Childress, Director of the DMVS, asking him to review the policy and see if he would allow our organization the opportunity to convince the DMVS Policy Board to change the policy towards trans people. After weeks of waiting for a reply, Trans=Action received a response from them saying, "We are comfortable keeping the policy as it is."

Despite evidence that trans people couldn't find work and faced violence and discrimination because of an incongruent sex marker, the DMVS still felt "comfortable" with their current policy. We planned to revisit the issue at a later date, but in 2005, the federal government passed the Real ID Act, which essentially created a national ID card, forcing states to standardize their driver's license policies. This made changing the sex marker in Georgia even more difficult.

Since some trans people had been harassed at DMVS offices by their agents, Trans=Action initiated the Buddy System. We suggested that whenever a trans person needed to make any changes to their driver's license, they should take along a friend or two. Dana, Pastor Paul and I discovered that when another person stood witness to what DMVS agents said, or even better took notes or held a camera, the DMVS agents kept their snide remarks to themselves.

In April, Trans=Action finally secured a meeting with the City of Atlanta's largest homeless shelter, the Atlanta Union Mission (AUM). Faced with the possibility that the people at AUM would be unreceptive and have a religious spin on their objections, Dana and I enlisted the help of Pastor Paul. He turned out to be a great asset for our organization because he brought a pastoral viewpoint to every issue that Trans=Action faced. Additionally, he had experience with homeless issues.

In May, I talked again with Lisa Mottet at the National Gay and Lesbian Task Force and she explained that the Atlanta non-discrimination law, passed in December 2000, covered public accommodations receiving city money, including homeless shelters. On May 16, I received confirmation from Doug Hall, of the City Council President's office, that the Atlanta non-discrimination law did indeed cover homeless shelters receiving funds, and had done so for 2.5 years. However, faith-based organizations operated all of the women's shelters in Atlanta and didn't receive any funding from the city. As such, they couldn't be forced to accept trans people.

In June, Dana, Pastor Paul, Cathy Brown-Owings and I attended a meeting of the Coalition for Homeless Providers, which had about 90 people in attendance. They gave Trans=Action some time to discuss the issues faced by trans homeless people in Atlanta, though it didn't have much effect. Some of those present even objected "for religious reasons" to allowing trans people to participate in the meeting at all.

At Atlanta Pride that year, I received the honor of speaking on the main stage and used the opportunity to talk about the trans homeless issue and urged everyone to register to vote for the next election.

In August, Trans=Action met with United Way to discuss the possibility for having Crossroads Ministry become an agent for United Way's voucher program. With this plan, a homeless trans woman could come to Crossroads Ministry and, if they qualified, Crossroads would provide them with a voucher to stay at an old hotel in downtown Atlanta, for up to two weeks. United Way agreed and some trans people later took advantage of the system we put in place. It became a small step in the right direction.

In October, Dana, Cathy, Pastor Paul and I met to discuss the need to take Trans=Action to the next level. As our outreach grew, we knew that for people to take the organization seriously, we needed to incorporate, apply for a tax-exempt status, and become a 501(c)3 organization. To do that, Trans=Action needed an official board, by-laws, operating procedures, a mission statement, a vision statement, a website and incorporation papers.

In November, and again in December, the word went out to the rest of the community to attend Trans=Action's first 'real' meeting in January 2004, when we would form a board.

2004

Fifteen people attended Trans=Action's organizational-forming meeting. All but two of them became board members. We elected Pastor Paul as the Board's first President and appointed me as the first official Executive Director.

Pastor Paul gave us a message that we carried with us into the future: "Transgender people shouldn't wait to be asked to sit at the table, but just take a seat and sit down." During the 2004 legislative session, that message struck home. Several of the board members and I took an active role in lobbying legislators against an amendment to ban same-sex marriage in Georgia. We watched as the bill made it through the Senate, initially be defeated in the House, but then finally pass the House in a second vote.

Up until that legislative session, other groups in the LGBT community typically forgot to include trans people in their thinking. Though gays and lesbians opposed the marriage-amendment, to the trans community it seemed like they thought that their families were the only ones that needed protecting. In truth however, the amendment would affect trans people in ways more drastic than anyone could imagine.

In response, Trans=Action provided legislators, community leaders and lawyers with a way to attack the amendment from a trans point of view. We suggested that if they wanted to 'avoid' same-sex couples from marrying, each person should pay to have their sex chromosomes tested. We thought this would appeal to the right, but in truth it was a spoiling tactic that would have added $850 to the cost of tying the knot and would have hopefully made the initiative unpopular.

Our 'allies' summarily dismissed every suggestion we made as not being good enough to try. Unsurprisingly, this caused resentment in the trans community, not least when, having already passed through the legislature, the amendment passed in the general election in November.

In early 2004, tragedy hit the trans community when, on February 29, an African-American trans woman by the name of Precious Armani was found shot to death in the front seat of her car, in the Buckhead area of Atlanta. This became the first transgender test for Atlanta's Community Liaison, Sgt. Connie Locke, and the new Chief of Police. They jumped on the case right away although to this day Armani's murder still hasn't been solved.

In March, the community held a candlelight vigil for Precious in one of Atlanta's parks, which received widespread and sympathetic press coverage. In July 2005, Fox 5 News would feature the Precious Armani case on their "Georgia's Most Wanted" segment, treating her story with unusual compassion.

I'm proud to have started TDOR in Atlanta, but eventually the event took its toll on Dana and me. Preparing for TDOR took a lot of time, planning and money. In 2004, Trans=Action offset some of the cost by holding their first ever fundraiser at Le Buzz, a local drag bar in Marietta. We took in $400 from tips to the entertainers, a cover charge and raffles. I even got up and did a drag number for the first and last time in my life.

2005

In January 2005, Trans=Action met with Atlanta's new City Council President, Lisa Borders, to see if the city could do anything about the trans homeless issue. She once again told us that the city had no control over faith-based facilities because they received their funding from private sources rather than the city. This meant they could discriminate as much as they wanted.

In response, Trans=Action met with a group that included United Way and several city officials and agencies, with the aim of figuring out a solution. The resulting effort seemed half-hearted to me however, and it soon became clear the Atlanta Union Mission, who were in attendance, and United Way had no intention of helping us.

In 2006, I resigned from Trans=Action and handed over my TDOR duties to someone else so that I could concentrate my time and efforts on TAVA. Trans=Action hung around for a short while in my absence, but not too long after closed its doors forever.

34 – NEW CHALLENGES

Toward the end of 2005, I met an amazing person at My Sisters Room, a lesbian club in Decatur. Her name was Del, short for Deloris, and she looked butch. We talked for a long time before she asked me to go back to her place with her. This surprised me because not many women would take a trans woman home. Normally no one asked me to go home with them.

Del and I spent a lot of time together over the next five months. I found out she had been married to another woman, but separated; she had a young daughter, and worked as a lawyer. I stayed at Del's house on Christmas Eve and spent Christmas morning with her and her daughter. The little girl got a child's makeup kit that morning and asked her mother to help her put it on. Del had no idea how to apply makeup, so I volunteered to help. Del appreciated that.

Early in 2006, I convinced my mother to come and visit me. Leading up to it, she looked forward to the trip. She also sent me some money so I could buy new hearing aids, since the ones I had no longer worked very well. She felt she wanted to give me something, since she had provided help to my other three siblings during the years we had been estranged.

We had a fantastic time when she came to Atlanta. I took her to Ruby Falls, near Chattanooga, the Atlanta Cyclorama, and Stone Mountain. We also went to the World of Coca Cola, the State Capitol, the CNN building, and the Jimmy Carter Presidential Library. I even took her to a drag show. The place she felt really excited to see however, was the Margaret Mitchell house, because she had been a big *Gone With the Wind* fan ever since the movie came out. We had lunch at a local gay restaurant and indulged in some real Southern cooking at the famous Mary Mac's Tea Room.

Since I was still dating Del at the time, we went with her and her daughter to the Aquarium. My mother stayed a week and seemed to have a great time. Shortly after my mother's visit however, Del and I broke up.

Around that time, I worked the mid shift at Sprint. The shift paid extra money, which I needed to pay off my debts to the IRS. However, the antisocial hours started to take a toll on my health. I couldn't get a lot done outside of work, which meant my activism suffered. I figured I needed to move out of my apartment and into one with two other people to reduce my monthly rent. As luck would have it, two friends of mine from Madison, Wisconsin, decided to move to Atlanta in search of better job opportunities. So, we decided to all move in together.

Not too long after Terrianne and Connie arrived, my left knee gave out. My knees had never been the same after flying over the handlebars of a dirt bike during a crash in the Arizona desert, back in 1972. When I had my left knee operated on in 1989, that doctor told me it would likely give out again at some point. And now it had.

I had the knee operated on, again. Once home, I had to be helped upstairs to my room, where I remained trapped in my bed for over a week, with a device on my right leg to help move the blood around. On my left leg, I had a different device that would periodically bend my knee. Terrianne and Connie brought me food on occasion, but at other times I had to disconnect the machines and stumble down the stairs to get something to eat. In my desperation, I remember eating cold peas out of the can. Unsurprisingly, I started losing weight.

When my mobility improved, I attended therapy sessions to improve my knee's flexibility. As luck would have it, the apartment complex I lived in had an exercise room with weights, treadmills and other machines that helped me to rehabilitate my leg. Since I didn't work, because of being on medical leave, I exercised a lot and made my leg much stronger. Combined with my previous forced dieting, I got down to 166 pounds, a weight I hadn't seen since before marriage. I got a chance to show off my smaller size at the next

Southern Comfort. I felt so good that I even had Mariette Pathy Allen take pictures of me in the nude.

After returning to work, I decided that working the mid shift had to end, in spite of the loss of income a change would mean. I took a day shift instead and felt much better for it. It meant I could sleep during the night and actually wake up feeling like I had rested.

In November, I decided to go home to spend some time with my family. The people who took over organizing Atlanta's TDOR from me, decided to hold that year's event on Saturday, November 18. I stayed in Atlanta to attend the event, but the next morning I flew to Phoenix. As it happened, the Phoenix group held their TDOR the night of Sunday, November 19, so my mother and I went to the memorial together.

Mom and I then planned to drive to San Diego the next day to see my son, but before we left, I found out that San Diego would be holding their TDOR the night of Monday, November 20. When the local group heard that I would be in town, they invited me to speak at the event. My mother and I stayed at my friend Autumn's house and, when we went to the San Diego TDOR, my eldest son, Robert, drove down from Camp Pendleton to be with us. 2006 became the only year I've attended three different TDORs, on three different nights, in three different cities.

As 2007 started, the 40th anniversary of my first model rocket launch fast approached. I started feeling the urge to get back into launching rockets. I joined the Southern Area Rocketry (SoAR) club to get back into the sport and felt happy to see how many adults enjoyed launching rockets as much as I did. That year I built ten rockets and had 11 launches. I launched my first on February 24, a month shy of the 40th anniversary of my first ever launch.

Afterwards, I stopped launching rockets until taking it up again in November 2011. This time I went all in. Over the next seven years, I built 88 rockets and had over 170 launches. I received my Level 1 Certification on June 22, 2014, allowing me to use the big "I" engines. One of my rockets that year stood over eight feet tall, had a 5.5-inch diameter and weighed over seven pounds. I sent up video cameras and altimeters, both with limited success. I had my share of spectacular crashes, including the eight-foot model I just mentioned. I specialized in scale models and odd shaped rockets, to see if I could fly them. I took a rest from the sport in 2018 to work on other projects, but I plan on getting back into it in 2019 or 2020.

2007 became a special year to me for another important reason. Around April, I began hearing a voice in my head saying, "You must buy a house." It came to me the same way I had heard, "You must leave Arizona." The housing boom was in full swing and finance companies had all kinds of creative ways help a person buy a home. I wanted to find one close to where I worked, but also in a quiet neighborhood. So, I contacted a realtor who knew the area.

The realtor first showed me a house that didn't suit my needs at all. Then she took me to a second house, on top of a hill and in a cul-de-sac. The street felt serene, which gave me a good feeling. As soon as I stepped inside and saw the interior, I knew I had found my house.

"I want this one."

Built in 1984, the house was actually the end home of a triplex. Inside, it measured 21' 4" by 27' 3", with two levels and a basement/garage. In total it had just over 1100 square feet of floor space. It boasted three bedrooms, although I found one so tiny that I turned it into a computer/entertainment room. The master bedroom had its own bathroom, and there existed another full bathroom upstairs. The main floor had a half bath, a long thin kitchen, and a combined living room/dining room. It even had a porch with a roof.

I loved the house and would later carve the words "Helms Deep" into an oak plank, which I then hung outside the front door. Helms Deep came from the *The Lord of the Rings* books. The basement wouldn't work as a garage but made an excellent workshop for my projects and a place to store my tools and rockets.

I had plans for the house, but first I had to qualify for and sign a mortgage. The lender worked out an adjustable-rate mortgage that I qualified for, where the rate remained fixed for the first four years. I had to jump through a number of hoops in order to get it, but I managed. Unlike the first two times I bought a house as a married man, I would be buying this one by myself as a trans woman.

I signed the mortgage on May 17, 2007. It felt good to be a homeowner once again and my timing was fortuitous. Two weeks later, I saw on the news that the housing bubble had burst and lenders had begun tightening the requirements for homebuyers. Had I waited any longer, I likely wouldn't have qualified and would have had to rent for several more years.

Over the years, I've made a lot of repairs and changes to the house. I had two dead trees removed, had a new roof put on, replaced the heating and AC units, and put in a tankless water heater. I also replaced two out of three toilets and have gone through three garbage disposals, two refrigerators and two gas stoves.

This house has been a respite for many of my weary trans friends who pass through the Atlanta area. They have stopped by, enjoyed a hot meal and rested for days, if they wanted, before continuing their journey. During Southern Comfort, I've invited several friends over to sample my Italian cooking. My grandmother and mother would have been proud. I maintain this house as much for my friends as I do for myself. It's their home away from home and I like that. I also like welcoming them to Helms Deep.

35 – HRC'S TREACHERY

HRC's The Workplace Project had been started in 2002 to assess companies on their LGBT acceptance. This included the Corporate Equality Index, which rated companies from zero to 100% on how well they treated their LGBT employees. They recomputed the rate each year, ensuring that companies maintained their standards or received a lower rating.

In 2003, HRC invited Jamison Green and Donna Rose to join HRC's Business Council, to assist with the trans part of the Corporate Equality Index. Later, Donna even joined HRC's Board. Avoiding HRC's politics, they worked on ways to improve the lives of the people in our community through the corporate and business world. However, HRC's infamous politics soon made itself felt in The Workplace Project.

Nevertheless, several people in the trans community became buddies with the HRC and someone even convinced Joe Solmonese, HRC's Executive Director, to come and speak at the 2007 Southern Comfort Conference. Not everyone at SCC wanted to see Solmonese there, me included, because of our community's history and mistrust of the organization he led.

Regardless, when Joe attended Southern Comfort, everyone who attended treated him with respect. Then it happened: Solmonese got up to speak. I sat there with nearly a thousand of my brothers, sisters and cis-allies to listen to what he said. The speech started smoothly. His words flowed like fresh cream. He held the attention of everyone in the room. Then he said it: "We absolutely do not support, and in fact oppose, any legislation that is not absolutely inclusive. And, we have sent that message loud and clear to the Hill."

Everyone in the audience cheered. After all these years, we had finally turned around the battleship HRC. It had finally decided to join all the other LGBT organizations in the 21st century. With the headline made, the question on everyone's lips was whether or not they would now walk the walk.

It took only two weeks before we got the answer. The House reintroduced ENDA and, thanks to the leadership of transphobic Barney Frank, didn't include any trans-inclusive language. Again.

Solmonese objected to the bill's reintroduction without the insertion of trans-friendly language, in keeping with the promise that he had made at SCC. My understanding is that Frank then told HRC that if they did not support the bill, he would no longer help them on the Hill. This rattled the HRC Board and they subsequently buckled. Joe Solmonese's promise disappeared like a sandcastle on a beach.

The reaction from the trans community was swift and harsh. Donna Rose's conscience compelled her to resign from the HRC Board, and even though the Business Council had advised the Board to support a trans-inclusive ENDA, she and Jamison Green resigned from the Business Council, too. HRC's politics had intruded into the only part of the organization that had been doing any good.

A few weeks after the betrayal, on October 9, HRC's National Dinner took place in D.C. Trans activists from all over the country mobilized in Washington that day. I drove up to North Carolina to meet Angela and together we drove into D.C. A large crowd gathered at the front of the dinner's hotel and heckled those arriving. A couple of our trans sisters attended the event itself, wearing 'Trans and Proud' buttons.

The hotel wouldn't allow protestors inside, but I ignored the security guards and took the Flag and a friend with a camera and entered the building. We managed to take a photo of me holding the Flag in front of a large HRC banner. They kicked us out right after that.

Two weeks later, Angela and I met in Charlotte, North Carolina, for HRC's dinner there. The two of us handed out flyers to attendees and held up protest signs at the venue entrance. Later, when the event had ended and everyone gathered in the hotel bar, I wandered in to see Joe Solmonese enjoying a drink. He knew me, so I walked up to him and said,

"Hello, Joe. Did you have a successful dinner tonight?"

"Yes, we did. Thank you for asking."

"You know, I think I should buy you a drink."

"Thank you."

"How about I get you a Southern Comfort... on the rocks?"

Solmonese gave me a dirty look and walked away.

Needless to say, the relationship between HRC and the trans community had been thoroughly trashed. Their treachery wiped out any goodwill they had built up with us since their last betrayal in 2004. As I write this, more than a decade later, HRC has only barely recovered from that event. They are now much better in supporting the trans community, and they have a lot of trans people working for them. However, there will always be members of the trans community who will never forget what they did. Some will never forgive. I still view the organization and its leadership with a healthy skepticism.

TAVA's Survey

At the end of 2007, TAVA's Board came up with the idea of having a survey of trans veterans and active duty members to understand their history and what issues they had with the military and the VA. We came up with 117 questions and released it to members online via SurveyMonkey, so that people all over the country could find and complete it.

TAVA went all out to advertise the survey, making sure that our trans veterans knew where to find it and urging them to take part. This became the first ever survey of the trans community, although it focused specifically on trans veterans.

The survey took place from December 13, 2007 to May 1, 2008. All told, 1001 trans people completed the survey, but since some of them didn't answer a specific question that verified whether they had served or were currently serving in the military, we cut the number down to 827. Four veterans who took the survey had served during WWII. Several current service members also took the survey. Notably, no Admirals or Generals participated.

The Palm Center in California compiled the results for us and came back with some disturbing findings. Ten percent of the people surveyed had been flatly turned down by the VA for help. In addition to discrimination, the group reported a high percentage of experience with violence while serving: 26% reported having been the victim of physical violence, while 16% reported having been raped.

From the findings:

"A full 38% reported that when they were in the military, people suspected or directly asked if they were gay. In addition, 14% had been questioned by an officer about their sexual orientation. For younger respondents (aged 18-35), all of whom had served under DADT, this finding was even more pronounced: 61% reported that when they were in the military, people suspected or directly asked if they were gay; 20% had been questioned by an officer about their sexual orientation. Such effects varied significantly by gender. Trans men were almost two times more likely to report they were suspected of being gay than trans women (72% vs. 37%). They were three times more likely than trans women to have been asked by an officer about their sexual orientation (33% vs. 11%)."

"There were many reports of interpersonal discrimination, via lack of respect from VA doctors (22%), non-medical staff (21%), and nurses (13%). These cases of interpersonal discrimination ranged from what many veterans describe as "typical" – refusing to change to gender-appropriate pronouns, failure to use a new name consistently – to the extreme – refusing to look at transgender patients, referring to them in dismissive ways, refusing to treat them for general medical care."

"One FTM respondent noted, "I was told by a religious clerk that I should just go away because I was an insult to the brave real men who were there for treatment.""

"One MTF respondent recounted the following experience: "A nurse pulled my partner out in the hall of the VA Hospital where I was an in-patient and said, 'You know that is really a man, don't you'?""

"Another MTF respondent noted, "I am asked about my genitals and my plans for SRS regardless of whether or not it has relevance to my treatment.""

In summary, we discovered what we knew all along; that the VA discriminated against trans veterans horribly and regularly. The results of the survey circulated far and wide on the Internet and even made it to the then current administration. President Bush's VA didn't treat any veteran very well, but all we asked was to be treated "equally crappy" as the rest of them. Thankfully, the Obama Administration later heard our cry.

IFGE Conference in Tucson

In 2008, the International Foundation for Gender Education (IFGE) scheduled its yearly conference for the end of March, in Tucson. I considered this to be great news because I could visit my family in Phoenix and then drive down to Tucson for the event.

After a day in Phoenix with my family, I rented a car and drove down to Tucson to the hotel where the IFGE conference took place. I paid for the trip with my tax refund, my first as a trans woman, made possible because my home ownership now factored into my tax return.

The hotel lobby quickly filled up with all kinds of friends of mine. The schedule included some great events. Jamison Green kicked off the conference with the first plenary session later that day. Since I had been elected a temporary IFGE board member I also had some duties to take care of.

While sitting in the lobby that first day, I noticed a woman walk in and sit down on the other side of the hall. I just had to meet her, so I walked over and struck up a conversation. Her name was Karen. She had a sweet smile, and a smattering of innocence that I found irresistible. We talked for a while and met up for lunch later in the day. We got to know each other through the course of the conference and vowed to see each other afterwards, even though she lived in Texas and I lived in Georgia.

The conference session that impacted me most was a panel titled Children of Trans Parents. I had seen this on the schedule prior to the conference and thought it would be a great chance for my two sons to tell their stories. So, I asked both of them to come to Tucson, which they did.

When the panel took place, I sat in the audience to listen to what they had to say. They started out explaining how my transition had affected them and how it had torn their lives apart. Their emotions appeared raw and painful, so much so that Bryan began to cry. I cried. I'm crying now as I write this. What parent wouldn't? I knew that I had thrown their lives into turmoil when I took the decision to transition, but hearing it from them that day brought me to a new level of understanding of what they went through. Apparently, I hadn't finished hurting them that day either. Later, at the outdoor lunch, I upset them further when they saw Karen and me being affectionate to one another. They thought my behavior inappropriate and childish. Looking back, I can see that they were right.

Karen came out to Atlanta to visit me about a month after the IFGE conference, but our relationship couldn't survive the long distance between our home lives and we drifted apart.

New VA Directive

In late 2008, shortly after the findings of TAVA's survey had been published, we heard rumors that the VA had sent out a draft of a new directive to improve how the VA treated trans veterans.

The VA had sent a copy of this new document to some trans veterans in Phoenix to solicit feedback. Upon hearing this, I immediately got on the phone with one of those people, who confirmed that she had indeed received a draft copy. She then told me it looked terrible. When she sent me a copy of the directive, I saw what she meant. Luckily, the directive never got implemented.

In 2009, Obama's VA decided they wanted to address the problem. They drafted a new directive and then sent it to Mara Keisling at NCTE. Mara contacted TAVA and said that they would be looking over the document and suggesting changes to the VA.

For a month, we went back and forth on the necessary language changes as well as other issues that the VA needed to address. Angela wanted to make sure that cross-dressers would also be covered, but since cross-dressers in general wouldn't visit the VA dressed as a woman, Angela quickly withdrew those proposals.

Having given the Obama Administration the revised document, we waited, and waited, and waited some more. I called Mara constantly for updates, but her White House contacts would always tell her they had nothing new to report. This went on for two years.

Eventually, I stopped calling Mara for updates. It seemed like the new Administration had blown us off.

Then, in early June 2011, the VA released a new document called "VHA Directive 2011-024, Providing Health Care for Transgender and Intersexed Veterans." The document didn't look perfect, and still didn't allow for SRS, but it helped to bring much-needed healthcare and respect to trans veterans. The day after the VA released the directive, a number of trans veterans contacted TAVA to tell us, "It worked!"

Thanks to Mara and NCTE, TAVA achieved the goal set out in its Mission Statement to fix the VA, eight and a half years after we started the organization. The result was a team effort and veterans should always be grateful to NCTE. Together we have actually saved lives.

I decided not to reproduce the directive here in my book because it is too long. I also understand that the Trump Administration is doing its best to destroy it and send healthcare for trans veterans back to the Stone Age. It is my fervent hope that responsible and patriotic people will stop this from happening. Trans veterans deserve better.

36 – DARLENE WAGNER

As 2009 came to a close, I felt good about how my life had progressed to date. The one hole in my existence however had to do with love. I felt frustrated at the lack of someone special to spend time with. At the age of 58, I had resigned myself to living the rest of my life alone.

Then in the middle of October, a friend sent me a message saying I should go to a gender-neutral contra dance being held at the UU Church in Atlanta. I didn't know what a contra dance was, but since the invitation had the words 'gender-neutral' and 'dance' in it, why would I say no?

For those of you who don't know, a contra dance is a folk dance, similar to a square dance, except instead of being in square formation, it is danced in lines of couples, with every other couple facing up or down the hall. It has mixed origins in English country dancing, Scottish and French dance styles from the 17th century, and a strong African-American influence from Appalachia.

As a teenager, and a sophomore in high school, my parents sent me to square dancing lessons for teens. I initially had fun, but soon tired of attending. Nevertheless, when I arrived at the contra dance, I noticed they used several square dance moves that I remembered. This made me confident I could do it.

While at the dance, I noticed a tall person, dressed androgynously, but who looked to me like being a trans woman. I saw she noticed me as well. After a short time, she approached me and asked, "Would you like to dance?"

"I don't know how to do this."

"Don't worry. I'll lead." I stood up. "My name is Darlene."

We danced together throughout the night, but because there is a lot of partner-switching that takes place in contra dances, I wasn't always Darlene's partner.

During a break we got to talk. She had lived in Georgia most of her life, had just begun her transition, hadn't changed her name yet, and worked on a Ph.D. in microbiology at Georgia Tech. I also found out her age. At 35, she was 23 years younger than me.

After the dance, we drove to a lesbian nightclub to enjoy a different kind of music. We danced, but after a while we just sat, talked, and stared at each other. She seemed to be shy when away from the familiar surroundings of the contra dance. Needless to say, I found her very intriguing.

We decided to meet up again the following weekend. Then, at the end of October, I stayed overnight at her tiny studio apartment during Pride weekend. From then on, we saw each other every weekend. In December, she had her name legally changed to Darlene Wagner.

One weekend, she even took me to meet her parents. Darlene's mother was only one year older than me. Her father was four years older. Her parents had a hard time adjusting to Darlene's new name, but they respected her decision to transition. They also seemed to get on well with me.

Darlene received a small stipend from Georgia Tech for being a grad student, but they barely gave her enough to cover her rent and food. So, in February, I asked her to move in with me to help her get through school with less stress on her personal finances. It would mean she would have to drive further to go to school, but she would also be able to save quite a bit of money.

We discovered that she and I had a lot in common. Importantly, we liked the same movies and some of the same music. In time, our sense of humors clicked to where today, we both have the same response when we hear a joke or a funny remark on the television.

However, that first year together was not all fun and games. We had issues that we had to work through, and I feared at one point we might break up. Thankfully, with the help of some counseling from Pastor Paul, we came out of that episode a much stronger couple.

Early on in our relationship, Darlene needed a new computer because she had an ancient and failing desktop. Dana Owings came through with a spare PC she had, and I got Darlene a used Linux desktop for her to use at home. Darlene would show me some of her written schoolwork on occasion. It contained words I had never seen before and certainly couldn't pronounce.

As time went on, Darlene became my domestic partner. I put her on my phone plan at Sprint and even added her to my health insurance policy. She saw the same doctor I saw, and her transition progressed steadily and happily. Her body started taking shape and she began to let her hair grow longer. Every year, she has gotten prettier and prettier and more and more confident. Eventually, her shyness disappeared, leaving a confident and outgoing woman.

We enjoyed doing things and going places together. We would go to the Ashville area, especially Chimney Rock Village. We hiked Kennesaw Mountain, launched model rockets at several locations, went to D.C. twice, and we visited several places in Georgia to take photos and shoot videos.

I also took Darlene to Phoenix twice, once shortly after Donna passed away and, in June 2018, for my Mother's 90th birthday. On the latter trip, we spent a whole week in Northern and Central Arizona taking pictures and video at the Grand Canyon, Sedona, Flagstaff, the Salt River, South Mountain, Slide Rock and Sunset Crater. We had an amazing time. Darlene and I can spend hours in the car together and not annoy one another. To me, that's a key test for a successful couple.

My Mother loves Darlene. The two times my Mother has spent time with us, she seemed to enjoy herself immensely. When we left to go home after our first visit, my mother told Darlene, "You can visit anytime. Oh, and you can bring Monica with you, if you want."

One of the things Darlene and I love to do together is canning fruits and vegetables. We will go to a farm and pick peaches to make peach jelly and preserves. Once a year, we go to a strawberry farm so we can make strawberry jelly. We've also made jelly from blueberries, blackberries, figs and nectarines. We tried canning pickles once, but they didn't turn out so great. Our specialty however is making condensed spaghetti sauce from fresh tomatoes. A jar of our sauce enhances any spaghetti dish and gives it a truly unique flavor, reminiscent of our home.

In December 2012, Darlene graduated from Georgia Tech with a Ph.D. in bioinformatics, a subset of microbiology. Over the years, I have known several trans people with Ph.Ds. Most of them received their doctorates before they transitioned, while others received theirs long after. Darlene seems unique in this respect. She started her transition right in the middle of her Ph.D., and in one of the most difficult sciences. Transitioning alone is stressful without all the academic work she undertook on top of it. In my opinion, she handled everything incredibly well. Darlene's timing was deliberate however. She waited to transition until she became a grad student, telling me, "They can't fire a grad student."

To help her get through her last years of study, Darlene worked at one of the local junior colleges teaching math and algebra. She has a Bachelor's in mathematics, so it came easy for her. It didn't pay much, but it helped to put food on the table for us.

Darlene had a dream to eventually work for the Centers for Disease Control and Prevention (CDC). She had contacts there and had talked to some of their people. They wanted to hire her, but initially the government had a hiring freeze, then later the obstructionist Republicans shut the government down for a short time. Altogether this kept Darlene from securing a position at the CDC for 15 months. Finally, the government lifted the roadblocks. Even then however, she couldn't be employed directly. Instead, the CDC sent her to one of its many subcontractors who supply the Center with people.

Darlene now works in the Enteric Diseases Laboratory Branch, where she processes the DNA of foodborne pathogen bacteria, such as *Salmonella, E. coli* and *Listeria*, along with other lesser-known diseases. She's on the frontline in the fight against microbes that want to make you sick. Having the CDC on her resume is golden. If she ever decided to move on, she would be hired in a heartbeat. I'm so proud of and happy for her. One day, she came home from work with a hoodie for me that read: "The CDC – Keeping the world safe from the Zombie Apocalypse since 1947." It always gets comments when I wear it.

One of Darlene's greatest desires is to become a mother. She wants to adopt and has now been working on this goal for over a year. Unlike me, she didn't get a chance to be a parent before starting her transition. She tried freezing her sperm so that she could have a child that would be biologically hers, but the ongoing expense eventually became prohibitive. We are now going through the adoption process together, jumping through all the appropriate hoops.

Darlene is spearheading the adoption, but I am supporting her and will do whatever it takes to make her happy. Becoming a parent in my late sixties is a little bit scary for me. Can I be a good parent this time around? I think I can, but I'm old. Will I have the energy to keep up with a child? No, but I'll do my best. We would like to adopt an eight- or nine-year-old and, if we can, a trans child. There are so many trans children who need a good home. Darlene and I think we would make perfect parents for one of them.

For the longest time, Darlene didn't want to get married. I had expressed my desire to marry her, but she refused. Finally however, she agreed. So, we planned our wedding for September 2016. We even bought matching rings earlier in the year. But she got cold feet as the date got nearer and didn't want to go through with it.

Then, Election Day came. November 8, 2016 should have been a day of celebration, but America elected the Orange Liar to be our next President. Darlene and I felt the Earth had slipped into a terrible alternate universe. Fearing that our world would collapse, and that the chances of us having a legal marriage might soon vanish, we visited Cobb County Courthouse on November 18, 2016, and were married along with a dozen other couples.

Darlene has taken on a leadership role in the Atlanta trans community. In 2017, she became the director of the Atlanta TDOR event. She worked hard and when the day arrived, people praised her for putting on an amazing event. Now, she is working on getting a 501(c)3 tax exemption status for the Atlanta TDOR.

I have not been this happy, for this long... ever. I had happy times with Donna, but they didn't last. I had thought I would die alone, without a job, and maybe even homeless. Right now, I may be retired, but I can truly call this the best time of my life. Darlene has made my life better and made me a better person. I cannot thank her enough.

37 – THE LAST FEW YEARS

In 2013, I decided to retire from activism and resign from TAVA. Angela became President for a short time before handing the baton over to the next generation of leadership. Today, TAVA has become a highly respected organization, one that has worked toward allowing trans service members to serve openly. That happened in 2017, but then Trump tried to backtrack on the policy when he became president. So far, lawsuits have kept the military from kicking trans service members out. Thanks to Evan Young, TAVA's current President, the organization has been at the forefront of the fight for trans military rights. Evan has made TAVA better than I ever could and I'm proud of the work he has done.

I resigned from TAVA because, after decades of activism, I just wanted to live my life. Building and launching model rockets started taking up a lot of my time, as did improving and maintaining the upkeep of my house. Once Darlene began working for the CDC, we were even able to start saving money. We just wanted to be a 'normal' couple.

At the beginning of 2015, Sprint did something unusual. In prior years, whenever they needed to lay people off, they would offer a large portion of them a severance package as an incentive for volunteers to come forward. I worked in a critical department however, so we never had a chance to take the offer. The argument always given by Sprint management was that "they needed us".

Then in January, they finally told our department we could apply for a severance package if any of us so wished. These packages gave each person two weeks of pay for every year they had worked for Sprint. That month I celebrated my 25th anniversary at Sprint, so if I took the severance package, I would get a whole year of pay without having to come to work. Soon, I would turn 64, so I applied for severance and felt grateful to later find out that they had accepted my application. For me, retirement had come early.

Later in 2015, my ex-wife Donna slipped and banged her head. She went into the hospital, but didn't recover. Instead, her condition worsened. She passed away in November, just after Thanksgiving. Understandably, my sons felt devastated. I cried at her passing too. No, we weren't close and no, she didn't want to talk to me, but she will always be special to me in ways that no one else ever could be. She gave me two wonderful sons who grew up and became better fathers than I ever had been to them. I hope Donna's soul is in a better place.

By the end of January 2016, my severance package had run out. Nevertheless, I continued to receive a small pension from Sprint. In March, I turned 65, so at that point I applied for Social Security and Medicare. The Medicare recently came in handy when I tripped on a sidewalk, fell and broke my nose. Together, Medicare and my supplemental health insurance policy paid for everything, except for fixing my teeth.

Initially, I felt elated when I left Sprint. Staying at home became fun and I got a lot done around the house with so much time on my hands. However, I still wanted to feel productive, so I looked at the courses various local schools offered to see if I could learn a new skill. After looking around, I found that Chattahoochee Tech offered an Associate of Arts (AA) degree program in Television Production. I could really sink my teeth into that. I already had two AA degrees, including one in Industrial Television, but I'd taken that back in 1987, during the tape and analogue days of television. This would give me the chance to learn about similar equipment in the digital age.

In August 2015, I started working toward my degree in the modern field of television and movies. I discovered that Atlanta has the third largest entertainment industry in the world, just ahead of London. Things happened all over Georgia that I could get involved with if I only had the skills.

So, for the next two and a half years, I took all the necessary classes, did all the required work and finished all the requisite projects to earn my AA degree. The college told students that the high quality of training provided by Chattahoochee Tech would mean we would be highly sought after in the business, once we graduated. All I hoped for was to get a part-time job or occasional contract work to bring in some extra money.

I met some great people during my time at Chattahoochee Tech and I learned a lot from them. Modesty aside, I became a good camera operator and an even better editor. I am also pretty skilled with 3D animated graphics.

Through the school, I received an intern job at Georgia Public Broadcasting as a camera operator and editor for a show called *Lawmakers*. The show only lasted through the Georgia legislative session of 40 days, but GPB hired me back again in 2019 as a contractor for the same show and two others.

In December 2017, I purchased a prosumer camera that allowed me to shoot video in 4K definition. Once I had it, I started visiting different places in Georgia to take nature footage and other images, and supplied them to stock footage companies. I've managed to sell about 20 of them and over 1000 of my clips have been accepted to date. It's rewarding, but it's not going to make me rich.

I've also been able to enjoy something of a celebrity status during my retirement. As the creator of the Trans Flag, I've been fortunate enough to be a Grand Marshall for San Francisco Pride, Charlotte Pride and Atlanta Pride.

San Francisco's Pride was particularly impressive. They really went all out in the way they treated their Grand Marshalls. The Parade itself went on for many hours, and the car I rode in had a giant Trans Flag draped across the hood. However, although the parade may have been big, the subsequent festival seemed to have fewer booths than Atlanta's equivalent event. Darlene and I particularly loved Charlotte Pride because it seemed smaller, friendlier, and generally more charming.

2019 should be a big year for me. Not only will I be publishing my autobiography, but it will be the 20th anniversary of the creation of the Trans Flag. I have been invited to be the Grand Marshall at Phoenix Pride in April, my old hometown, and Montreal Pride in August. But there will also be an even bigger honor. 2019 is the 50th anniversary of the Stonewall Riots. In honor of that, I have been invited to be one of the Grand Marshalls for New York City's Pride March, which this year also doubles as World Pride.

I'm hoping 2019 will be the year the Smithsonian finally puts the original Trans Flag on display and, if they do, I hope to make the trip up to Washington, D.C, to see it, for what might be the last time.

38 – THE END FOR NOW

To the readers of *More Than Just A Flag*, I would like to say how much I appreciate you making it this far through my book. Thank you for staying the course as I've recalled the various events that collectively make up my life to date. It may look like I went through a lot of shit, but in reality all I did was experience life.

The journey from a young, snot-nosed, virginal, naive, newbie sailor to an old, worn-out, cynical, trans woman came with many highs and lows. Life smacked me down more than a few times, but also blessed me with amazing highs, a host of wonderful friends, and a loving wife. For the most part however, I have played the role of an unsuspecting traveler who just dealt with whatever she encountered. Writing this book has been like pulling into a rest stop mid-road trip and looking at the videos and photos that I've taken so far. I know my journey isn't over however, and my camera battery remains fully charged.

My complicated and, some would argue, overactive love life brought me periods of joy and, finally, a lasting companionship with another woman. It also introduced me to gut-wrenching periods of love lost and female vengeance, two things I could have done without, but which doubtless made me a stronger person. Far above many of these fleeting relationships however, was the feeling of twice holding a new life in my hands and of the unconditional love I have given to and received from my sons.

During my life, my gender identity has played havoc with my

emotions. Many times, I felt confused and lost, which often sent me traveling down the wrong path. Other times I felt as if a huge burden had been lifted from my shoulders because I had finally figured things out. My transgenderism had people turn their backs on me, embrace me for my courage, and accept me back after years of shunning me. I've been discriminated against, scorned, vilified, preached to and condemned to Hell, but it's also caused me to be admired, loved, honored, cheered and respected.

My activism was enhanced by my Navy career, my writing, my sales experience, my speaking skills, my people skills, but more broadly my love for others. Biology made me trans, but life made me an activist. Time made me a woman, but love made me human. I have talked to more politicians then I can count and even made friends with some of them. Many know me when they see me, but not all of them are happy when I appear.

My friendships with other trans people have been extraordinarily rich. Principally this is because we have shared experiences that involve some of life's most extreme moments.

I often wonder what my life would have been like if Mother Nature had given me a body to match my brain at birth. How many children and grandchildren would I have? How old would they be? Would I be a strong woman or a weak one? What occupation would I have and would I have advanced very far? What medical problems would I face today? Would I be straight or a lesbian? I know it's all unanswerable, but I ponder it nonetheless.

The trans community is more diverse than any other community I have known. Some in the trans community embrace these differences and build bridges, while others construct elaborate hierarchies designed to put other people down and create a false sense of superiority. The horizontal cruelty in our community knows no boundaries and sadly, at times, I have contributed to it. Yet, we are a community. We have more in common with each other than we have differences, and when it comes to overcoming societal prejudice and achieving equality for our misunderstood brothers and sisters, we are stronger together.

Nevertheless, some believe that, while trans activists say they want equality for all trans people, in reality they are only working to advance the rights of trans people who have surgery. Some famous trans women think that in order to be considered a 'true transsexual' you have to get SRS. This is wrong. To these 'purists' the pain in starting transition, losing family, friends, places of worship and jobs means nothing, in spite of the fact that, unfortunately, these days such experiences go hand in hand with transgenderism. The idea that you have to have a vagina or you aren't committed to being a woman is, in my humble opinion, ridiculous.

Another issue in our community bothers me. There are people who have little or no experience in grassroots activism and yet they think they can dictate to the rest of the community what we should or should not do. Life has taught me that those who listen to others tend to be best informed. It seems to me that listening is a forgotten skill these days, eclipsed by the need for everyone to have their say, regardless of whether or not they know what they are talking about.

Some in the community blindly support organizations based on inconclusive evidence, saying those organizations fought for us. Others perpetuate hatred toward those same organizations, also based on inconclusive evidence that the organizations didn't support us. Both sides argue the issue excessively, recalling anecdotes as conclusive evidence that they are right. Things are not all black and white. One must step back and look at the big picture to get a clearer view of the situation. My advice is to always maintain healthy skepticism.

Another challenge our community faces is how to build bridges among races. I have African American trans friends who express frustration at how white trans people seem to look down on trans people of color. I have seen this kind of racism first hand and it disgusts me. Classism is another problem our community needs to face, an issue that often seems to piggyback on racism. As a community that sees so much hate and discrimination, we should be bringing everyone closer together, for our own collective safety, rather than pushing each other apart.

Over the years, I have discovered that a sense of humor is a rare commodity in the trans community, but that those who actually possess one seem to make the best trans activists. Why is that? For me, a sense of humor helps to put things into perspective. Those who cannot laugh in certain situations tend to burn out quickly. A good activist has to be flexible, be able to bend with the wind, and laugh at the ridiculous when presented with it. Especially when they find it staring back at them in the mirror.

Looking ahead, I have many hopes for the future. I want my sons to grow old and have grandchildren of their own, on a planet that can sustain them. I want to grow old with Darlene and know that the child we adopt will have a great life after I'm gone. Ideally, I'd like to live long enough to see a man, or a woman, walk on Mars.

I'm so happy to have found a partner as amazing as Darlene. In the beginning of the book, I mentioned my "soulmate". As time goes on, I know her to be exactly that. It amazes me that we found each other and that our love keeps growing.

I now come to the end of my book. Now that it's published, I expect to get emails, text messages and phone calls relaying all kinds of criticism and corrections. So, if I got something wrong or remembered an event inaccurately, please forgive me. I'm 67 and those brownies I ate back in 1976 are only now wearing off.

Some names in this book have been changed to protect the guilty, but the account I have given is very much real. I suspect some people may even enjoy reading it.

Life is not a bowl of cherries or a box of chocolates, but more like a gold mine. Sometimes you'll find that rare nugget that makes life worth living. However, most of the time, you get the shaft. You just gotta live with it. I have.

AFTERWORD

Monica Helms declared the day I was born, March 8, 1978, to be the worst birthday of her life. She says as much in Chapter 15. However, despite us sharing the same birthday, 27 years apart, she knew nothing of me until I contacted her in 2017 and asked to interview her. I flew out to Atlanta and quizzed her on her activism and, of course, her creation of the Trans Flag.

Subsequently, I became aware that she had written an autobiography and asked if I could be involved. We came to an arrangement whereby I would edit her manuscript, and the result is the tome you are holding now.

As Monica notes, she will principally be remembered as the creator of the Trans Flag. If you are reading this, chances are you already knew who she was. Initially, I didn't. Over the past 20 years I have traveled to every country in the world and seen the Trans Flag and Gilbert Baker's Rainbow Flag in various countries, on six continents. They seemed like they had existed forever. It didn't occur to me that they were invented in my lifetime, and yet they were. The Rainbow Flag was created for San Francisco's June 1978 Pride, and the Trans Flag was created by Monica in August 1999.

That these two designs became globally synonymous with the gay and transgender communities respectively, within their inventor's lifetime, speaks to the brilliance of their design, and the breakneck speed with which we are nowadays able to coalesce and communicate. As I write this, both look likely to remain indelible and defining symbols for ages to come. The silver lining of living in an age in which civil rights are infringed upon is living in an age when civil rights leaders make history.

I remember asking Monica if she had ever met Gilbert Baker, whom I had been fortunate enough to interview a few weeks prior to her and my first meeting.

"He was mean to me." She told me.

"How so?" I asked.

"Well, we met one another at San Francisco Pride in 2015. Someone introduced me to him, explaining that I was the inventor of the Trans Flag and his reaction to me was snide and aloof. 'Oh. Do you sew?' Of course, I didn't, and I said as much. That seemed to diminish me in his eyes."

The episode obviously hurt Monica's feelings, but she and Gilbert subsequently became Facebook friends and were able to salvage a respectful friendship from that initially rocky start. Of course, it would have been lovely if these two historical figures had hit it off, but sometimes real life isn't the fairytale we want it to be.

For me, the story of Gilbert and Monica's first meeting is a microcosm for the relationship between the LGB and T communities. In my view, the former has treated the latter badly. Prior to interviewing Chaz Bono, in 2011, I knew remarkably little about trans people, despite identifying as LGBT for my entire adult life. I have heard my gay friends express frustration at the inclusion of transgender people under the LGBT umbrella. "They're not like us." "I don't get what we have in common." Well, for those of you who don't get it, allow me to enlighten you.

Transgenderism is about identity, rather than sexual orientation. A trans person doesn't change gender in order to better sleep with the sex they are attracted to, instead they transition because their body doesn't match their true gender. Moreover, the gender a trans person is attracted to doesn't normally change because of their transition. So, if a trans man was attracted to women before he transitioned, he will more than likely still be attracted to women afterwards. If a trans woman was attracted to women before she transitioned, most of the time she will still be attracted to women afterwards. From these two limited examples, readers should be able to see that, in the former case the trans man 'started out' as a lesbian (using commonly accepted societal definitions), and in the latter example the trans woman 'became' a lesbian. So, in a nutshell, what the T has in common with the LGB is that, in most cases, prior to or after their transition, transgender men and women would be labeled 'gay'.

Not surprisingly then, given their vested interest in gay rights, transgender men and women have been at the forefront of the fight for LGBT equality. Yet, as this book details, gays and lesbians have not always been at the forefront of the fight for transgender rights, and this is something we should be ashamed of. Moreover, this needs to change. Part of my motivation in helping Monica publish this book has been to help educate society on what it means to be transgender, along with the hardships and prejudices that so many trans people endure.

What you won't find in this book is a step-by-step description of Monica's physical transition. Why? Well, because she regards the details of her body as her business and nobody else's. The non-transgender world might be fascinated by the surgeries sometimes involved in transitioning, but that doesn't mean we have a right to know the workings of anyone else's physiology. Also, by overly obsessing on surgery, we set ourselves up to lesser understand the broader issues of hardship, discrimination, and the journey to true self.

What have I learned from working with Monica on her book (other than the fact she can cuss like the sailor she is)? My eyes have been opened to a community that has suffered far greater hardship than I myself have faced as a gay man. At any given point in my life, the option of keeping my sexuality under wraps has always been an option. Not so for the transgender community. They are a minority that shares much in common with the lesbian and gay communities, but which has to date been held back by that association rather than helped. At the heart of the transgender disposition is, as far as I can see, simply a desire to be and be loved. That is something we should all be able to empathize with.

To Monica, thank you for letting me be part of your story, for challenging me, and for occasionally letting me get my own way.

Laurence Watts

ABOUT THE AUTHOR

Monica F. Helms is a transgender activist, author, and veteran of the United States Navy, having served on two submarines.

She created the Transgender Pride Flag in 1999 and subsequently donated the original flag to the Smithsonian Institution in 2014.

In 2003, she co-founded the Transgender American Veterans Association where she was president for ten years.

In 2004, she was elected as a delegate from Georgia to the Democratic National Convention.

In addition to her autobiography *More Than Just A Flag*, published in 2019, Monica is the author of the novels *Valhalla* (1997), *Blue and Gold* (1999), *Time Hostages* (2000), *The Wayward Star* (2003), *Tales from a Two-Gendered Mind* (2006), and *The Straits of Hell* (2012).

Her hobbies include launching model rockets and making video clips for a stock footage company. She has earned three AA degrees.

Monica has two sons and three grandsons.

In 2016, she married Darlene Wagner, Ph.D. They are currently working on adopting a child.

Made in the USA
Lexington, KY
04 July 2019